Poetry towards Novel

POETRY TOWARDS NOVEL

by
JOHN SPEIRS

NEW YORK UNIVERSITY PRESS
New York

Copyright © 1971 John Speirs

Library of Congress Catalogue Card Number: 72–169252

SBN: 8147–7755–4

Manufactured in Great Britain

TO RUTH, LOGAN AND HEATHER

CONTENTS

1. Blake, Coleridge, Keats and Shakespeare   *page* 11

2. Wordsworth: The Tales of *Margaret* and
   Michael   49

3. Wordsworth: *The Prelude*   79

4. Wordsworth: Poems Contemporary with
   The Prelude and Later   140

5. Crabbe: *Tales in Verse*   153

6. Byron: *Beppo, The Vision of Judgment* and
   Don Juan   200

7. Poetry into Novel   283

   Index   334

BLAKE, COLERIDGE, KEATS AND SHAKESPEARE

I

If we ask ourselves what distinguishes the novelists of the 19th century from those of the 18th our first answer might well be their poetic imaginativeness. The remarkable development of introspectiveness, interest in the individual and psychological insight which equally distinguishes the 19th-century novelists is closely associated with their poetic imaginativeness and is furthered by it. The recovery and renewal of an exploratory-creative (or poetic) use of language, which began with Blake, after the deliberately and consciously prosaic cultivation of the 18th century, is an essential part of these remarkable new developments in the novel. Dickens and George Eliot (along with the Brontës, and, in New England, Hawthorne and Melville) are at least as much successors of the English poets as of the 18th-century novelists. The great 19th-century novels are a development out of the whole of English language and literature from Chaucer and Shakespeare and, more immediately, from the original and exploring poets of the beginning of the century. Jane Austen is not simply an early 19th-century Richardson, Dickens not simply a 19th-century Smollet. The novelists did not only read novelists. The novel, as part of the 19th-century developments in consciousness, took on a new dimension of greatness. In the depth and breadth of their handling of human life, Dickens, George Eliot, James, Conrad, Lawrence are, in their different ways (as is now at last recognized), the great successors of Shakespeare. This is not simply a matter of influences. But the influence of Shakespeare on the great 19th-century novelists – especially on George Eliot, and also, in quite different ways, on Dickens – is so profound and pervasive as to be, though unmistakable, strictly immeasurable. It is a creative influence which has worked both directly through reading (as well as witnessing

popular theatrical performances) of Shakespeare, but also in-
directly through the greater English poets.

II

We may have agreed that the great successors of Shakespeare in
the depth and breadth of their handling of life are the great
novelists of the 19th century (and beginning of the 20th). But
already in certain of the poets of around 1800, beginning with
Blake, the creative or re-creative effect of Shakespeare (and of the
poets of the 17th century, his immediate successors) becomes per-
vasive and profound, specifically in the imaginative-creative way
in which the English language again begins to be used. Of the
poets of the 18th century, an age of great prose authors, only Pope
himself shows occasionally a comparable imaginativeness,
especially in his last major poem, the last book of the *Dunciad*.
('Never had I more excited, passionate, fantastical imagination'
might at least as appropriately have been said by the ageing Pope
as by the ageing Yeats.)

The unorthodox new things which Blake did also with the
Bible and with Milton are certainly a matter of interest and
curiosity for the understanding of his great original achievement.
The 18th-century poets before Blake had been, of course, also
much under the spell of Milton. But what they chiefly took from
Milton was 'style'. For them Milton was the model of the 'grand
manner' in English. They learned how to apply the Miltonic style
to lend dignity to subjects not necessarily in themselves sublime,
such as descriptions of landscape, often as background to the
human figure, who is still in his pensive meditations or Horatian
retirements 'social man'. The descriptions of morning and evening
in Eden – and in general the pastoral passages – in *Paradise Lost*,
as well as *Il Penseroso* and the other minor poems of Milton, are
imitated in minor 18th-century verse on such conventional poetical
subjects as the evening walk (which occasionally takes one round
by the churchyard). But, if it was 'style' which the 18th-century
men of 'polite letters' principally found in Milton, there is
evidence that the English 'people' – or such of them as read books
– read *Paradise Lost* as they read their Bible and *Pilgrim's Progress*
as a religious book. This is certainly more nearly the way in
which Blake read it and in which it affected his individual vision.

There are certain affinities, as well as the obvious differences, between Blake and Bunyan. Both men, in their different centuries, shared the culture of the 'people' (Blake early apprenticed to a London engraver). Bunyan did so fully: the surprising thing is that Blake also could still, to some extent, do so, partly because he happened to be outside the 18th-century circle of 'polite letters'. The seeing of visions, for example, so 'Gothic' to the 'polite' rational mind, would surely not have seemed so odd among a people whose books, even in the 18th century, were still the Bible and *Pilgrim's Progress* and among whom evangelism had taken a renewed hold on the religious imagination. Blake's visions are exceptional simply in being Blake's, his individual way of seeing things imaginatively and, therefore, shockingly unorthodox. It is not the seeing of visions but the visions themselves, Blake's original insights, that are startlingly new. Bunyan's *Pilgrim's Progress* is fully and profoundly traditional, as was his whole popular culture out of which that English classic comes. There is more of the kind of thing that the *Pilgrim's Progress* is, more of the nature of allegory, symbolism or metaphor, more poetry in the great 19th-century novels – more noticeably so, perhaps, in the New England authors, Hawthorne and Melville – than had been assumed until some modern Shakespearian criticism perhaps began to open the eyes of readers to it. We may go much further and assert that in the great 19th-century novels there is more of the kind of thing Shakespeare is than had been assumed before Mr. Leavis's essays on the novelists appeared in *Scrutiny*.

But what concerns me here is to point out the way in which Blake in his great poems (the *Songs of Experience* and one or two other short poems and fragments) is using language not only in a way uncharacteristic of the 18th century but in an imaginative-creative (or Shakespearean) way. In his *Poetical Sketches* (printed in 1783) already the youthful Blake's responsiveness to Shakespeare is apparent as one of his main sources of literary inspiration. The three songs, *Memory, hither come, My silks and fine array* and the *Mad Song*, are instances of the effects of literary inspiration at its purest[1] on the imagination of a truly original poet. Blake's

---

[1] One or two of Collins's poems are less remarkable instances of the same kind, simply because Collins is a much less remarkable poet, a delicately conventional 18th-century minor poet.

personal responses to particular plays of Shakespeare become transmuted in his memory and imagination into poems that are unmistakably Blake's and entirely original. *Memory, hither come* is a song that is surely what has become in Blake's imagination of his recollections of *As You Like It*, in particular the melancholy fancies of Jaques beside a brook in the forest of Arden.

> I'll pore upon the stream
> Where sighing lovers dream
> And fish for fancies as they pass
> Within the watery glass.

My silks and fine array could be a song for Ophelia. Recollections of the mad Ophelia and of the grave-diggers' scene in *Hamlet* (as well as of later Jacobean plays and songs) have surely become transmuted into this Blake poem. It could still, however, be mistaken for a Jacobean song. *Mad Song* could not. There is no poem in *Poetical Sketches* in which the voice, as well as the quality of the imagery, is already more utterly characteristic of the great Blake of *Songs of Experience* than the *Mad Song*. Again, it might be a song for Lear. Recollections of the mad Lear in the tempest, the scene of Cordelia's restoration to Lear's awakening consciousness, with its recognitions and discoveries, and the theme of blindness in the same play, have surely all been fused and transmuted into what is, nonetheless, a new, truly unique poem of Blake (expressing a frightening, indeed sublime, sense of a blinding illumination or revelation, the recognition that men can endure but a little consciousness, 'cannot bear very much reality').

How much Blake's responses to Shakespeare have had to do with his *Songs of Innocence* (1789) is less easy to apprehend. The *Songs of Innocence* are, of course, uniquely Blake. They could not be by anyone else; they come directly from Blake's new imaginative vision of man which begins from his new vision of the child – 'On a cloud I saw a child' (cf. 'Pity like a naked new-born babe striding the blast,'). But the nearest to that distinctive note of a pristine or recovered primal innocence in our imaginative literature is surely to be found not in any other simple ballads or songs but occasionally in the last plays of Shakespeare, recurring in the midst of their complex poetry. There is, early in that disturbing first Act of *A Winter's Tale*, preceding its crashing dissonances, a glimpse of an age of innocence (the childhoods of Leontes and Polixenes recollected).

> We were as twinn'd lambs that did frisk i' the sun,
> And bleat the one at the other; what we changed
> Was innocence for innocence; we knew not
> The doctrine of ill-doing, nor dreamed
> That any did.

Certainly the *Songs of Innocence* are not simply a new version of pastoralism made out of Blake's Elizabethan and 17th-century reading any more than they are simply the scene on the English village-green as observed by the 'corporal eye'. *The Echoing Green*, for example, is an imaginative vision in which 'Old John with white hair' is just as much in an Age of Innocence, after a rich full summer-day fulfilment, as are the children playing on the green. The *Songs of Innocence* are Blake's unique imaginative vision not simply of a lost Garden of Eden or a Golden Age recovered but of a particular state of being. What has been transmuted into Blake's imaginative vision is partly, of course, the Bible ('The lion and the lamb shall lie down together' and partly perhaps Spenser's Una and the Lion) but more essentially (I think) Shakespeare.

> And there the lion's ruddy eyes
> Shall flow with tears of gold . . .
> From his eyes of flame
> Ruby tears there came.

Whatever further interpretations may be relevant in the contexts of the particular poems, these tears are precious primarily because they are the overflowing of love, abundant and generous, as are for example the tears of Cordelia.

> You have seen
> Sunshine and rain at once; her smiles and tears
> Were like a better way: those happy smilets
> That play'd on her ripe lip, seem'd not to know
> What guests were in her eyes; which parted thence
> As pearls from diamonds dropt.

As in the last plays there is the daughter lost and found (Perdita, Marina) and there are metamorphoses or transformations ('Those are pearls that were his eyes' cf. 'When this corruptible shall put on in corruption ... we shall be changed') so also there are in Blake's *The Little Girl Lost and Found* (two poems which were at first among the *Songs of Innocence*, though later placed by Blake with the *Songs of Experience*).

> And wondering behold
> A spirit armed in gold.

The lost child is in reality not lost. The tigers of the night that beset her change into guardian and gentle beings, as our fears sometimes do when confronted – as in that later poem of Blake.

> The sun is freed from fears
> And with soft grateful tears
> Ascends the sky.

There are such strange events – parallel also in their significances – in the last plays of Shakespeare, whether or not Blake consciously recollected them.

But it is in the greater *Songs of Experience* that for the first time in the 18th century we come upon what may be described as again a fully Shakespearian poetic use of language. Already in the Introductory poems, *Hear the voice of the bard* (the poet chanting as solemn prophet or seer), words are used not simply to elude any simple or orthodox conception of the Fall (e.g. 'the ancient trees' here suggest the Druid grove rather than the Garden of Eden) but with a fully poetic use of language, a wide range and variety of suggestion and association uncharacteristic of the 18th century. Where else in English poetry since the 17th-century poets, the immediate successors of Shakespeare (unless, unexpectedly enough, occasionally in some passages in Pope that transcend his Augustan mode), do we find such a fully poetic use of language before Blake?

The transmutation of the observed facts of the London streets –

> And mark in every face I meet
> marks of weakness, marks of woe –

into imaginative vision in the poem *London* culminates in a concentration and fusion of diverse images that may properly be described as Shakespearian.

> How the chimney sweeper's cry
> Every black'ning church appals
> And the hapless soldier's sigh
> Runs in blood down palace walls.
>
> But most through midnight streets I hear
> How the youthful harlot's curse
> Blasts the new-born infant's tear
> And blights with plagues the marriage hearse.

The blood that runs down palace walls is in fact shed by the hapless soldier on the battlefield. But the blood-guilt of that event is, in the vision of the poem, seen as fatally associated with the palace. The churches in London were, no doubt, as a matter of observed fact turning black from the soot that falls from chimneys.[1] But, in the Blakeian imaginative vision, the blackness, like that of the 'midnight streets', becomes that of the curse drawn upon them by the oppression of the child 'chimney sweeper'. There are three oppressed human creatures in the poem, the 'chimney sweeper', the 'hapless soldier' and the 'youthful harlot'. The blood which the Macbeths cannot wash from their hands and the 'secret, black and midnight hags' of the Shakespearian tragedy belong to the same kind of tragic vision as Blake's in this poem and may well have had something to do with its formation and formulation. In the final stanza the 'marriage hearse' is a combination of opposites like 'lilies that fester' (and there are marriage hearses, too, or their equivalents, in *Hamlet* and earlier, *Romeo and Juliet*). Marriage, in this perverted order, instead of being a source of joy and life has become a death. 'Plagues', in this imaginatively magnified vision of universal disaster, suggests whole cities and nations blighted. The youthful harlot's 'curse' heard in the 'midnight streets' expands into the curse of the consequences of the wrong done to her. The charged rhythm of the lines and the explosive force (in their context) of the alliterated words ('blasts', 'blights', 'plagues', following 'black'ning',

---

[1] Cf. in the dead Dombey Street – 'two gaunt trees with blackened trunks and branches, rattled rather than rustled, their leaves were so smoke-dried.'

'blood', 'appals', 'palace') can be paralleled by many Shakespearian passages ('that but this blow might be the be-all and the end-all here'). The force of the words 'blastments' and 'blasted' in the following passages in *Hamlet* is a characteristic instance.

> (Laertes) And in the morn and liquid dew of youth
>   Contagious blastments.
> (Ophelia) that unmatch'd form and feature of blown youth
>   Blasted.

Milton's youthful lines about a dead infant

> no sooner blown but blasted
> Soft silken primrose fading timelessly

are, in contrast, more simply a melodious arrangement of word sounds on a sad theme.

The Sick Rose is another Shakespearian fusion and concentration of diverse images into a complex simplicity. The poem seems to happen in a flash (the short poem can be read through in a single breath), an almost instantaneous moment of vision, as clear and coherent as it is intense. 'O Rose thou art sick' (cf. again 'Lilies that fester') instantly carries the poem out of the category of conventional poems about roses, Elizabethan or other. The poem that swiftly follows communicates a single unified vision of the sources of life (Original Innocence) corrupted. As such it attains a symbolic significance beyond, for example, the Shakespearian parallel in *Twelfth Night*

> let concealment like a worm i' the bud
> Feed on her damask cheek.

The worm becomes in Blake's poem no ordinary canker worm. It is 'invisible' and 'flies in the night'. Insects do so, but here the words convey the further suggestion of a power of darkness and death, the Angel of Death. The 'howling storm' has here the suggestion of a demonic power. 'Crimson joy' (cf. Marvell's 'green thought in a green shade') transmutes abstract joy into the full, rich, glowing exuberance of life the crimson-petalled rose is. But 'love' which should give life and joy is here (cf. 'marriage hearse') the destructive love of the worm, because or therefore

clandestine ('dark, secret'). (Secrecy is associated in Blake with evil in contrast with spontaneity and frankness, e.g. *I was angry with my friend*.)

The Shakespearian use of the strength of the English language in these poems of Blake should make it less easy to read *Ah Sunflower*, when we come to it, as if it were a nostalgic pre-Raphaelite poem. The Blake poem expresses not simply a longing to be done with life. It expresses something stronger, characteristically of Blake, a need to burst the bonds, to be freed from the fears, prohibitions and inhibitions which are as graves.

> Where the youth pined away with desire
> And the pale virgin shrouded in snow
> Arise from their graves and aspire . . .

The phrase 'weary of time' here suggests an aspiration towards a timeless realm (the realm the 'imaginative eye' sees) beyond the mechanical, mathematical temporal realm (in which the 'corporal eye' and Newtonian Physics imprison us). Certainly the poem expresses, as other poems of Blake do, an aspiration towards a joyous liberation of the human being from imprisoning states of mind, fears and inhibitions, which are as graves or tombs –

> The sun is freed from fears
> And with soft, grateful tears
> Ascends the sky.

The new-born infant of *Infant Sorrow* is already (like the youth and virgin) bound. No poem more completely shows Blake's originality, his power to distinguish what he really thought and felt from what he might conventionally be supposed to think and feel about his subject, in this instance a new-born infant. The primal energy of the new life that has entered the world is expressed in the words 'leapt', 'struggling', 'striving against'. A mysterious demonic power, its voice is not as yet recognizably human

> piping loud
> Like a fiend hid in a cloud.

The image of the 'naked new-born babe striding the blast' surely did, consciously or unconsciously, work with peculiar power on Blake's imagination. In the line

> Into the dangerous world I leapt

the stress falls equally on 'dangerous' and 'leapt'. The oppressive material mass of the world opposes the energy of life bursting in upon it. Yet, despite its inner power of life the new-born infant is 'helpless, naked' in the physical world, its freedom already impeded and restricted. The father's hands holding it, the swaddling bands binding it are already oppressive constrictions – foreshadowing the compulsions and coercions of adult experience, the chains and tombs spoken of in other poems of Blake.[1]

> Bound and weary I thought best
> To sulk upon my mother's breast.

The stress falls with particular emphasis on 'sulk'. 'Sulk' is unusually shocking here as being 'upon my mother's breast', where the infant is supposed to find content – and, no doubt, naturally does, as in the great passage about the mother and infant in Book 2 of *The Prelude*.

Clearly then Blake – the Blake of the great *Songs of Experience* – takes his place somewhere between Shakespeare and not only the poet Wordsworth but the later great English novelists, in particular Dickens and Lawrence. The remarkable originality of Blake shows itself specifically in the recovery of an imaginative-creative (or Shakespearian) use of the English language in what was still the 18th century.

III

Coleridge's imagination, too, we can see from some of his poetry, as well as from his criticism, was profoundly affected by Shakespeare. The comparison between Coleridge's criticism (with which we may associate De Quincey's Note on the Knocking at the Gate

---

[1] Cf. Mr Dombey, the man of money, weighed down with his 'heavy gold watch-chain' at the funereal christening of his son, or Mr Barnacle – 'He wound and wound folds of white cravat round his neck as he wound and wound folds of tape and paper round the neck of his country' – or the great financier Merdle feeling his cuffs as if conscious that they are, or should be, hand-cuffs, or Pip uncannily conscious of a prison taint hanging about himself, even when set up as a 'London gentleman'. There are no end of images of similar significance in Dickens.

in *Macbeth*) and Johnson's reveals the change. Coleridge read Shakespeare with new kinds of interest and insight. It had become possible to read Shakespeare more imaginatively, unconstricted by 18th-century preconceptions about language. Coleridge read Shakespeare not only with his new kind of introspective interest, his interest in the workings of the mind, in particular the creative process itself, but also with his imaginative insight into the metaphorical nature of Shakespearian poetry and in consequence a perception of the kind of unity, an 'organic unity', which is characteristic of a Shakespearian dramatic poem.

But there is the evidence also of some of Coleridge's own poetry. Shakespeare has (I think) had at least as much to do with *The Ancient Mariner*, with the workings of Coleridge's imagination in that poem, as have the ballads and tales of voyages of exploration and discovery. The exploration that interests Coleridge here is, of course, as much into strange regions of the mind as into distant seas and far latitudes. The Mariner's hallucinations have clearly the same cause as Macbeth's, the sense of guilt working on the imagination.

That the shooting of the bird should be felt as a crime, a fell deed that cannot be undone, and as somehow a sacrilegious act, is surely not difficult to understand. Blake, who said 'Everything that lives is holy', would have felt it to be so. Several of Blake's moments of vision in *Auguries of Innocence* express imaginatively, in sharply compact proverbial form, horror at the killing of even the minutest living creature, the apprehension that such an act will inevitably produce repercussions throughout the universe, Judgement from the Heavens.

> Kill not the moth or butterfly
> For the Last Judgement draweth nigh.

The bird that breaks the isolation of the ship in the region of ice and snow, offering companionship, is a living creature, the mystery of life (not simply a sociable presence).

> As if it had been a Christian soul
> We hailed it in God's name.

Of course, Coleridge's own deep-rooted personal sense of loneliness, his need for love and companionship, must have had much to do with the feeling in the poem ('Alone, alone, all all alone . . .'). That sense of personal loneliness comes out in several of his most intimate informal poems (*This Lime-Tree Bower my Prison*, *Frost at Midnight*). The Albatross is another such 'companionable form' as is the 'fluttering stranger' in the grate in *Frost at Midnight* which (as he recollects in that poem) had once had a portentous significance for himself as a boy at school 'in the great city pent', an orphan deprived of his childhood home in his native village of Ottery St. Mary. The image of a lost child ('upon a lonesome wild') crops up unexpectedly again in the great *Dejection Ode*. The lost or orphan or oppressed child recurs throughout the novels as well as the poetry of the 19th century, one of the symbols of the individual life in the world.

The Mariner's crime, however, finally produces, as Macbeth's does, a more radical isolation than anything the Mariner had experienced before, even when the ship was isolated in the region of ice. Not only does his crime separate him from his fellow-men on the ship but his sense of guilt produces in himself a revulsion against life itself, the miracle of life he has violated, a nightmarish horror and disgust for living creatures.

> Yea, slimy things did crawl with legs
> Upon the slimy sea.

It is no doubt these same sea-creatures that by an accident of moonlight are suddenly seen (our eyes opened – cf. *Biographia Literaria*, chapter 14) as strangely beautiful and lovable, releasing the springs of love.

> O happy living things! no tongue
> Their beauty might declare;
> A spring of love gushed from my heart
> And I blessed them unaware . . .
> The self-same moment I could pray.

Simultaneously the slain body of the Albatross, the burden of his guilt, falls from the Mariner, as in the *Pilgrim's Progress* (perhaps another unconscious reminiscence) the burden falls from Christian. These particular events are more like some of the miraculous events in the last plays of Shakespeare than they are like anything in *Macbeth*.

We recall, however, 'Macbeth doth murder sleep' and Macbeth's lines about sleep, when we find again in Coleridge's poem, as in Shakespeare, that sleep is associated with spiritual, as well as physical, healing, restoration and re-creation and is spoken of as a blessed gift from Heaven. The being is renewed or re-born in 'natural' sleep.

> O sleep it is a gentle thing
> Beloved from pole to pole
> To Mary queen the praise be given
> She sent the gentle sleep from Heaven
> That slid into my soul.

It is followed by the refreshing and restoring rain. Again, as in the strange restoration scenes in *Lear* and in the last plays, we find that the influence of sleep is assisted by the therapeutic influence of music – heard (as in *The Tempest*[1]) in the air. There could be no such singing birds over the tropic seas except in a dream or vision.

> Sometimes a'dropping from the sky
> I heard the sky-lark sing;
> Sometimes all little birds that are,
> How they seemed to fill the sea and air
> With their sweet jargoning.
>
> And now 'twas like all instruments
> Now like a lovely flute;
> And now it is an angel's song
> That makes the heavens be mute.

Yet Coleridge's Mariner, it seems, is never entirely freed. The agony returns again and again, nightmare states of horror and sense of unreality. His experience proves less purgatorial than (as in *Macbeth*) a recurring Hell from which there seems to be no deliverance. Coleridge's deep-seated personal trouble, perhaps, could not be resolved by him in the poem – though, at the end, the Mariner returns to his own country, recognized joyfully as familiar –

---

[1] Cf. also the strange things that happen to the ship in *The Tempest* (e.g. the Boatswain's narration in the last scene of the play).

> Oh! dream of joy! is this indeed
> The light-house top I see?
> Is this the hill? is this the kirk?
> Is this mine own country? —

returns also (in wish-fulfilment at least) to the traditional pieties
of the village community (Ottery St. Mary?)

> To walk together to the kirk
> In a goodly company!

In the line of the great novels the successor of *The Ancient
Mariner* is, in some of its aspects, Conrad's *The Shadow Line*.
The Shadow Line is the greater imaginative achievement, more
complex and subtle and, in its insight into the human mind and
situation, more searching. The essential interest in both works is
psychological and not simply an interest in happenings that
appear to be supernatural. But in *The Shadow Line* the youthful
Captain's shock of sensing that there is something queer about
his first command and the eerie atmosphere about the ship that
later develops ominously are traced and subtly analysed as the
effects of something in the minds of some of the crew. The feeling
that the becalmed and fever-stricken ship in the tropical Gulf of
Siam is under a spell or curse is discovered to be reducible to their
simple sailors' superstitious feelings about that rum customer, the
previous Captain, down there at the bottom of the China sea
exerting a sinister influence still on the fortunes of the ship. This
dreadful unnerving feeling (his successor, the youthful Captain,
discovers) has to be vigorously combated if the ship is to be
brought through the perils of the Gulf. The ship is brought
through, in the end, against all the odds, through inconceivable
horrors, by strength of character, traditional discipline, loyalty of
man to man and to the ship, a hard-won triumph of the human
spirit. In both works — poems, I had almost said — the ship be-
calmed on the tropic sea is as if enchanted, arousing certainly a
'feeling analogous to the supernatural', though a natural physical
phenomenon not uncommon in the days of sailing-ships.

> Day after day, day after day,
> We stuck, nor breath nor motion;

> As idle as a painted ship
> Upon a painted ocean.

It may be less certain, but not perhaps fanciful, to suggest that the ghost scenes in *Hamlet* have had something to do with some of the details producing the uncanny 'atmosphere' of *Christabel* ('Is the night chilly and dark?' 'the crowing cock'), the shudder from both the icy cold and the apprehension of ghostliness, the heightened attention to minute details ('the one red leaf, the last of its clan,' that dances a ghostly dance in the air), the sense of the presence of something that may conceivably be menacingly evil. Coleridge knows also how to make use of vagueness; our vague fears are the most unmanageable and, therefore, powerful.[1] Coleridge's own commentary on the ghost scenes in *Hamlet* is especially interesting in relation to the new 'romantic' poetry he was inaugurating.

'... the ghost-seers were in a state of cold or chilling damp from without, and of anxiety inwardly. It has been with all of them as with Francisco on his guard, – alone, in the depth and silence of the night; – 'twas bitter cold, and they were sick at heart, and *not a mouse stirring*. The attention to minute sounds, – naturally associated with the recollection of minute objects, and the more familiar and trifling, the more impressive from the unusualness of their producing any impression at all – gives a philosophic pertinency to that last image; but it has likewise its dramatic use and purpose. For its commonness in ordinary conversation tends to produce the sense of reality ...'

It seems that the dream poetry of the 19th century, poetry 'made out of our dreams' (as Yeats said), began with Coleridge's opium dreams or reveries (e.g. *The Circassian Love Chant* and *Kubla Khan*), as also did the notion of poetry as magic, having its ancient origin in the practice of magic, chants and incantations, trances and prophesies, words thought of as having magical (as well as musical) powers. But the dream poetry of the 19th century is another matter. What concerns me here is to suggest that the

---

[1] Cf. in *The Ancient Mariner*, the line

> The mariners gave it biscuit-worms

was deliberately altered by Coleridge to

> It ate the food it ne'er had ate.

new poetry around 1800 extended the conception of the nature of the human mind and thereby opened up new possibilities for the novel. Wordsworth could speak of 'the mystery, the depth of human souls' and Coleridge, too, makes a creative analysis of his own state of mind, the nature and causes of his dejection, in the great *Dejection Ode*. We find the great novels of the 19th century exploring states of mind, human experience in depth, the motivation and perplexities of human individuals, beyond anything in 18th century literature (though Richardson and Rousseau are certainly pioneers) or in any literature since Shakespeare (unless, perhaps, Racine).

Note on *Dejection: an Ode*

Coleridge's *Dejection: an Ode* begins in the tone of familiar easy conversation. In its closeness throughout to the idiom and movement of living speech it is much more Shakespearian than Miltonic, and it is Coleridge's most complete expression of a whole complex state of mind, the presence of analytic thought, the presence of deep feeling about (paradoxically) his inability to feel, to respond as formerly to the beauty of external nature, which is nevertheless as exquisitely perceived as ever. A storm in nature (the signs of the imminence of which he notes in the sky, 'its peculiar tint of yellow green') might, he hopes, rouse him, if anything could, from his dejection, a lethargy of soul, a dull heavy damp depression (described by him very particularly).

> Might startle this dull pain, and make it move and live.

His perception of the details of external nature, like his description of his inner condition, is as exact and as delicately sensitive as ever. But

> I see, not feel, how beautiful they are.

The fountains, the sources of life and joy, are in himself and are blocked. He diagnoses his condition as a failure of the imagination – 'my shaping spirit of Imagination'. The storm in nature, when it breaks out and rages, a grand performance, like some universal symphony or tragic spectacle on the stage of a universal theatre, fails to rouse him, leaves him unmoved. His last hope gone, himself past cure, he wishes the 'Lady' the joy which only the pure and innocent heart can know. But, paradoxically, in expressing the poet's personal sense of failure, the poem itself is (as I said) Coleridge's completest expression of his whole mind and being, the whole man speaking, and it expresses also his fundamental faith in the imagination. The poem is a great example of a poetic triumph wrung from a sense of personal defeat.

IV

The Shakespearian characteristics developing in Keats's poetry up to its climax (in the *Ode to Autumn* and, finally, in the great fragment of a revised *Hyperion*) are generally acknowledged. They show themselves specifically as the way Keats is drawing more and more on the strength of the language. It is a development not only out of the Spenserian or Miltonic modes but out of the luxuriating ('the pleasant smotherings') of the larger proportion of his early poetry into a use of language that may justly be described as more Shakespearian – or more fully and strongly Keatsian, a wonderfully quick maturing.

In the early poems up to and including *Endymion* (if we can speak of early and late in regard to the poetic production of so short a time as Keats was granted) the reader is first amazed by the richness of the poet's sensuous endowment, a sensibility that shows itself in a wealth of sensuous perceptiveness comparable only to that of the young Shakespeare or of Lawrence. The resemblances in this respect between Keats and Lawrence are as notable as those other resemblances between Blake and Lawrence. But in the early poems of Keats this sensuous wealth, in contrast to the young Shakespeare's, is more of a split profusion, a waste fertility, indulged and, as yet, undisciplined. The reader, at first delighted, soon finds he has had enough for the time being, cannot go on reading for long at one time because of this too muchness. In the youthful plays of Shakespeare there is already more variety and surprise, more force and vitality, more 'wit' in the copiousness and fertility of the imagery itself, as well as, of course, an organizing and controlling dramatic purpose and a wide range of comic and tragic scenes of human life. Nevertheless, the resemblances between Keats and Shakespeare have begun to show already in the early Keats as some of the qualities that are about to develop so suddenly into those of the greater Keats. They are not simply a matter of conscious or unconscious reminiscence of Shakespeare. They arise from the emergence of a Keatsian individuality (character and intelligence, as has often been re-marked, as well as sensibility), which the Spenserian spell (as later, in the first *Hyperion*, also the Miltonic) to some extent arrests and impedes rather than fosters. We remember that the young Shakespeare, too, was susceptible to the Spenserian music. But we need only place side by side some of the lines from *A Midsummer Night's Dream* (or from *Love's Labour's Lost* or *Romeo and Juliet*) to show that the youthful Keats and the youthful Shakespeare are often more like one another than they are like Spenser.

Here are a few lines from *A Midsummer Night's Dream* that will recall whole passages of the poetry of that play.

> More tuneable than lark to shepherd's ear
> When wheat is green, when hawthorn buds appear . . .
> The seasons alter; hoary headed frosts
> Fall on the fresh lap of the crimson rose . . .
> And sometimes lurk I in a gossip's bowl,
> In very likeness of a roasted crab;
> And when she drinks, against her lips, I bob,
> And on her wither'd dewlap pour the ale . . .
> As wild geese that the creeping fowler eye
> Or russet-pated choughs many in sort
> Rising and cawing at the gun's report.

Here (rather more fully) are some lines extracted from the early Keats that have already something of a Shakespearian quality – in the movement as much as in the imagery.

> Large dock leaves, spiral foxgloves, or the glow
> Of the wild cat's eyes, or the silvery stems
> Of delicate birch trees . . . (*Calidore*)
> A pigeon tumbling in clear summer air;
> A laughing school-boy, without grief or care,
> Riding the springy branches of an elm . . . (*Sleep and Poetry*)
> On one side is a field of drooping oats,
> Through which the poppies show their scarlet coats;

So pert and useless, that they bring to mind
The scarlet coats that pester human-kind.

(Epistle to My Brother George)

From *Endymion, Book I*

Trees old, and young, sprouting a shady boon
For simple sheep; and such are daffodils
With the green world they live in . . .
                                    while the willow trails
Its delicate amber; and the dairy pails
Bring home increase of milk . . .
Are not our lowing heifers sleeker than
Night-swollen mushrooms? Are not our wide plains
Speckled with countless fleeces? Have not rains
Green'd over April's lap? . . .
Broad leaved fig trees even now foredoom
Their ripen'd fruitage; yellow girted bees
Their golden honeycombs; our village leas
Their fairest blossom'd beans and poppied corn;
The chuckling linnet its five young unborn,
To sing for thee; low creeping strawberries
Their summer coolness; pent up butterflies
Their freckled wings; yea, the fresh budding year
All its completions . . .

From *Endymion, Book IV* the Titianesque triumph of Bacchus
and Ariadne, with its rush and energy, as well as glowing colours,
will come to mind – the whole passage.

Like to a moving vintage down they came,
Crown'd with green leaves, and faces all on flame.

These passages of the young Shakespeare and the young Keats
have in common, besides their wealth of sensuous perceptiveness,
a youthful buoyancy, vitality, high spirits, gaiety that contrast
with the languorous music and dreamlike imagery of Spenser. The
actuality of the English country, in its seasons, breaks through the
Spenserian dream-world of Greek mythology or medieval ro-
mance, introduces a note of cool freshness that relieves the heavy
intoxicating atmosphere, the cloying luxuriousness and lushness

of so much of the early Keats. The stronger side of Keats's wonderful sensuous perceptiveness shows itself already occasionally in the language (as, for example, in the passages quoted above as comparable with the early Shakespeare) the immediate presence of the tangible and graspable, the sense of solidity and body, physical effort and movement, as well as rich, deep colours. Here already are the beginnings of Keats's firm, as well as sensitive, apprehension of the shapes and forms of the organic and inorganic things of the three-dimensional external world.

Keats's classic achievement is, of course, the *Odes*. These differ from the 18th century grandiloquent Miltonic odes in much the way in which Coleridge's *Dejection Ode* does. They express, discover or explore states of mind of the poet, as these change or develop in response to outward things and events, and in this respect they are in the same line of development as Coleridge's *Ode* and as passages in *The Prelude*. The *Ode to Autumn* should be regarded as yet a further development from the other *Odes* of Keats, requiring to some extent a different account, as presentation of the poet's sense of his subject as an object outside himself. But it can be said of all the *Odes* of Keats that, out of the trouble and perplexity of his personal existence – including the shadow of his brother's, if not his own, suffering and death – as well as out of his own immense capacity for enjoyment of life, Keats has made these works of art. They are so fine as art – as choice and arrangements of words – in being so fine as renderings of the inner pressures and tensions of his personal experience. (Coleridge's 'the balance and reconciliation of opposite and discordant qualities' would seen to apply with special felicity to the *Odes* of Keats – as it does also to Yeats's *Sailing to Byzantium*.) As already the *Dejection Ode* does, the *Odes* of Keats may justly be said to anticipate the analysis or, rather, the embodyings of complex states of mind in the great novels of the 19th century. There is a relationship here again between some of the poetry of the early 19th century and both the Shakespearian soliloquys on the one hand and the inner debates in the great novels on the other.

Blake, Wordsworth and Coleridge had already invoked what they called the Imagination. Keats further explores, in and through the poetry of the *Ode on a Grecian Urn* and the *Ode to a Nightingale*, the problems of what the Imagination can and cannot do.

The poet contemplates the urn, in itself a lifeless object, motionless, silent, cold to the touch and, as he does so, the pictures on it come to life in his imagination. This is then how art works – on the imagination. Perplexing questions both of the nature of art and of life are aroused. The poem develops as a delicate balancing and weighing up of art and life over against one another (in a way that may remind the modern reader of the tension and difficult poise between opposites in Yeats's *Sailing to Byzantium*). The relationship between art and life is, if not worked out, exhibited in its subtle complexity in the *Ode on a Grecian Urn*. The poem leaves us with its problem or at least with the urn that teases us 'out of thought' – and also with the sad sense that neither art nor life can be completely satisfying. The urn remains, having a certain permanence. But so also does the sad recognition of the transience of life.

> When old age shall this generation waste
> Thou shalt remain.

Hence the elegiac note in the poem, especially towards the end. The urn with its pictures is, after all, a 'cold pastoral'.

Keats is, of course, no 'aesthete'. What he 'experiences as beauty' is, judging from his poetry, much more like Blake's 'Exuberance is beauty' than the languorous, often deathlike beauty of the pre-Raphaelite and other poets of the late 19th century. In the *Ode on a Grecian Urn* Keats is not simply expressing a wish to substitute Art for Life. He recognizes a living relationship between the two, and it is this relationship he is exploring and testing in the poem. The relationship is there discovered to depend on the workings of the imagination, the creative power that the human mind had been discovered (or rediscovered) to have. It is by means of the imagination that art, in some sense, liberates us from the temporal, transcends or defeats time. But it proves to be an equivocal victory. Art is discovered to have its limitations also, though they are different from those of life. The imagination can only do so much, and also it easily slips into becoming indistinguishable from mere fancy. The truth of the imagination can lapse into the deceptions of fancy, when not controlled by the perceived facts of existence, the recognition that things are as they are.

It may be worth looking again here at this poem in some detail.
The picture on the urn, then (to go back to the beginning of the
Ode), comes to life in the imagination and, in so far as it does so,
is no longer simply a picture. The motionless and silent picture
has already communicated something beyond itself, the sense of
life, the movement, the turmoil, the turbulence of active physical
life –

> What mad pursuit? What struggle to escape?

– though we do not know what it is about. Again, the unheard
music, the music the silent pipes on the silent picture are imagined
to be playing, is imagined to be sweeter than any music the sensual
ear is capable of hearing. (Cf. 'The unheard music hidden in the
shrubbery' in *Burnt Norton* – as well as the passage, which Keats
himself would have known, about the music of the spheres in *The
Merchant of Venice* – 'We cannot hear it.') The imagination is
here conceived as superior to the senses – as Blake, Wordsworth
and Coleridge had already conceived.

Further, the pictures on the urn, with the urn itself, have lasted
through centuries of change ('slow time'), outlasted generations
of the living. The moment of life arrested in the picture has been
given a certain permanence. The spring season has become an
eternal spring by having been made a picture – so long as the urn
lasts, at least, and there are human imaginations for the picture to
work on. The trees, because pictures of trees, are unfading, can
'never be bare'. Even so, there is that continuing note of sadness
in the poem, the presence of the consciousness of the transience
of our life. Still, art is discovered in the poetry to have (unlike
human life) an eternal quality or at least to suggest a notion of
eternity.

But there would be disadvantages in being a picture – even if it
were possible to be both alive and at the same time a picture as the
young lovers are here imagined (or fancied) to be.

> Bold Lover, never, never canst thou kiss,
> Though winning near the goal.

There can be no fulfilment such as is possible in life, no fulfilment
of that kind.

> Yet, do not grieve;
> She cannot fade, though thou hast not thy bliss,
> For ever wilt thou love, and she be fair!

The compensation is that she will be eternally young and he will eternally love. At least, in the imagination of the poet who contemplates their picture on the urn, they are so. There is, therefore, a sense in which art transcends the temporal. But, as the poem goes on to discover, this victory won by art over time is only partial as well as equivocal. The lovers are in fact long dead and 'old age shall this generation waste'.

For a few glorious lines, indeed (in stanza 3), the note of the poetry becomes fully triumphant.

> Ah, happy, happy boughs! that cannot shed
> Your leaves, nor ever bid the Spring adieu;
> And, happy melodist, unwearied,
> For ever piping songs for ever new;
> More happy love! more happy, happy love!
> For ever warm and still to be enjoy'd,
> For ever panting, and for ever young.

The trees are eternally in their spring beauty, the musician ('unwearied') will never be subject to the fatigues of the flesh, and above all the girl will be 'for ever young'. We have forgotten we are looking at a picture – such is the power of art working on the imagination. The lovers on the urn are momentarily imagined to enjoy all the advantages with none of the disadvantages, both of being art and of being fully alive. Indeed in this realm of the imagination (or the imagination losing itself in pure fancy) they seem to have passed beyond both all the limitations of art and all the limitations of life.

The note of triumph is there, certainly, in this poem, but also, never far absent in this same poem, the elegiac note. We who contemplate the urn (poet and readers) are unlike the pictures on the urn, subject to time and change. Even as the poet is saying 'For ever wilt thou love, and she be fair' he evidently knows well enough that for mortal creatures it cannot be so.

But for the moment the poet has forgotten or would wish to forget the girl is a picture. She has changed into a living, breathing creature, 'warm' and 'panting'. She has, in his imagination, broken away from the urn which nevertheless remains cold to the touch. Such is the power of the work of art – or of the imagination responding to the work of art – that in the imagination she has become 'life' not 'art'. But whoever lives and enjoys must pay the penalties of living, must suffer the ills that flesh is heir to – 'a burning forehead and a parching tongue' – must also suffer satiety ('cloyed'). So this wonderful stanza ends with that disenchanting recognition, an abrupt return to the actualities of the human condition. (Cf. the conclusion of the *Ode to a Nightingale*.)

But there is another picture on the urn. The poet (as it were) walks round the urn or turns it to look at the picture, on the other side, of the ritual procession. The priest in this picture is 'mysterious' not simply because priests, at least ancient ones, are so, to the romantic imagination, but because the poet who contemplates the priest of the picture does not know who that priest is or anything about him or about anyone in that procession.

> Who are these coming to the sacrifice?
> To what green altar, O mysterious priest.

The people in the procession (with the soundless 'heifer lowing') have no existence outside the picture. We can know nothing of their background. They have no background; they exist only on the surface of the urn. It would be as irrelevant and as futile to ask about their family or social background as to ask 'How many children had Lady Macbeth?' If they were living people (the people, perhaps, who were originally portrayed in the picture) they would have come from some town (not in the picture) to which they would return. To imagine such a town (as the poet proceeds to do in the poem) is to imagine it deserted of its inhabitants, empty and silent. Once again, in this poem, the note of sadness, elegiac and nostalgic, comes uppermost. The inhabitants of the little town, the people visible in the picture, will never return to it, never find home, remain for ever, as if enchanted figures in a picture, frozen in an eternity of art. The little town, not in the picture, will remain for ever emptied and deserted. This is the condition in which the poet sadly imagines it. Of course, the actual people portrayed in the picture 2,000 years ago, if they were actual people, would no doubt have returned to their town after the festival. Even so, these people of 2,000 years ago and their 'little town' would have long since dissolved into dust. Only the urn remains.

So we are back with the urn and with the perplexing problems of the relationship between art and life which it stirs. The lifeless object, silent and cold does, nevertheless, 'tease us out of thought as doth eternity', beyond where thinking can go (possibly, to a reality of imagination beyond the mere abstractions of thought).

> When old age shall this generation waste
> Thou shalt remain.

(Cf. 'No hungry generations tread thee down.') But if we recall the whole poem, what remains is not only the 'silent form', 'the cold pastoral', which at the end we return to, but the poem itself, the effect of the pictures on the urn on the imagination, the un-heard music heard by the imagination, the lovers who become in the imagination 'for ever young', the spring trees for ever unfading. The silent and cold object will continue to have this power to set the imagination going, to produce poetry. Though 'old age shall this generation waste', the work of art can save something from time, can catch a moment of life and lift it out of the stream of transience into the realm of the creative imagination. Much is lost, but it would have been lost in any case inevitably. The artist seizes those aspects of his subject or object which strike him as its essential aspects and by making them into art gives them such permanence as art has. These moments of life can be brought if not to life again, to imagined life.

The assertion with which the *Ode on a Grecian Urn* concludes – 'Beauty is Truth, Truth Beauty' – appears to have attracted as much attention or at least discussion as the whole poem. By itself the phrase seems to say no more than Keats says in the prose of one of his letters, 'What the imagination seizes as beauty must be truth.' It makes explicit what might be gathered from the whole poem, that Keats's conception of the imagination is more in accord with that of Blake, Wordsworth and Coleridge, and with what Lawrence says about art as being 'the truth about the real world', than with 'art for art's sake', 'beauty for beauty's sake'.

Clearly, then, the *Ode on a Grecian Urn* comes from – has its place in – the early 19th-century development of introspective-ness, the inner debate, which has, in its turn, partly to do also with the great novels that were to follow.

The same may be said of the *Ode to the Nightingale*, another Keatsian exploration into what the imagination can and cannot do. There is no point in attempting to go over again Mr. Leavis's analysis of this *Ode* (with his analysis of the other *Odes* in his *Scrutiny* essay), which for the first time revealed its complexity, the balancing in its poetry of alternating and contrary impulses. The impulse towards oblivion and extinction and the contrary impulse towards a possible fuller and richer conscious life equally derive their force from the poet's consciousness of the limitations and disabilities inseparable from the human condition, his acute consciousness of suffering and death. Keats in the *Odes* is still seeking to discover what can be done to evade or, perhaps, in some way 'transcend' the harsher facts of human existence that are only fully faced in tragedy, supremely so in the great Shake-spearian tragedies.

I am here mainly concerned, however, with noticing the recovery and renewal of Shakespearian elements and qualities in this poetry of the early 19th century that precedes the great novels. To begin with there are again discernible specific recol-lections of Shakespearian dramatic poetry transmuted (as in certain of Blake's poems) in Keats's poems. I do not think it fanciful to suggest that in the *Ode to a Nightingale* recollections of *Antony and Cleopatra* – or at least of the poetry of Cleopatra's luxurious dying – have been incorporated in Keats's total imaginative experience –

> Now more than ever seems it rich to die.

There is the interplay on 'mortal' and 'immortal' in that Shake-spearian scene which begins with the 'blunder' of the clown (the countryman with his basket of figs) in warning of the deadly asp ('his biting is immortal') and which is developed in Cleopatra's dying speech –

> I have
> Immortal longings in me.

In Keats's *Ode* it has been caught up (it may be suggested) in

Thou wast not born for death, immortal bird.

(Likewise, the Clown and 'Royal Egypt, Empress' may have been, at least unconsciously, recalled in Keats's

In ancient days by Emperor and Clown.)

There is Cleopatra's

Now no more
The juice of Egypt's grape shall moist this lip.

which so poignantly, in the imminence of death, evokes the fullness of sensuous life, the life of the earth (with 'the basket of figs', etc.). The line may certainly be paralleled by

Can burst joy's grape against his palate fine

in the *Ode on Melancholy*, another Keatsian poem in which the death wish is powerful. But it may also be paralleled, in its total developed effect, by almost the whole of the second stanza of the *Ode to a Nightingale*

O, for a draught of vintage! that hath been
Cool'd a long age in the deep-delvèd earth,
Tasting of Flora and the country green,
Dance, and Provençal song, and sunburnt mirth!
O for a beaker full of the warm South,
Full of the true, the blushful Hippocrene,
With beaded bubbles winking at the brim,
And purple-stainèd mouth.

The 'draught of vintage' or the 'beaker full of the warm South' is at first like Cleopatra's 'juice of Egypt's grape', the sensuous fullness of life, the life of the earth, and it evokes with it the peasants dancing in the grape-harvest of the Mediterranean South. It is so, at least, until the conclusion of the same stanza when it changes abruptly into its opposite, an intoxication that sinks us into oblivion ('dissolve and quite forget').

What it is from which the poet should so intensely wish to 'fade far away, dissolve and quite forget' becomes present, as actuality, in the unenchanted poetry of the third stanza – growing old, falling sick and dying and having to witness these painful conditions in others, the world as one great hospital (as some part of it always in fact is). This is what accounts for the intense concern in the poem to find a possible avenue of escape or liberation from the pain and suffering that attends human life, not simply the poet's personal suffering but that of others who are dear to him. Hence, again, the concern in the poem with what the imagination may be able, or not able, to do – 'Though the dull brain perplexes and retards' – in relation not only to the fact of suffering but also to the human capacity to live and enjoy. In this testing of the capabilities of the imagination, Keats seems to arrive, through the poetry of the *Ode*, somewhere near the kind of distinction Coleridge makes between the Fancy (which 'cheats') and the Imagination (as truthful insight into a given real state of things).

For example, in stanza 5, the poet standing in darkness 'cannot see what flowers are at my feet'. Yet his imagination, as he listens in darkness to the nightingale singing 'of summer', evokes at this point in the poem the actual English summer that he cannot in fact see, not a dream or a fairyland, but summer as it actually is in the meadows and woods. (In this respect this stanza recalls from the first stanza the 'plot of beechen green and shadows numberless' in which the bird sings 'of summer'.) The unseen flowers and their surroundings are seen, not with the corporal eye, but with the imaginative eye, seen as they actually are in summer. They are in fact actually there, at his feet, though unseen.

> The grass, the thicket, and the fruit-tree wild;
>   White hawthorn, and the pastoral eglantine;
>   Fast fading violets cover'd up in leaves;
>   And mid-May's eldest child,
>   The coming musk-rose, full of dewy wine,
>   The murmurous haunt of flies on summer eves.

This is no dream or fantasy but the rich full reality of summer (though again there is the suggestion at its end of drowsiness or intoxication as an effect of the atmosphere of summer eves).

The *Ode to a Nightingale* has, of course, also its suggestions of faery-land, its magic. The bird itself has become for the poet, at least momentarily, a faery-spirit ('light-winged Dryad of the trees') leading him on by its singing into an otherworld realm.

There is the note of enchantment recurring throughout the poem. There is the recurrent hypnotic music. But there is actuality also, never far absent or for long – painful in stanza 3 (the world as a hospital), delightful in stanza 2 (the Mediterranean peasants dancing) and stanza 5 (the English summer). Even though the delightful actualities are elsewhere or out of sight, they become momentarily vivid and immediate to the imagination. Finally there is, after the maximum enchantment of the concluding lines of the penultimate stanza (stanza 7), the desolating utter disenchantment of the return to the actual present in the last stanza.

It is peculiarly significant that it is exactly at that moment earlier in the poem, at the conclusion of stanza 5, when the sense of the rich fullness of actual summer in the meadows and woods is at its maximum that the death wish reasserts itself (at the beginning of stanza 6) with its maximum compulsive power.

> Now more than ever seems it rich to die.

There is here, perhaps, something of Othello's

> If it were now to die
> 'Twere now to be most happy; for I fear
> My soul hath her content so absolute
> That not another comfort like to this
> Succeeds an unknown fate.

We remember that Othello, too, has his magic and his Othello music. But the resemblance is much more with the poetry of Cleopatra's dying. To die a Cleopatra-like death, listening to the singing of the nightingale, would be to experience a kind of luxury in dying. It would be a conscious experiencing of dying, but (significantly) 'without pain'. To be experiencing is, of course, still to be living. It would in fact be an experiencing not of dying but of dreamily sinking into oblivion listening to the singing of the nightingale. Then comes the sudden recognition in the poem that to be in fact dead would be no longer to be conscious, no longer to hear the nightingale, to have 'ears in vain', to have become a senseless 'sod'. (Cf. Yeats's 'deafer and dumber and deader than a fish'.)

But Cleopatra (we may recall) has 'immortal longings', her death is to be for her a marriage in death, or beyond death, with

Antony. Keats, too, at this point in the poem, appears to seek some possibility of some way of transcending death and to find that the nightingale does so. So strong indeed is his wish that the mortal bird becomes an 'immortal bird'. Is this again the imagination lapsing into merely the fancy (that 'cheats')?

> Thou wast not born for death, immortal bird
> No hungry generations tread thee down.

The assertion is at least to this extent true (and not fancy) that in every century 'those dying generations' (in Yeats's phrase) the 'birds in the trees' are 'at their song'.

> (And sang within the bloody wood
> Where Agamemnon cried aloud.)

The singing of nightingales – though not these same nightingales – will continue, as the Grecian urn will 'remain',

> When old age shall this generation waste.

For Keats, however, the nightingale the poem is addressed to, the nightingale that 'Singest of summer in full-throated ease', has done more. It has worked on the poet's imagination to assist the creation of the poem. It may be said to have been productive of some cheating fancies as well as true imaginative insights. There are moments in the wonderful poem, indeed, when it works magic spells – or rather when the poet under its influence works magic with words –

> Charm'd magic casements, opening on the foam
> Of perilous seas, in faery lands forlorn.

There is in those lines, at its maximum, the note of enchantment that has haunted and bemused readers of this *Ode*. But already the word 'forlorn' (repeated in the final stanza with its sense of 'utterly lost') sounds the knell of its disintegration. The enchantment proves momentary only and breaks. As the nightingale flies away and is lost in the woods of night, as its music recedes into silence, the magic fails and leaves the poet himself 'forlorn', like one who has awakened out of a strangely beautiful dream or trance. He is brought back painfully to the actual present that seems left desolate, the hard bare world of fact. 'The Fancy cannot cheat so well . . . deceiving elf.' It is as if the bird itself becomes identified with fancy – a flight of fancy.

The word in the poem is Fancy, not Imagination. But, we may ask, is this fair to the poem itself as a whole? Have we not, we may ask, in the poem a work of imagination, 'the truth of the imagination', as well as within it, as one element in its structure, an interweaving play of fancy? Does not the poem itself arrive at the recognition that as soon as the imagination moves out of relation to actuality it becomes a mere play of fancy which then sooner or later inevitably collapses in what may prove to be a harsh and disagreeable disenchantment? But the strength of the *Ode to a Nightingale* is that it takes the reader who experiences it through the cycle that ends, within itself, in the disenchantment. The magic by means of which for enchanted moments the poet eludes (or transcends) his painful sense of the limitations and disabilities of the mortal condition is recognized within the poem itself before its end as having been illusory. Not that by any means all of the poem before the final stanza is simply enchantment. There are those strongly imagined actualities in it (including the enjoyments of the Mediterranean peasants dancing and the English summer).

Yet even in this final stanza of the *Ode to a Nightingale* there is a question or doubt which seems to permit a partial hope.

> Was it a vision, or a waking dream?
> Fled in that music: – Do I wake or sleep?

Was it merely fancy after all or was there in it, perhaps, something of 'the truth of the imagination'. (Cf. the concluding lines of *Prufrock* in which the return to what is ordinarily regarded as 'consciousness' after the dream or vision of the mermaids – or sirens – is a kind of death, a drowning.)

It may be said, at least, that the fact that the poet can ask these questions in the final stanza of the *Ode* shows that the waking consciousness has recovered, or is recovering, control. But the perfection of the 'art', the felicitous exactitude of the selection and arrangement of the words, everywhere throughout the whole poem, indicates that the poet has in these respects never lost control, that he has indeed been throughout in conscious control of his ever-changing experience, whether or not we are to describe it as more an imaginative experience than a flight of fancy. The 'art' is such that it could not have been 'done from the outside' as we may feel about some of the 18th-century Odes. It does not show that kind of artistic manipulation. The imagery and rhythms of Keats's *Ode*, within its strict form of formal ode, could only have arisen from his inner responses, from the pressures of living complex experience. A 'classic' art of this order could only be the expression of an inner maturity of mind, at least in process of formation, that has developed remarkably early in Keats (if we compare the *Odes* with Keats's earlier poetry). The *Ode to a Nightingale* is itself something like the flight of a bird, rising and falling, controlled by the life within, fluctuating with 'the strange irregular rhythm of life' which Henry James describes the novelist, too, as seeking to reproduce in his art.

But more significant than any recollections of Shakespearian poetry transmuted in the Keatsian imagination (such as we may also detect in Blake's *Poetical Sketches* or Coleridge's *Ancient Mariner*) is the development in Keats's poetry, as in Blake's *Songs of Experience*, of a Shakespearian creative use of the English language itself such as is un-characteristic of the 18th century, as well as of Milton, whom the 18th century imitated. This development in Keats's poetry culminates most impressively in the great fragment of a revised *Hyperion* which has the authentic note of great tragic poetry so rare since Shakespeare's. Among the *Odes* this Shakespearian (or English) strength in the creative use of language shows itself with most vigour and body in the *Ode to Autumn*.

But even in the *Ode on Melancholy* we find it coming out unexpectedly in the second stanza.

> But when the melancholy fit shall fall
> Sudden from heaven like a weeping cloud,
> That fosters the droop-headed flowers all,
> And hides the green hill in an April shroud.

'April shroud' (like Blake's 'marriage hearse' or 'sick rose') is the kind of startling combination of opposites that we recognize as also characteristically Shakespearian. The 'weeping cloud' is suddenly changed from being merely melancholy. As April rain, it 'fosters the droop-headed flowers', becomes refreshing, brings greenness. Though it 'hides' the hill, the hill is 'green'. The spring associations of April come together with the deathly associations of 'shroud'. The wonderful lines follow almost as a result of these suggestions of new life.

> Then glut thy sorrow on a morning rose,
> Or on the rainbow of the salt sand-wave,
> Or on the wealth of globed peonies.

'Glut' is not a musical word such as Tennyson would have chosen there, but it has vigour and it lends added force (two lines later) to 'globed' which in its turn gives a three-dimensional solidity to the image of peonies. 'Salt', too, gives a suggestion of savour to the freshness, airiness and colour of 'the rainbow of the salt sand-wave'. (Cf. *Ash-Wednesday*, 'the salt savour of the sandy earth'. Perhaps also there is here a recollection of Ariel's song, 'Come unto these yellow sands'.)

Though the *Ode on Melancholy* opens with the injunction 'No, no, go not to Lethe' the whole impulsion, the movement of the poetry itself, in the opening stanza is Lethewards. The effect the poetry produces, with its sleepy music and its imagery, is that of a heavy, drugged sensation, a poisonous beauty, a Garden of Proserpine night atmosphere (that recalls Spenser's rendering from Ovid of that classical garden in *The Faerie Queene*, Book 2, Canto 7) irresistibly compelling the senses towards sleep and death. It is repeated in the stanza that the effort must be to resist this, to keep awake, not allow 'the wakeful anguish of the soul' to be drowned. But the poetry itself is exactly what makes it hard to resist. The reader would have to resist the poetry itself, which overcomes him, drawing him overpoweringly downward with it, sinking luxuriously towards death and oblivion. The reversal in the second stanza is, therefore, the more surprising, the recovery of the life-ward impulse as it asserts itself in the sudden Shakespearian vitality of the language there. This vitality, this sense of a sensuous wealth of living experience, persists even in the concluding stanza, particularly in the gusto of

> his strenuous tongue
> Can burst Joy's grape against his palate fine.

The poem thus, on a smaller scale, embodies again the same conflict of mind, the same contrary impulsions, deathward and lifeward, of the *Ode to a Nightingale*.

The Shakespearian full-bodied vitality of the language informing and forming the imagery and movement of the *Ode to Autumn* was brought out in Mr. Leavis's analysis. There are other 19th-century poems about autumn in which that season is made an occasion for the poet's expressing his own personal melancholy moods. Tennyson's poems – and recurrent passages in poems – about late autumn, with its mouldering garden flowers, are musical expressions of his own somewhat morbid melancholia. Keats's *Ode to Autumn*, on the other hand, is the Ode which appears to be most completely not about himself. The poet's absorption in his subject here is such as to exclude his consciousness of his personal self (contrast 'My heart aches', etc.). We are presented not with the personal feelings of John Keats but with the autumn season as he observes it outside himself, a phase in the process of the year, the changing phenomena of the external world.

Yet this impersonal or objective strength of the *Ode to Autumn* is of the kind that implies Keats's personal acceptance of the fact not only of the cycle of the natural year but, with it, the whole process of change which inevitably involves death as well as birth. There is (in the first stanza) the fruition of late summer and early autumn, the abundance and weight of the ripening fruits of the earth. There are (in the second stanza) the labours of harvest, the countryman's and countrywoman's occupations, and rest after labour. There is (in the final stanza) already winter in the air, the clearing of the air and the bareness of the earth which are, in their turn, welcomed after the heavily rich atmosphere, the charged sense of earth's fruitfulness. We are made more conscious of the sky and less of the earth. But I have wondered why, in reading this final stanza about autumn changing into winter, I have found myself aware also of spring, as it seemed to me irrelevantly. I have found that other readers say this happens with them also. It is not surprising. It is not simply a misreading. Spring is in fact subtly suggested in the words of the text. When it is said

Speak not of spring, thou hast thy music too

we inevitably do think also of spring, the coming spring and its music, and cannot entirely dismiss it from our mind. The lambs spoken of in the text are now 'full-grown', but we inevitably think also of lambs, the new-born lambs of spring. When the birds are spoken of, even though they are the migrating birds of late autumn (and though late autumn has 'its music too') we can scarcely not think also of the birds of the spring and the music they make. When the poem introduces the small creatures ('the small gnats mourn') in the declining day of the declining year, the effect may naturally be to suggest further those other multitudes of tiny lives that, though in themselves ephemeral, will appear again in the new season. The clearance of the winter prepares also for new creation and (it is felt) has its place in the unending cycle. We may justly conclude, therefore, that in the *Ode to Autumn* Keats has put death in its place, without ignoring the fact of it, in the whole natural process. There is the autumn fulfilment, the year's maturing and fruition. There is thereafter the decline that follows harvest. But with the movement of the year into winter, a season which also has its characteristic beauty and splendour, there are (as expressed in that last stanza of the *Ode*), even while it is the beauty of the declining year which is being celebrated, hints and intimations also of the promise of spring again. The *Ode to Autumn*, in its rare kind of objectivity, its freedom from self-regardingness, may therefore truly be said to be as much a triumph of self-conquest as an artistic triumph, the purest and fullest celebration of autumn, as what in itself it is, in the English language.

But a still greater Keatsian triumph is the fragment of the revised *Hyperion*. Though only a fragment, broken off, it has the authentic note of great tragic poetry. The poets of the beginning of the 19th century have indeed the right to have it said of them that they brought the tragic note back again into English literature, if only occasionally, at moments in Blake, Wordsworth and here in Keats. This recovered presence of tragic experience is developed further in one or two of the great novels that followed in the 19th century, in *Wuthering Heights* and in the novels of George Eliot. It had been almost wholly absent from English literature since the great Shakespearian tragedies (though Johnson's view of the human condition at least verges on the tragic). Before working on his revised *Hyperion* Keats had, of course, been reading Dante (as Shelley also had been doing before his last remarkable fragment, *The Triumph of Life*), and his reading of Dante has noticeably had a good deal to do with its achieved freedom from the Miltonic mode which dominates the earlier *Hyperion*. But the note is at least as much like that of Shakespearian tragic poetry as it is Dantean. Keats's use of the English language here is the Keatsian equivalent of the characteristically Shakespearian, felt especially in the verse movement.

The passage I am thinking of particularly is, of course, the vision of Moneta. There are, for example, again those combinations of words with opposing associations – 'bright-blanched' (with, later in the passage, 'blank splendour'), 'an immortal sickness', 'a constant change', 'happy death'. These combinations of opposites are creative in their contexts in that a new perception is born from each, different from anything suggested by either of the two component words separately.

> Then saw I a wan face,
> Not pin'd by human sorrows, but bright-blanch'd
> By an immortal sickness which kills not;
> It works a constant change, which happy death
> Can put no end to; deathwards progressing
> To no death was that visage; it had past
> The lily and the snow.

The complex qualities focused in the vision of the face and, especially, the eyes of the goddess (later in the passage) are given poetic definition, the unimaginable becoming imaginable. The goddess of the vision chills with fear or would do so but for the luminous quality of her eyes which, though sightless, are felt to be compassionate. Her non-humanness is suggested partly through her associations with the planets and the non-human energies of the universe ('globed brain', 'electral changing', 'an immortal's sphered words', 'planetary eyes'). On the other hand, her associations with the moon contribute to suggest her mild or benignant aspects. Thus, though the poet would have 'fled away' from fear, he is 'held back' by the 'benignant light' of her eyes, the counteracting suggestion of pity (whether or not Keats was here conscious of the Aristotelian 'pity and fear').

> But for her eyes I should have fled away.
> They held me back, with a benignant light,
> Soft mitigated by divinest lids
> Half-closed, and visionless entire they seem'd
> Of all external things; – they saw me not,
> But in blank splendour, beam'd like the mild moon,
> Who comforts those she sees not, who knows not
> What eyes are upward cast.

There is throughout the whole passage a subtle interplay of the associations again of 'mortal' and 'immortal'. The face and eyes, as well as the words spoken by the goddess, are those of an immortal. Yet they are not dissociated altogether from tender human feelings (those of a mother).

> As near as an immortal's sphered words
> Could to a mother's soften . . .

Though the goddess is 'not pin'd by human sorrows' she is pined as humans are by sorrows. This much at least the immortal and the mortal have in common. Though the sorrows of an immortal are beyond the range of anything it is possible for a mortal to imagine, they both experience sorrows. Though the goddess suffers 'an immortal sickness which kills not', and though the sickness which mortals suffer kills, the goddess does suffer, as mortals do, sickness. As an immortal she is 'not born for death', but that is no happiness for an immortal sufferer; on the contrary, death for such a sufferer would indeed be 'happy death'.

If we say of this poetry that it is Shakespearian we are not implying that it is not wholly Keatsian; on the contrary it is more fully Keatsian than anything of the earlier Keats, more completely the whole man speaking from the whole of himself. There is a new authority in the voice, a new power and weight in the words and in their controlled movement which (as in great dramatic poetry) keeps close to that of spoken language. What has brought about this further maturing of Keatsian poetic art is certainly a further maturing of mind and character, an objectifying or depersonalizing of profoundly disturbing and painful personal experience, the attainment of a tragic vision of life. The poetry here is an authentic response, the product of the poet's complete exposure not only to the fact of his own personal suffering and the contemplated sufferings of others near to him, but, beyond these, to the fact of suffering humankind and indeed, ultimately, to suffering simply as a fact in the universe, a fact in the very nature of things.

The unveiled face of the goddess may perhaps have been suggested by – as it suggests – an ancient tragic mask or an ancient sculpture of a goddess or tragic muse (with a stone sculpture's blank eyes), an impersonation of Tragedy itself, in its essence, to the imaginative vision. But to discuss the passage in this way, as if it simply projected a visual image, a face with blank eyes, would be to leave out the complexity of the poetry, its subtly powerful communication of the sense of what we are accustomed to call 'tragic experience'. The poetry (as has been recognized) is that of a poet who has become able to view suffering and death as facts detached from his personal self and fate, to contemplate them (that is) as tragic art. Though what got written of this poem is a fragment, it is a fragment of greatness, a greater greatness than the classic *Odes*, perfect as (within their limits) these are.

CHAPTER TWO

WORDSWORTH: THE TALES OF *MARGARET* AND *MICHAEL*

'Cataracts and mountains are good occasional society,
but they will not do for constant companions.'
(Wordsworth – Letter to William Matthews,
November 7th, 1794)

I

Almost all of Wordsworth's living poetry was composed, or at least originated, in a single decade, between about 1795 and 1805 (the year in which the original version of *The Prelude* was completed). Though the tale of *Margaret* or *The Ruined Cottage*, one of Wordsworth's great poems, was incorporated in Book I of *The Excursion* (published 1814) it was composed in 1797–8, before the *Lyrical Ballads* (1798). Blake, of course, came even earlier, *The Songs of Innocence* (1789) and, his greatest poems, *The Songs of Experience* (1794). In their poems of original genius, Blake and Wordsworth (with whom we should associate also Coleridge) express a new vision not only of Nature but of Human Nature. Not only the work of the early 19th-century poets, Shelley, Keats, Byron, but the great achievements, later, of the novelists, Dickens, George Eliot and Lawrence became possible.

There is also, of course, the testimony of the accumulations of Wordsworthian nature verse – and prose. Much of it simply recalled for imprisoned urban dwellers the countryside and childhood. A small amount of it, including Arnold's and Tennyson's, is truly distinguished in a minor way, sensitive, delicate observation steeped in their personal moods. Hopkins's nature poems stand out, within their frame of dogmatic belief, as having their unique quality and value, though they are his lesser poems.[1] Hardy's poems, too, stand out, such is the integrity of Hardy's very individual character. In general it is evident that Wordsworth's poetry altered the way in which people look at nature.

[1] Hopkins's greater poems are those sonnets which render inner debate.

Nineteenth-century people, whether they themselves read Words-worth's poetry or not, became, without necessarily knowing it, Wordsworthians more or less.

But, more important, it is evident that around 1800 there was a remarkable development of interest in the individual and of intro-spectiveness, an exploratory interest in the workings of the individual mind. We need only compare Coleridge's criticism with Johnson's to see the difference. We find this change not only in the poets but in the development of the novel from the 18th-century novelists into an important modern art in *Mansfield Park* and *Emma*. It is not simply because it analysed but because it created a new conception of human nature that the poetry of Blake and Wordsworth (and some of the insights of Coleridge) had its most profound effect, as is borne out in the work of the great novelists.

II

The poems in which Wordsworth's poetry begins to break through, individual experience beginning to find individual expression, are *Guilt and Sorrow* (about 1794), *Lines left upon a Seat in a Yew-Tree* (1795) and *The Borderers* (1795–6). It is particularly in a Macbeth-like sense of a disturbed conscience and a consequent desolation of spirit that some of this poetry comes closer than Wordsworth's poetry as a whole does to an immediate sense of suffering, the sense of a mind that has undergone some recent painful and unsettling trouble.

The opening stanzas of *Guilt and Sorrow* produce for the first time in Wordsworth's poetry the sense of an individual imagina-tive experience. 'My rambles over Salisbury Plain (in 1793) put me ... upon writing this poem, and left on my mind imaginative impressions the force of which I have felt to this day.' The bleak wastes of moorland traversed by the solitary itinerant, the lines of road extending to the horizon, become symbolism; the outer desolation corresponds to an inner desolation associated with a sense of guilt, the haunting memory of a crime committed, driving the man on.

> On he must pace, perchance 'till night descend,
> Where'er the dreary roads their bare white lines extend.

There is his sense of lost bearings, the landmarks gone – the spire associated with the traditional faith of the community of his upbringing –

> the distant spire,
> Which oft as he looked back had fixed his eye,
> Was lost, though still he looked, in the blank sky.
> Perplexed and comfortless he gazed around.

There are images of sterility and of stormy darkness, as in *Macbeth*.

> And so he sent a feeble shout – in vain;
> No voice made answer, he could only hear
> Winds rustling over plots of unripe grain,
> Or whistling thro' thin grass along the unfurrowed plain.
> The crows rushed by in eddies.

There is the shock of coming upon a gibbet in a desolate place (a recollection of something that happened to the poet himself as a child, as recorded in *The Prelude*, Book 12).

> All he had feared from man, but roused a train
> Of the mind's phantoms.

Wordsworth had known these 'mind's phantoms' as Johnson had known the 'Melancholy's phantoms' of *The Vanity of Human Wishes*. The bustard 'Forced hard against the wind a thick unwieldy flight', an energy of individual life forcing itself through a resistant element (besides the particular and exact observation of 'thick unwieldy flight') is an image comparable to that of the girl with the pitcher[1] who 'seemed with difficult steps to force her way against the blowing wind'. There is no hint in *Guilt and Sorrow* – significant title – of the later Wordsworthian consolations, nature as a source of tranquillity and joy.

> All, all was cheerless to the horizon's bound.

In *Lines left upon a Seat in a Yew-Tree* (1795) there is again a sense of a wasted, sterile life finding, however, some kind of satisfaction in a desolate place and the absence of human companionship.

---

[1] Again *The Prelude*, Book 12.

> And with the food of pride sustained his soul
> In solitude . . .
> His only visitants a straggling sheep,
> The stone-chat, or the glancing sand-piper:
> And on these barren rocks, with fern and heath,
> And juniper and thistle, sprinkled o'er,
> Fixing his downcast eye, he many an hour
> A morbid pleasure nourished, tracing here
> An emblem of his own unfruitful life.

A landscape is largely what the imaginative eye makes it. In the poetry here, the delicately sensitive selection and noting of particular features of the observed place and its 'visitants' make of it 'an emblem of his own unfruitful life'.[1] The kind of pleasure is, however, marked self-critically – there is surely a relationship here between the Solitary and the poet himself – as, so far, 'a morbid pleasure' of a kind not to be indulged (cf. the melancholy Jaques in the forest of Arden).

> Stranger! these gloomy boughs
> Had charms for him.

But, as the poem goes on, 'the more distant scene', as he looks up and contemplates it, entering his mind from outside himself, is discovered to have a beneficent influence even on the morbid self-centred Solitary.

> And, lifting up his head, he then would gaze
> On the more distant scene, – how lovely 'tis
> Thou seest, – and he would gaze till it became
> Far lovelier, and his heart could not sustain
> The beauty, still more beauteous!

For a mind not narrowed and inhibited by pride and contempt arising from some shock of disillusion and loss of faith in his fellow-men, there is the possibility of becoming open to receive these influences –

> When nature had subdued him to herself –

[1] Cf. Edward Thomas.

influences of joy in natural beauty breaking through egoism, awakening the sympathies, restoring a sense of the true dignity of man. These impulses of joy, recorded throughout Wordsworth's poetry, often come as surprises, taking him unaware – 'My heart leaps up,' 'Surprised by joy' – though joy is 'in widest commonality spread'. It is only necessary to be open to receive them when they come – to cultivate 'a wise passiveness'. After the 18th-century emphasis on the 'social man' and conversation, Wordsworth is rediscovering the uses of solitude and contemplation for the individual soul – provided they are not of a morbid kind and restore, not narrow, the human sympathies.

The Borderers (1795–6) is Wordsworth's early attempt at a Shakespearian tragedy. As such it is inevitably a failure. But there are memorable lines and fragments of poetry in it which evidently come directly from the same disturbance of mind as *Guilt and Sorrow*. Reminiscent though these passages are of the great dramatic poetry of *Macbeth* and *Lear*, they are not simply so, they have an individual quality recognizable again as that of Wordsworth's earliest original poetry.

'Much about the same time, but a little after, Coleridge was employed in writing his tragedy of *Remorse*.' (Wordsworth's Preface to *The Borderers*.) Remorse is largely the subject also of *The Borderers*.

'As to the scene and period of action, little more was required for my purpose than the absence of established law and government, so that the agents might be enabled to act on their own impulses.'

In a later note to *The Borderers* Wordsworth says

'. . . there are no limits to the hardening of the heart and the perversion of the understanding to which they may carry their slaves. During my long residence in France, while the Revolution was rapidly advancing to its extreme of wickedness, I had frequent opportunities of being an eye-witness of this process and it was while that knowledge was fresh upon my memory that the tragedy of *The Borderers* was composed.'

The Godwinian rationalist Oswald exerts a fatal persuasiveness over the hero, Marmaduke, inducing him to crime.

> Companionship with One of crooked ways,
> From whose perverted soul . . .
>   I have heard
> Of some dark deed to which in early life
> His passion drove him.[1]

His attitude towards his dupe is unhumanly contemptuous.

> These fools of feeling are mere birds of winter
> That haunt some barren island of the north,
> Where, if a famishing man stretch forth his hand,
> They think it is to feed them.[2]

Wordsworth's personal sense of things having gone wrong, the
times out-of-joint, occasionally comes through the Shakespearian
(not here Miltonic) expression and movement with an authentic
and disturbing force.

> And yet, in plumbing the abyss for judgment,
> Something I strike upon which turns my mind
> Back on herself . . .
> Just as we left the glen a clap of thunder
> Burst on the mountains with hell-rousing force.
> This is a time, said he, when guilt may shudder . . .
>   Lacy! we look
> But at the surfaces of things; we hear
> Of towns in flames, fields ravaged, young and old
> Driven out in troops to want and nakedness;
> Then grasp our swords and rush upon a cure
> That flatters us, because it asks not thought:
> The deeper malady is better hid;
> The world is poisoned at the heart.[3]

A characteristically Wordsworthian episode, introducing a
trembling note of hopefulness in the midst of this despair, is that
of a beggar woman, the earliest of Wordsworth's vagrants, who
finds in the darkness a glow-worm.

> The darkness overtook me – wind and rain
> Beat hard upon my head – and yet I saw

---

[1] Act 1.   [2] Act 2.   [3] Act 2, Marmaduke speaking.

> A glow-worm, through the covert of the furze,
> Shine calmly as if nothing ailed the sky.

Desolate moorland is again congenial to the mood of the charac-
ters (and, as we may suppose, of the poet). Occasionally, minute
details and features of these moorland places register themselves
on the consciousness, coming directly from Wordsworth's
particular observation.

> Hush! – 'tis the feeble and earth-loving wind
> That creeps along the bells of the crisp heather.
> Alas! 'tis cold – I shiver in the sunshine...
> Here is a tree, ragged, and bent, and bare,
> That turns its goat's-beard flakes of pea-green moss
> From the stern breathing of the rough sea-wind;
> This have we, but no other company.

The recognition that 'what's done cannot be undone', that a
momentary act can have permanent and inescapable conse-
quences – nemesis – is expressed with an individual power in one
of the most striking passages, as if it had been experienced over
again in the poet's own life and imagination – as it is again to be
experienced and explored in the novels of George Eliot.

> Action is transitory – a step, a blow,
> The motion of a muscle – this way or that –
> 'Tis done, and in the after-vacancy
> We wonder at ourselves like men betrayed:
> Suffering is permanent, obscure and dark,
> And shares the nature of infinity.[1]

In contradiction to what Oswald goes on to say, the poetry in
which he says it expresses the power of remorse which cannot, as
he says it can, be willed away or be dissolved by 'thinking'.

> Remorse –
> It cannot live with thought; think on, think on,
> And it will die. What! in this universe,
> Where the least things control the greatest, where
> The faintest breath that breathes can move a world;

[1] Act 3.

What! feel remorse, where, if a cat had sneezed,
A leaf had fallen, the thing had never been
Whose very shadow gnaws us to the vitals.[1]

Two lines (spoken by Marmaduke) express the tormented mind that finds no end to its searching (cf. 'O the mind, the mind has mountains . . .').

Three sleepless nights I passed in sounding on,
Through words and things, a dim and perilous way.

These lines, which reappear, slightly modified, years later in *The Excursion* spoken there by the Solitary, come unmistakably out of Wordsworth's personal experience at a time when he himself had 'yielded up moral questions in despair' (cf. *The Prelude*, Book 12). At the conclusion of *The Borderers*, Marmaduke becomes a wanderer haunted Orestes-like by his guilt.

III

By the time he had completed *The Borderers*, however, Wordsworth was at work on his first great poetic achievement, the tale of *Margaret* or *The Ruined Cottage*. Originally composed 1797-8, it is another of the poems which precede the *Lyrical Ballads*. Much later it was incorporated in the first book of *The Excursion*.[2]

Already (even in the original version) there has been some distancing of the fact and actuality of the tragedy. There is no mistaking that the tale of the woman's sufferings has deeply affected the poet, such is the poignancy of the poetry, though there is no longer (as there is in *Guilt and Sorrow* and *The Borderers*) a near-identification of the character with the poet himself. Yet the tragedy has been made bearable, can be contemplated steadily, because it has receded into the past, become a tale of things remembered by an old man. There is the influence of

---

[1] Act 3.

[2] The passages quoted are taken from the poem as it now stands in *The Excursion*. Though not chosen for that reason, it cannot be an accident that they almost all prove to be passages that have remained very little altered by Wordsworth from what they were in the original 1797-8 version. (In a note dated 1843 Wordsworth says he was composing the poem as early as 1795, but after nearly 50 years even Wordsworth's memory can hardly be relied on. The evidence indicates 1797-8.)

the tranquil old man and there is the influence of the tranquil and
beautiful place. These influences calm the disturbed mind, as the
young man (the poet) listens to the old man telling his memories
of the place where there is a ruined cottage, the scene once of a
human tragedy. The tale is thus told by a tranquil old man in a
tranquil place where these things happened in the past. There is,
further, the weight and value of the contrast between the old man,
to whom the years have brought 'the philosophic mind', and the
young man still subject to 'wild varieties of joy and grief', not yet
grown into maturity, though the experience which is made into
the poem becomes itself part of his growth towards maturity.

The foreground, the immediate present in the poem, is there-
fore the experience of a place and the presence there of an old man.

> Unnoticed did I stand some minutes' space.
> At length I hailed him, seeing that his hat
> Was moist with water-drops, as if the brim
> Had newly scooped a running stream. He rose . . .[1]
>
>   'Tis,' said I, 'a burning day:
> My lips are parched with thirst, but you, it seems
> Have somewhere found relief.' He, at the word,
> Pointing towards a sweet-briar, bade me climb
> The fence where that aspiring shrub looked out
> Upon the public way.[2]

Besides the discovery of the well, the old man will provide re-
freshment and relief for the spirit also. But first the poetry conveys
the features and character of a particular place that has acquired a
special value because human lives have been lived there and have
left their traces. The plot of ground, now overgrown, has once
been cultivated by human hands. It yields some fruits still and the
now half-hidden well – 'shrouded with willow-flowers' – still
yields 'cool refreshment'.

>   It was a plot
> Of garden ground run wild, its matted weeds
> Marked with the steps of those, whom, as they passed
> The gooseberry trees that shot in long lank slips,

---

[1] *The Excursion*, Book 1. 443–6.
[2] 448–53. (Not in the 1797–8 version.)

> Or currants, hanging from their leafless stems,
> In scanty strings, had tempted to o'erleap
> The broken wall. I looked around, and there,
> Where two tall hedgerows of thick alder boughs
> Joined in a cold damp nook, espied a well
> Shrouded with willow-flowers and plumy fern.
> My thirst I slaked.[1]

The human associations of the place begin to re-assume form and definition in the old man's recollections.

>   'I see around me here
> Things which you cannot see: we die, my Friend,
> Nor we alone, but that which each man loved
> And prized in his peculiar nook of earth
> Dies with him, or is changed; and very soon
> Even of the good is no memorial left . . .'[2]

>   Beside yon spring I stood,
> And eyed its waters till we seemed to feel
> One sadness, they and I. For them a bond
> Of brotherhood is broken: time has been
> When, every day, the touch of human hand
> Dislodged the natural sleep that binds them up
> In mortal stillness; and they ministered
> To human comfort. Stooping down to drink,
> Upon the slimy foot-stone I espied
> The useless fragment of a wooden bowl,
> Green with the moss of years, and subject only
> To the soft handling of the elements.[3]

Change is felt deeply here, and this is characteristic of Wordsworth. It has to do with his feeling for stable and permanent things – e.g. the enduring hills – and his sense of a connection between each individual man and his 'peculiar nook of earth'. There is tragedy in the severance of the connection, the breaking of 'the bond of brotherhood'. In particular, objects made and daily handled by people, especially by more than one generation, acquire human associations and value by such use and custom.

[1] 453–63. (Very little altered from 1797–8 version.)
[2] 469–74. (Very little altered.)   [3] 484–95. (Very little altered.)

The now 'useless fragment of a wooden bowl' has once been in daily use; it has felt 'the touch of human hand', though now subject 'only to the soft handling of the elements'. The 'natural sleep', 'the mortal stillness' of the water of the now 'shrouded' well has at one time been awakened daily to life, as if by magic from sleep or death, at 'the touch of human hand', to yield living refreshment. By such delicately rendered minute particulars (e.g. the play on 'hand', 'handling' and 'mortal', 'shrouded') the poetry communicates a sense of the 'bond of brotherhood' between man and nature there had been in a particular place. The bond has been broken by death, but nature with the lapse of time has dealt gently ('silent overgrowings') with the traces of human habitation that remain. This is much more a poetry of individual experience than the (in a good sense) conventional 18th-century elegies, very distinguished as one or two of these are.

The story of the ruined cottage is the story of Margaret, one of the tragedies of humble lives towards which Wordsworth directed the consciousness of his time.

> Many a passenger
> Hath blessed poor Margaret for her gentle looks,
> When she upheld the cool refreshment drawn
> From that forsaken spring; and no one came
> But he was welcome; no one went away
> But that it seemed she loved him. She is dead,
> The light extinguished of her lonely hut,
> The hut itself abandoned to decay,
> And she forgotten in the quiet grave – [1]

'forgotten' except in the memory of the old man who tells her story. The human tragedy of *The Ruined Cottage*, like that of *Michael*, has for its circumstances the economic and consequent social dislocation of the time, reaching even into remote places among the hills. Margaret struggles on alone at the cottage with her two children, expecting from day to day her husband's return and is gradually, painfully, over the years, defeated.

The old man, a pedlar by the public way that passes her cottage,

---

[1] 502–10. (Unchanged except for the last 3 lines which, though very moving, have lost some of the immediacy of the lines in the 1797–8 version which they have replaced.)

pieces together her story, as having been a witness of it, from his recollections of his recurrent visits, successive glimpses at intervals of years of the gradual decline and final extinction of her life and the life of her cottage.

There is a glimpse of an early time of married happiness and cheerful industry in these natural surroundings.

> She with pride would tell
> That he was often seated at his loom,
> In summer, ere the mower was abroad
> Among the dewy grass – in early spring,
> Ere the last star had vanished. – They who passed
> At evening, from behind the garden fence
> Might hear his busy spade.[1]

This settled life is interrupted by 'two blighting seasons' and 'the plague of war', the effects of which in the lives of people were witnessed by the old man.

> I, with my freight of winter raiment, saw
> The hardships of that season: many rich
> Sank down, as in a dream, among the poor;
> And of the poor did many cease to be,
> And their place knew them not.[2]

The Biblical phrases come naturally in the old man's speech. They are not 'literary'. They must already have become part of the speech of the people, the speech that Wordsworth listened to and himself spoke. 'And their place knew them not' expresses a deeply felt and specific sense of these tragedies of common life, displacements, vanishings from their 'peculiar nook of earth'. The unsettling of the traditional life through the intrusion of external events, the uprooting of people and breaking of family and local ties, bring hardships that have to be endured also by those left behind without a helpmate to çarry on an unequal struggle in the accustomed place. This is the tragedy of Margaret (as of Michael). The only excuse her demoralized husband conveys to her for his despairing desertion is that he would not take her from 'her place' to share the wandering existence of a soldier in foreign places. The old man's wanderings, as an itinerant pedlar, are

---

[1] 523–9. (Little altered.)   [2] 542–6. (Little altered.)

purposeful, useful to the scattered communities and isolated cottages among the hills, linking them together. His journeyings take him with a certain regularity by accustomed ways and familiar places and faces, in contrast to the drifting unemployed.

> shoals of artisans
> From ill-requited labour turned adrift
> Sought daily bread from public charity.[1]

A pause in the old man's tale allows the consciousness to take in the beauty and tranquillity of surrounding nature. This partially absorbs the disturbing effect of the tale of things that have happened in that same place, distancing and proportioning the tragedy.

It happens to have been midsummer when next the Wanderer passed by the cottage. It 'wears its customary look' except that Margaret herself is absent. As he awaits her return, he looks curiously (as Crabbe might have done) at the plant-life of the garden.

> Her cottage, then a cheerful object, wore
> Its customary look – only, it seemed,
> The honeysuckle, crowding round the porch,
> Hung down in heavier tufts; and that bright weed,
> The yellow stone-crop, suffered to take root
> Along the window's edge, profusely grew,
> Blinding the lower panes. I turned aside,
> And strolled into her garden. It appeared
> To lag behind the season, and had lost
> Its pride of neatness. Daisy-flowers and thrift
> Had broken their trim border-lines, and straggled
> O'er paths they used to deck: carnations, once
> Prized for surpassing beauty, and no less
> For the peculiar pains they had required,
> Declined their languid heads, wanting support.
> The cumbrous bind-weed, with its wreaths and bells,
> Had twined about her two small rows of peas,
> And dragged them to the earth.[2]

[1] 559–61. (Little altered.)
[2] 713–30. This passage has been considerably developed from the original 1797–8 version, on the whole felicitously.

It is the wild luxuriance of neglect, nature running riot, unchecked, uncontrolled. The forebodings it arouses are confirmed when Margaret appears. Her face and figure show marks of suffering, deprivation, distraction, aggravated by her inability to relieve her infant's hunger.

Though it is spring when the Wanderer next returns, the place does not look springlike. It reflects a further stage of decline, the garden barren and desolate because untended, uncultivated, uncared for, the bond between man and nature visibly broken. The telltale signs are noted (again as Crabbe might have done).

> Saw
> More plainly still, that poverty and grief
> Were now come nearer to her: weeds defaced
> The hardened soil, and knots of withered grass:
> No ridges there appeared of clear black mould,
> No winter greenness; of her herbs and flowers,
> It seemed the better part was gnawed away
> Or trampled into earth; a chain of straw,
> Which had been twined about the slender stem
> Of a young apple-tree, lay at its root;
> The bark was nibbled round by truant sheep.[1]

A later return reveals the grim reality – rendered in the verse with a Shakespearian directness and control, in the movement of living speech, though as spoken by the tranquil old man the note is even here subtly elegiac – the final stage of her tragedy.

> Meanwhile her poor Hut
> Sank to decay; for he was gone, whose hand,
> At the first nipping of October frost,
> Closed up each chink, and with fresh bands of straw
> Chequered the green-grown thatch. And so she lived
> Through the long winter, reckless and alone;
> Until her house by frost, and thaw, and rain,
> Was sapped; and while she slept, the nightly damps
> Did chill her breast; and in the stormy day
> Her tattered clothes were ruffled by the wind,
> Even at the side of her own fire. Yet still
> She loved this wretched spot, nor would for worlds

---

[1] 832–42. (Little altered.)

Have parted hence; and still that length of road,
And this rude bench, one torturing hope endeared,
Fast rooted at her heart.[1]

What consolation can be found for such tragedies? The
direction in which Wordsworth's poetry is beginning to move
becomes apparent not only in the way the tragedy of Margaret is
presented but, notably, in the conclusion of the poem. The young
man (the poet) has been deeply disturbed by the old man's tale.
It has awakened an impulse of love towards the woman who once
lived in that place. His movement of sympathy, though impotent,
his sense of kinship with her, though he has never seen her, bring
a measure of relief – at least to the sympathizer.

> The old man ceased: he saw that I was moved;
> From that low bench, rising instinctively
> I turned aside in weakness, nor had power
> To thank him for the tale which he had told.
> I stood, and leaning o'er the garden wall
> Reviewed that Woman's sufferings; and it seemed
> To comfort me while with a brother's love
> I blessed her in the impotence of grief.[2]

But, mainly, the answer to the disturbing question, 'What
possible consolation can be found?' is simply the old one that time
heals, that mercifully with the passage of the years we forget and,
more positively, that life goes on almost imperceptively renewing
itself. What comes from Wordsworth's individual experience,
making his poetry new, is the way nature is associated with time
and promotes the gradual healing and perpetually renewing
action.

> Then towards the cottage I returned; and traced
> Fondly, though with an interest more mild,
> That secret spirit of humanity
> Which, 'mid the calm oblivious tendencies
> Of nature, 'mid her plants, and weeds, and flowers,
> And silent overgrowings, still survived.[3]

[1] 900–14. (Unaltered.)
[2] 917–24. (Unaltered, except 'garden wall' for 'garden gate'.)
[3] 925–30. (Unaltered, except for minor changes in the first two lines.)

Further, amid 'the calm oblivious tendencies' and 'silent over-growings' of nature, 'that secret spirit of humanity . . . still sur-vived.' It has become, as it were, the spirit of the place and one with its tranquillity. The place has acquired an identity and a value, almost a sanctity, from the human life that has been lived, the sufferings that have been borne there. These sufferings in their turn have been finally absorbed into the tranquillity of the place.[1]

It is the tranquil old man, not the disturbed young man, who speaks the final words in Wordsworth's poem.

> She sleeps in the calm earth, and peace is here.
> I well remember that those very plumes,
> Those weeds, and the high spear-grass on that wall,
> By mist and silent rain-drops silvered o'er,
> As once I passed, into my heart conveyed
> So still an image of tranquillity.[2]

The references to Christ and the Cross in the passage as it now stands in *The Excursion* are interpolations from Wordsworth's later Anglicanism. What we have in the original version is simply the imagery of unusual delicacy and tenderness suggesting 'the calm oblivious tendencies of nature' –

> Those weeds, and the high spear-grass on that wall,
> By mist and silent rain-drops silvered o'er.

With the slow lapse of time the 'silent overgrowings' softly cover the place that has been devastated or ruined. By such influences the hurt mind is also healed. These images are among the earliest hints in Wordsworth's poetry of a healing power in nature. There is nothing particularly metaphysical as yet about what nature is

---

[1] The concluding passage of the poem is comparable to the tranquil close of *Wuthering Heights*:

'I lingered around them under that benign sky; watched the moths fluttering among the heath and harebells, listening to the soft breathing through the grass and wondered how anyone could ever imagine unquiet slumbers for the sleepers in that quiet earth.'

There are resemblances, certainly not accidental, between Emily Brontë's whole imaginative experience, for all its element of wilder passionateness, and Words-worth's.

[2] 941–6. (Unaltered.)

coming to mean in Wordsworth's poetry, no reference to a philo-
sophical system, though the old man from his years of experience
has his 'philosophy' in an old sense of the word. There is simply
the experienced fact of the slow, silent, scarcely perceptible
processes of growth and renewal that go on continually through
time in nature and in man. The place has a kind of permanence in
change.

> So calm and still, and looked so beautiful
> Amid the uneasy thoughts which filled my mind,
> That what we feel of sorrow and despair
> From ruin and from change, and all the grief
> That passing shows of Being leave behind,
> Appeared an idle dream.[1]

It is the old man speaking. But it is his tranquillity that the young
Wordsworth would attain, if he could, and does attain in the end
in his poetry. If he arrived through his poetry at tranquillity it
was evidently because, at least at one time in his life, he desper-
ately needed to do so.

The effect of the later setting of the tale of Margaret in *The
Excursion* is to give added weight to the tranquillity. The charac-
ter of the old man, the Wanderer of *The Excursion*, is enlarged
upon.

> But still he loved to pace the public roads
> . . . he was a man,
> Whom no one could have passed without remark.

But the best poetry was already there in the original 1797–8
version, and more has perhaps been lost than gained within the
amplifications of the later setting. The clarity of the outline of the
original tale has been blurred.

The Wanderer is, of course, one in Wordsworth's succession
of old men met with among the hills. The Old Cumberland
Beggar, Michael, the Leechgatherer, the Old Soldier, are others.
But in their cases we are made more immediately conscious of the
suffering they themselves endure and have endured and, conse-
quently, of a strength of endurance in them which is an essential
part of their human dignity. We are therefore more deeply

[1] 947–52. (Unaltered.)

convinced that they have earned the serenity they possess. To what extent such characters were the effect of lives lived in natural surroundings, solitary occupations and meditations among the permanent objects of nature (as Wordsworth believed) it would be hard to say exactly. The Old Soldier, for example, had been 'away'. At least equally important must have been the effect of upbringing in those communities among the hills with their traditional way of life. The Biblical element in the speech of these characters could only have come from an upbringing among a pious people whose speech was also theirs. Certainly a combination of all these influences, together with the experience of their years, made them what they were. The fact remains there are or have been such characters. Wordsworth had met them among the hills, shepherds, pedlars and others. They are the ground of his recognition that wisdom is not a matter of urbanity or sophistication. He had himself come to recognize the value, for example, of being alone with nature for promoting truth of thought and feeling about fundamental things. Wordsworth would clearly wish to be such a man as his Wanderer. The old man is partly an ideal to be attained, but related firmly to real characters whom Wordsworth had actually met (cf. Yeats's Fisherman).

IV

Wordsworth's other masterpiece among his tales, the tale of *Michael* (1800), though composed a few years later, and after the *Lyrical Ballads*, might well be read together with the tale of *Margaret* (though its companion piece is, of course, *The Brothers*). The tragedy of Michael has again for its circumstances and part cause the changes, the displacements, the dislocations in the traditional life of the people, even in remote places, brought about by external economic, political and social events and forces. Michael, like Margaret, is deprived of the helpmate he needs for his place, his only son and heir, upon whom all his hopes depended. In his letter to Charles James Fox (January 14th, 1801) Wordsworth himself says the relevant things.

'But recently by the spreading of manufacture through every part of the country . . . the bonds of domestic feeling . . . have been weakened . . . parents are separated from their children, and children from their parents; the wife no longer prepares with her own hands a meal for her husband, the produce of his labour.

'In the two poems, *The Brothers* and *Michael*, I have attempted to draw a picture of the domestic affections as I know they exist amongst a class of men who are now almost confined to the North of England. They are small independent *proprietors* of land here called statesmen, men of respectable education who daily labour on their own little properties. The domestic affections will always be strong amongst men who live in a country not crowded with population, if these men are placed above poverty. But if they are proprietors of small estates, which have descended to them from their ancestors, the power which these affections will acquire among such men is inconceivable by those who have only had an opportunity of observing hired labourers, farmers, and the manufacturing Poor. Their little tract of land serves as a kind of permanent rallying point for their domestic feelings, as a tablet upon which they are written which makes them objects of memory in a thousand instances when they would otherwise be forgotten. It is a fountain fitted to the nature of social man from which supplies of affection, as pure as his heart was intended for, are daily drawn. This class of man is rapidly disappearing.'

The tragedy of *Michael* reveals the strength, even in external defeat, of some of the deepest instincts of human nature, the instincts for family, place and inheritance, often inhumanly ignored by utilitarian reformers and revolutionaries. In so far as it illustrates the ties of inherited land and of 'the domestic affections', particularly those that bind parents and children, the tale runs counter to the Revolutionary theories of Wordsworth's own time. In this tragedy of common life, as in Greek and Shakespearian tragedies, we are shown a breaking of the 'natural bonds'.

In *Michael*, as in *Margaret*, a place is discovered to have a character of its own and a tragic memory associated with it. The tale of this particular place is the tale of the old shepherd, Michael, one of those 'domestic tales',

> that spake to me
> Of shepherds, dwellers in the valleys, men
> Whom I already loved.

Loved for the sake, he adds, of

> the fields and hills
> Where was their occupation and abode.[1]

In these places nature and the human lot are, and have long been, linked.

The tale begins and ends with a heap of stones, evidently assembled by human hands in a desolate place where there are no other visible signs of human life.

> No habitation can be seen; but they
> Who journey thither find themselves alone
> With a few sheep, with rocks and stones, and kites
> That overhead are sailing in the sky . . .
> But for one object which you might pass by,
> Might see and notice not. Beside the brook
> Appears a straggling heap of unhewn stones.[2]

The character of the old man, Michael, who placed them there, is thus introduced, a character of a Biblical simplicity and grandeur shaped, in part at least, by his occupation as a mountain shepherd. The various notes of the wind, for example, are interpreted by him not idly but according to what they may portend for his sheep, his constant care.

> Hence had he learned the meaning of all winds,
> Of blasts of every tone; and, oftentimes,
> When others heeded not, he heard the South
> Make subterraneous music, like the noise
> Of bagpipers on distant Highland hills.
> The Shepherd, at such warning, of his flock
> Bethought him, and he to himself would say,
> 'The winds are now devising work for me!'[3]

In such ways his 'affections' have become connected with the various aspects and changing moods of nature in his particular region, the world of weather there, the sense of distances and spaces.

[1] 22–6.   [2] 9–17.   [3] 48–55.

Up to the mountains: he had been alone
Amid the heart of many thousand mists . . .
So many incidents upon his mind . . .
Which, like a book, preserved the memory
Of the dumb animals, whom he had saved . . .
Those fields, those hills – what could they less? had laid
Strong hold on his affections . . .
The pleasure which there is in life itself.[1]

But Michael, a patriarchal figure, has an anchorage also in his domestic life, his cottage where his wife, his 'help-mate', lives a daily round of cheerful industry. The value of this anchorage in his life is delineated with beautiful clarity. Furthermore, the cottage has acquired a significance for the whole neighbourhood. It has become known as The Evening Star because of the lamp, 'an aged utensil', that for so many years has shone from it far into the night and become 'a public symbol'.

But life, as Wordsworth knew, needs hope. Michael's hopes are centred on his only son and heir, born to the hitherto childless couple when Michael had already grown conscious of the years beginning to tell on him. A child

brings hope with it, and forward-looking thoughts.[2]

The companionship of father and son is portrayed tenderly and tactfully, with no sentimentality, with exactly the right note.

objects which the Shepherd loved before
Were dearer now . . .
. . . the old man's heart seemed born again.[3]

He hopes to hand on his ancestral place and occupation to his son, Luke, as he had inherited them from his father and forefathers. But, though it had so been from generation to generation, it is here unexpectedly that Michael is vulnerable. Unforeseen misfortunes break in (as in *Margaret*) from outside, and these

took

More hope out of his life than he supposed
That any old man ever could have lost[4]

[1] From 58–77.   [2] 148.   [3] 199, 203.   [4] 218–20.

– because his hope has had its roots in those strong human instincts about land, inheritance and family.

> Yet if these fields of ours
> Should pass into a stranger's hand, I think
> That I could not lie quiet in my grave.
> Our lot is a hard lot . . .[1]

There is clearly an affinity which is not simply 'literary', not a matter of conscious or unconscious echoes, between Wordsworth's old shepherd and Shakespeare's in *A Winter's Tale* (and elsewhere in the plays). These shepherds come not from pastoral poetry but the real life of England. The affinities can be felt in the way the English language is being used and in the verse movement. The old man, addressing his son, recalls his own parents.

> Both of them sleep together: here they lived,
> As all their Forefathers had done; and when
> At length their time was come, they were not loth
> To give their bodies to the family mould.
> I wished that thou should'st live the life they lived.[2]

But the traditional pattern is broken. Luke is forced to leave his native place to join a kinsman, 'a prosperous man thriving in trade', in the great city, 'the dissolute city', where he succumbs to its corruptions.[3] Thus tragedy comes on the old man. There is nevertheless discovered to be a stoic strength of character, a power of endurance in the stricken old man that is heroic and does honour to human nature. In particular the strength of the connection of his affections with his native place and with his whole life's occupations there supports him to the end.

---

[1] 230–3.   [2] 367–71.

[3] This is a subject which is treated also in Crabbe's tale, *The Learned Boy*, but the difference in treatment between Crabbe and Wordsworth is again characteristic. In *The Learned Boy* – he learns among other things that the Bible is now an old-fashioned book about which one may be condescending – the boy is initiated into the ways and pleasures of 'the world' by his fellow-clerks, his experienced seniors. The process is represented in detail (though with a sharp-edged classic economy), as an astringent little comedy, from Crabbe's shrewdly humorous observation and knowledge of human weakness. But Wordsworth's subject, treated wholly seriously, is the tragedy which comes on the old man and the dignity with which he endures it even in extreme old age.

There is a comfort in the strength of love;
'Twill make a thing endurable, which else
Would overset the brain, or break the heart:
I have conversed with more than one who well
Remember the old Man, and what he was
Years after he had heard this heavy news.
His bodily frame had been from youth to age
Of an unusual strength. Among the rocks
He went, and still looked up to sun and cloud,
And listened to the wind; and, as before,
Performed all kinds of labour for his sheep,
And for the land, his small inheritance.
And to that hollow dell from time to time
Did he repair, to build the Fold of which
His flock had need. 'Tis not forgotten yet
The pity which was then in every heart
For the old Man – and 'tis believed by all
That many and many a day he thither went,
And never lifted up a single stone.[1]

In that last line the whole tragedy is implied,[2] as in those abso-
lutely simple lines that come, at moments, in *Lear* and other great
tragedies, that go straight to the heart and seem to count far more
than all the rhetoric.

His fields do in fact 'pass into a stranger's hand' after the death
of the old couple. The ploughshare has been through the ground
on which the cottage stood. But the poem does not end on this
note of impermanence and change. The heaped stones of the
unfinished sheepfold have outlasted the cottage and remain a
natural memorial of the old man.[3] Wordsworth, who looks
always for permanence in the midst of change, has found a sign
of it in a not accidental heap of stones.

The effect of the poem depends of course on its purity of style,
its unity of simplicity and nobility in perfect correspondence with
its subject. It is the summit of Wordsworth's achievement in this

[1] 448–66.
[2] Arnold quotes the line as one of his touchstones. The effect of the line
depends, however, upon its context in the whole poem.
[3] '. . . at every turn and angle, human remembrances and memorials of time-
honoured affections' (De Quincey, *Recollections of the Lake Poets*).

respect and had been anticipated already before the *Lyrical Ballads* in *Margaret*. Its kind of simplicity is neither naïve nor self-conscious, not a fake simplicity, but entirely right, with no false note. It is a style that does neither less nor more, and nothing other than exactly convey its grave and dignified subject. The reader's imagination is made entirely possessed of that subject, and he is not aware of the style as something separate or added to it. The pure transparency of the style is indeed such that there appears to be an absence of style. This is its distinction. Its simple nobility is that of its subject, the old man's character and tragedy. This is the greatness of art, that, not recognizing it as art, we say (as Arnold said of Tolstoy) this is not art, this is reality.

V

The Old Cumberland Beggar and *The Brothers*

Composed in 1798, though not published till 1800, there is another poem, *The Old Cumberland Beggar*, which expresses Wordsworth's recognition of the 'still sad music of humanity' as having 'power to chasten and subdue'. There is little to recall the pomp and splendour of Miltonic verse in this poetry which, though grave and solemn, is quiet and unemphatic.[1] The verse movement, as well as the diction and idiom, is again close to that of someone talking, in this respect more Shakespearian than Miltonic. There are here two main interests, a contemplation of the condition of extreme old age (cf. *Animal Tranquillity and Decay*, also 1798) and, secondly, a pondering of the humanizing effect the aged beggar has on the people in the countryside, simply by being what he is.

> Surrounded by those wild unpeopled hills,
> He sat, and ate his food in solitude.[2]

A figure of Biblical simplicity, described in language of a Biblical simplicity, he scatters crumbs on the wayside, but merely out of physical frailty, involuntarily a providence for birds.

> and the small mountain birds,
> Not venturing yet to peck their destined meal,
> Approached within the length of half his staff.[3]

---

[1] Cf. the poetry of Edward Thomas in this respect.　[2] 14–15.　[3] 19–21.

This is different from either the idealization of 18th-century pastoral poetry or from the degree of formal stylization with which other 18th century poets, even Cowper, set the human figure in the landscape as background to it, or from the realism of Crabbe too conscious of the imperfections of human nature and the human lot to idealize. If the aged Cumberland beggar, despite his decrepitude, has become a figure of human dignity it is because Wordsworth really saw him so. The particularity and exactitude with which the old man and the natural scene are recalled preclude idealization. Though he is a familiar figure in the countryside, and has been so since the poet's memories of him in childhood, he is more than simply that; he too fulfils the destiny of man, travelling on in solitude as if timelessly.

> Him from my childhood have I known; and then
> He was so old, he seems not older now;
> He travels on, a solitary Man . . .[1]
> His age has no companion.[2]

In the feebleness of extreme age, his eyes bent perpetually on the ground now distinguish only the trivial objects that lie there. But he is not therefore become useless.

> an implement
> Worn out and worthless.[3]

Simply by his need he evokes charity, is a humanizing and moral force in the land, keeps awake feelings of humanity among the people of the hill communities through which 'he travels on'.

Thus, in its unassuming manner, the poem comes directly and authentically from Wordsworth's personal observation of what it is like to be very old; and it communicates the sense of our common humanity, the dignity of individual man and the mystery of life – 'he travels on, a solitary Man' (cf. *Stepping Westward*, 1803).

> And while in that vast solitude to which
> The tide of things has borne him . . .[4]
> And, long as he can wander, let him breathe

---

[1] 22–4.   [2] 45.   [3] 86.   [4] 163–4.

> The freshness of the valleys; let his blood
> Struggle with frosty air and winter snows.[1]

Never to be shut up in the work-house.

> Be his the natural silence of old age!
> Let him be free of mountain solitudes.[2]

Published in the same year (1800) as *The Old Cumberland
Beggar* and as the greater poem *Michael*, with which Words-
worth himself associated it in his letter to Charles James Fox, is
the tale of *The Brothers*. It differs, much as *Margaret* does, from
what we may conventionally think of as a narrative poem. The
past and the present come together in a particular place and in a
dialogue. The simple tale is pieced together, mostly as 'recol-
lections', in the dialogue between the 'homely priest' and the
native who returns to his place, after the absence of a life-time, to
find there have been changes. He has spent his life at sea; his
brother has remained among his native hills. But when the sea-
farer returns he finds that his brother is dead, buried in the
churchyard.

His native region had accompanied the seafarer on the sea;
visions of his native hills, those 'permanent objects', had super-
imposed themselves on the fluctuating element and its depths.

> Oft in the piping shrouds had Leonard heard
> The tones of waterfalls . . .[3]
> Even with the organs of his bodily eye,
> Below him, in the bosom of the deep,
> Saw mountains; saw the forms of sheep that grazed
> On verdant hills – with dwellings among trees.[4]

The poetry here expresses something more, or other, than home-
sickness – a need for the kind of stability his native place repre-
sented in his life, a foundation of permanence in a world of
perpetual turmoil and change. Yet when the brother returns it
seems to him, disturbingly, that the appearances of things have
changed.

[1] 172–4.   [2] 182–3.   [3] 47–8.   [4] 60–3.

And, looking round, imagined that he saw
Strange alteration wrought on every side
Among the woods and fields, and that the rocks
And everlasting hills themselves were changed . . .[1]
'And yet, some changes must have taken place among you:
And you, who dwell here, even among these rocks,
Can trace the finger of mortality . . .'[2]

The fact of change must itself be accepted as an inevitable condition of mortal life. It is the Priest who speaks the most memorable passage in the poem, a passage having a Shakespearian actuality, about changes and tragic accidents among the hills. The hills themselves are after all perilous as the sea is.

For accidents and changes such as these,
We want not store of them; a water-spout
Will bring down half a mountain; what a feast
For folks that wander up and down like you,
To see an acre's breadth of that wide cliff
One roaring cataract! a sharp May-storm
Will come with loads of January snow,
And in one night send twenty score of sheep
To feed the ravens; or a shepherd dies
By some untoward death among the rocks:
The ice breaks up and sweeps away a bridge;
A wood is felled: – and then for our own homes!
A child is born or christened, a field ploughed,
A daughter sent to service, a web spun,
The old house-clock is decked with a new face;
And hence, so far from wanting facts or dates
To chronicle the time, we all have here
A pair of diaries, – one serving, Sir,
For the whole dale, and one for each fireside –
Yours was a stranger's judgment: for historians,
Commend me to these valleys![3]

The communities among the hills have their intimate and homely memories and pieties which form part of their enduring strength and coherence.

[1] 96–9.   [2] 127–9.   [3] 146–67.

We have no need of names and epitaphs;
We talk about the dead by our firesides.[1]

The Shakespearian qualities of this Wordsworthian poetry can
again be felt in the language and verse movement. Wordsworth
is here sharing, in his individual way, the strength of a common
spoken English language and tradition.

> I warrant, every corner
> Among these rocks, and every hollow place
> That venturous foot could reach, to one or both
> Was known as well as to the flowers that grow there.
> Like roe-bucks they went bounding o'er the hill;
> They played like two young ravens on the crags.[2]
> . . . to this hour
> Leonard had never handled rope or shroud:
> For the boy loved the life which we lead here
> And though of unripe years, a stripling only,
> His soul was knit to this his native soil.[3]
> . . . he would return,
> To live in peace upon his father's land,
> And lay his bones among us.[4]

As in *Michael* (to which *The Brothers* is a companion-piece)
there is here a Wordsworthian sense of a man's ties with his
paternal land and inheritance, the place where he was born and
grew up and where he would wish to live and die in the ways of
his father before him.

VI

Those meetings in waste places and on moorland roads between
himself and individuals, old experienced men with a power of
endurance and a grave wisdom, have become an important ele-
ment in Wordsworth's poetry. But like Wordsworth himself it
may be supposed these solitary individuals, even the itinerants,
also came from and returned to the settled, if scattered, com-
munities among the hills. There was this anchorage to their lives,
a long-established order, with its inherited occupations, customs

[1] 178–9.   [2] 273–88.   [3] 294–8.   [4] 323–5.

and pieties, morality and religion, a traditional way of life. The young man from this northern region who descended on Cambridge, London and Paris towards the end of the 18th century brought with him a capacity for 'communion with nature' and for possessing his soul in solitude even in a crowd. But he also brought with him, as a part of his individual life, a knowledge of another kind of community from that of the 18th-century urban 'polite' society, a community of independent sheep-farmers and all those who were closely-knit or connected with them, a provincial rural society older than the 18th century, though still existing in it, a people with an experience and wisdom distinct from that which could be acquired from 'polite letters and conversation'. He could contrast this real pastoral order with that of 'pastoral poetry'.

The hillsmen and dalesmen among whom – as well as among the objects of nature in those parts – he had grown up, men of independent mind and character, had made a permanent impression on him. His recognition of the intrinsic worth and wisdom of individuals among them corrects the conventional 18th-century regard for urbane cultivation, elegance and refinement – and in this again he accords not only with Burns but with Johnson:

> Yet still he fills affection's eye,
>   Obscurely wise and coarsely kind
> Nor lettered arrogance deny
>   Thy praise to merit unrefined.[1]

Wordsworth shared the developing democratic spirit of the age particularly as himself a countryman of Cumberland and Westmorland where the individual counted a great deal. The men of 'humble and rustic life' whom he best knew, though many of them were men of solitary occupation, were none the less members of a community and had their homes on the sheep-farms and in the villages in the dales. They were men of religious upbringing, their lives and speech deeply influenced by the Bible and shaped by the same traditions and customs as Wordsworth himself had been. His own speech out of which he made his poetry must have been basically that of the people of his native region. He was and remained basically one of them. His subject (as he

[1] Lines on Dr. Levet.

says in a letter to James Tobin, 6th March 1798) is 'Nature, Man and Society'. The difference is that Wordsworth's society (cf. Crabbe's provincial society) is not the urban polite society of the 18th century.

The Horatianism of the 18th century had, of course, made much of the corruptions of the city, but had still on the whole assumed that the city was the centre of civilization. To withdraw from the corruptions and madding passions of the city, to retire to a quiet country place, live simply and moderately there, entertain and converse with a few well-chosen cultivated friends might restore a man's peace of mind, offer him indeed the possibility of living in some ways a more civilized life. But the assumption remained that he took his civilized values, as he took his books, with him into the country, and that these values had been originally the creation of the city (as the words 'urbanity' and 'politeness' themselves imply). Wordsworth, on the other hand, had found a centre of humane life and wisdom in his remote native region as well as a source of creative power in the association of the individual mind with nature. One of the effects of the 'false taste' engendered in cities, he says, is the corruption of language itself.

'... the medium through which in poetry the heart is to be affected is language; a thing subject to endless fluctuations and arbitrary associations ... And how does it survive but through the People?' (Preface to the *Lyrical Ballads*.)

He makes here an important distinction between the Public and the People.

'Still more lamentable is his error who can believe that there is anything of divine infallibility in the clamour of that small though loud portion of the community, ever governed by factitious influence, which, under the name of the Public, passes itself upon the unthinking for the People.' (Preface to the *Lyrical Ballads*.)

Wordsworth is essentially right. The language out of which the great poets, Chaucer, Shakespeare, made their poetry was the speech of a whole people, not merely of a section of it, however sophisticated, and this has clearly to do with their range and centrality.

CHAPTER THREE

WORDSWORTH: *THE PRELUDE*

I

The *Prelude* was intended to be the prelude to a much larger poem. Its alternative title, *The Growth of a Poet's Mind*, is more descriptive of its subject, which is not simply landscape but

> the Mind of Man
> My haunt and the main region of my song.[1]

Further, the subject is the 'growth' of the mind. The implication, which the poem itself bears out, is of an organic development in the human individual from childhood to manhood ('The child is father of the man') and that if we are to understand the nature of a man we must endeavour to trace his development from his origins in childhood. How new this conception was it is difficult for us now to realize so long after the event and when it has become a commonplace. (Rousseau, of course, had had much to do with its origination.) The poem is Wordsworth's attempt to search back through recollection to sources and origins, to trace the process of development from earliest childhood to maturity, as the way to discover the nature of the man whom the child has developed into. Still further, the subject is a 'Poet's Mind', that is to say, the creative mind – the Imagination as Wordsworth and Coleridge (as Blake before them) were rediscovering it after the 18th century emphasis on Reason. Indeed, Wordsworth's conception of the human mind is that in its essential nature it is creative.

Since the mind which it is most possible for an individual to explore is his own, it need not be regarded as a sign of egoism that Wordsworth's poem should be an essay in essential autobiography, that the development he should attempt to trace should be his own, that he should attempt to discover through his own recollections the foundations of the moral and imaginative life of

[1] Fragment of *The Recluse*.

a man. The creative part played in his own development by the influences of external nature in the region where he grew up is inevitably one of the main themes of his poem. His subject further turns out, therefore, very largely to be the human mind in its creative relationship with the non-human universe.

> How exquisitely the individual Mind
> ... to the external world
> Is fitted: – and how exquisitely, too ...
> The external World is fitted to the Mind.[1]

By seeking first to know the nature of his own mind he is seeking to know the nature of the human mind. This ('Know thyself') is nothing new. What is new in the poem is the depth of Wordsworth's introspectiveness, his recognition of an organic development from childhood to manhood and his insight into his experiences of a creative relationship between the individual mind and the external world.

But men other than himself, including those solitary wanderers met with among the hills, play a part as creative as that of nature in his development and in the poem. There was (as I have said) a community of people among whom, as well as among the hills, he grew up and this has, perhaps, had as much as had 'nature' to do with the poem being what it is.

The Prelude, then, is as much a poem on the nature of man as on the nature that is not man. It is a poem 'On Man, on Nature and on Human Life'. These subjects are intimately associated, inseparable in the poetry. Indeed, the poem's subject is their creative association.

But if we say that the interest in *The Prelude*, as in Wordsworth's poetry as a whole, is essentially psychological, an interest in the workings of the mind, the word 'psychological', because of its more recent popular scientific associations, needs enlargement. For one thing, the Wordsworthian interest in the workings of the mind is accompanied by a sense of reverence, a recognition of the natural dignity of each man, a recognition of the mind as a creative power (the imagination) working on nature as nature works on it, a recognition of unknown, therefore mysterious, depths in man and in the universe.

[1] Fragment of *The Recluse*.

The Prelude and, later, *The Excursion* are the only completed
parts of the vast planned whole. The reason why Wordsworth
never completed the planned whole was, we may guess, because
he no longer needed to. He had already completed what was there
for him to complete, or the greater part of it, when he completed
the original version of *The Prelude*. In *The Excursion* the inspira-
tion is drying up, and the enormous protraction of that compara-
tively prosaic poem becomes wearisome for most readers. *The
Excursion* modifies and qualifies Wordsworth's attitude to his
original body of experience but scarcely extends it except in the
pejorative sense of drawing it out at too great length. *The
Prelude* itself remains the fullest and completest poetic expression
of Wordsworth's most living experience. It is itself the whole, or
the greater part of it, and not merely the prelude to it. It contains
a very large proportion of Wordsworth's greater poetry.

Arnold perhaps encouraged the view that in *The Prelude* the
poetry is a matter of great passages, though these are more
frequent and abundant than in *The Excursion*. But *The Prelude* is
a whole, and my experience is that much is lost by not reading it
(and indeed also *The Excursion*) consecutively through. The
passages of great poetry themselves lose by not being come upon
in their contexts in the whole. *The Prelude* is, somehow, greater
than the great passages read separately. It is equally true that the
greatness of the whole *Prelude* does depend on the great poetry
that rises again and again from its general level.[1]

Arnold (as I said) may have encouraged the view that all that
need be done is to extract the passages of great poetry. Neverthe-
less, when he said of Wordsworth, 'His poetry is the reality, his
philosophy . . . the illusion', he was expressing a fact about the
reader's experience (and not only the reader who was himself).
The philosophic passages in *The Prelude* are often hard to para-
phrase, harder than a poem of Donne.

The ideas and their logical or associative progression or evo-
lution in a poem of Donne are often ingenious and subtle, fine-
spun and intricate. But they are definite and exact and they can,

---

[1] Some of those passages were in fact composed separately – virtually as
separate poems – before being incorporated in the whole poem. One such
passage is the meeting with the Old Soldier (now forming the conclusion of
Book 4).

with some painstaking, be unravelled and extracted from the poetry by paraphrase.[1] The difficulty for the reader of Wordsworth is different. The philosophic passages in *The Prelude* often come in between, and are themselves separable from, the poetry which is embodiment of experience. The philosophic passages have the appearance of offering thought. But when the reader attempts by paraphrase to extract the thought, he often finds that it is curiously ungraspable, nebulous. It turns out to be hard to say what the 'thought' and, therefore, the 'philosophy' exactly is; it eludes exact statement, prose definition. The reader may then begin to wonder how philosophic the philosophic passages are, which are neither philosophic prose nor poetry.

The poetry in *The Prelude* is another matter. The passages which are poetry are instantly recognizable when the reader comes upon them. The imagery is distinct, solid and definite, the rhythm varied and subtle as living speech, tense and taut. By comparison with this poetic definition, or imaginative verbal recreation, of experience the semi-abstract philosophic passages are vague and blurred, the rhythm flat and slack or sometimes, to compensate, mechanically heightened by an application of the Miltonic style. In the great passages of poetry the selection and

---

[1] The real difficulty with Donne is, rather, that the reader who is intent upon isolating and pursuing 'the ideas' may lose the poem. He may cease to respond to the varying rhythms, the changing movement of what is often passionate speech as in Shakespearian dramatic verse. He may miss the shifting emphases, the surprising turns, as well as the force of the often startling images. He may find the hyperboles merely extravagant ('frigid conceits'), missing the passionate intensities that produce them (as if it were not 'natural' for the imagination to exaggerate and magnify under the stress of passion). He may lose the sense of the whole dramatic situation and its moments of crisis, its climaxes – for example, in *A Valediction: of Weeping*, the grief of parting, the apprehension of a separation which could reduce each to a nothingness in the absence of the other, which could prove to be the final parting, he being about to cross the dangerous sea to the farther shore. The paraphrasing reader, abstracting the concepts ('conceits'), may lose the cumulative power and weight of the poem experienced only when the imagery and the rhythm take hold and are fully responded to, e.g. the force of the rhythmical emphasis on 'drown' 'dead' 'sea' 'do' in that final stanza.

> . . . So you and I are nothing then when on a divers shore.
> 　　　　　　　O more than Moon
> Draw not up tears to drown me in thy sphere
> Weep me not dead in thine arms but forbear
> To teach the sea what it may do too soon.

arrangement of words have a precision and rightness and are felt
to have happened so, with a profound inevitability, as an outcome
of the creative process. This is an aspect of Wordsworth's best
poetry – the poetry of imaginative embodiment of experience –
which is still perhaps not given its adequate recognition.

The Wordsworth who composed the original *Prelude* was a
mature man of about thirty. The experiences recollected had
happened years before, in childhood, boyhood and youth or early
manhood. They are imaginatively lived through in the poetry
with remarkable vividness and particularity as if they were
actually happening again as they originally did. The nearest
parallel is, perhaps, the fullness and richness of George Eliot's
recollections of the provincial English life of the Warwickshire of
her childhood and youth out of which she began making her
novels when, at the age of forty, detached now by time and place
– the intervening years and her London life – she discovered
herself as a novelist. In the poetry of Wordsworth, as in the
novels of George Eliot and Dickens, these memories of child-
hood and youth flow back into the consciousness with unusual
distinctness and abundance. But, though recollected experiences
form the substance of the poetry of *The Prelude* (as of the novels
of George Eliot) it is what is made of that substance that is the
poetry (or that is the novel). A great deal has necessarily happened
to the original experiences in being recollected and transmuted
into poetry, and indeed throughout the whole period of years,
before they were again at the time of composition 'recollected'.
They have not only been brooded and pondered over. They have
become part of the developing life of a man who, in those inter-
vening years, had experienced many other things, had known and
witnessed tragic events, had observed, felt and thought deeply.
The poet himself is necessarily in many ways no longer the same
person as the child or youth to whom these things originally
happened. He is and he is not the same, though he recognizes
that he is the kind of man he now is partly as a result of those
childhood and boyhood experiences. Those experiences are not
simply repossessed in the imagination of the mature Words-
worth, becoming objects there of his contemplation, they have
been transmuted in the words, recreated, converted into the new
imaginative experiences which are the poetry of *The Prelude*. The

meanings which the mature mind of the poet now sees in them are inseparable from them as they now are in the poetry.

> We had the experience but missed the meaning
> And approach to the meaning restores the experience
> In a different form.
>
> *(Dry Salvages)*

The meaning of an experience – or the meaning it can be seen or made to have – can break upon the reflective or creative mind, perhaps years after. The experience now shares the quality and insight of the mind that recollects it. So in *The Prelude* the meaning of an experience has become as much part of the poetry as the experience itself. The meaning and the experience are now one thing, and that thing is the poetry.[1]

II

The succession of recollected childhood and boyhood experiences are what stands out from Book 1. Whatever else these are about, they are basically about the disturbed conscience and an order of things outside himself forcing itself upon the consciousness. At the root of at least two of these experiences a Macbeth-like sense of guilt works on the boy's imagination, transforming the shapes of the outer world into menacing presences, powers threatening retribution. The meaning of these experiences for the mature mind of the poet has come to be that 'nature' has had something to do with the awakening and development of the moral sense. The boy has been forced to experience an obscure, but definite and powerful, sense of an order of things outside himself which may be violated, but not with impunity. In some of his early experiences already, therefore, nature has become for Wordsworth (as he recollects) associated, if not identified, with the

---

[1] The passages quoted in what follows are taken from Wordsworth's final version of *The Prelude* – the text as published after his death in 1850. They should be compared, of course, with the original 1805 text (now also readily available). Wordsworth tended not to alter his best passages much. They are substantially there from the beginning. The 1805 version is more of an effusion, in that sense 'fresher' and more immediate in places. But the final text – the text in which most people mostly read the poem – seems to me on the whole the best to read. Most of the alterations made over many years are stylistic only (but in the best sense), most are improvements, some not.

moral order. Nature may be benevolent (as Wordsworth seems to feel); but certainly in the imagination of the wrongdoer it may appear to react (as an outraged parent might) frighteningly, as if not easily to be appeased. It has become identified in the imagination with the unappeased conscience. The familiar, accustomed world seems suddenly unfamiliar, is felt to have been alienated and estranged. It seems to pursue the conscience-stricken individual, a haunting impersonation of his own sense of guilt. In these particular experiences in *The Prelude*, fear abruptly predominates and submerges the boy's natural joy. These sudden frights overcome the boy's delight in his solitary activities and adventures, his movements as a free agent among the hills. But common to all these experiences – not only those rooted in a sense of his having done something wrong – there is the boy's discovery that even when he is alone, unconscious of human companionship, he is not alone; that there is a reality outside himself, other than himself and other than anything human, with which he is, nevertheless, somehow connected. These experiences, therefore, are relevations for Wordsworth, not only of the awakening of a moral sense but of a religious sense. The 'feeling analogous to the supernatural' that is here aroused is a feeling of nature itself as being (paradoxically) supernatural. Hence the sense of awe in the presence of 'nature' as not only the external world but a largely unknown power outside himself, a reality and a mystery; hence the 'dim and undetermined sense of unknown modes of being' hence the

> Fallings from us, vanishings
> Blank misgivings of a Creature
> Moving about in worlds not realised.[1]

The first of these episodes in Book 1 is the snaring episode.

> Ere I had told
> Ten birth-days, when among the mountain slopes
> Frost, and the breath of frosty wind, had snapped
> The last autumnal crocus, 'twas my joy
> With store of springes o'er my shoulder hung
> To range the open heights where woodcocks run

---

[1] *Ode on Intimations of Immortality from Recollections of Early Childhood.*

Along the smooth green turf. Through half the night,
Scudding away from snare to snare, I plied
That anxious visitation; – moon and stars
Were shining o'er my head. I was alone,
And seemed to be a trouble to the peace
That dwelt among them. Sometimes it befell
In these night wanderings, that a strong desire
O'erpowered my better reason, and the bird
Which was the captive of another's toil
Became my prey; and when the deed was done
I heard among the solitary hills
Low breathings coming after me, and sounds
Of undistinguishable motion, steps
Almost as silent as the turf they trod.[1]

The boy's joy in his solitary activity, his free movement through the frosty night on the heights, under the moon and stars, becomes a troubled joy – 'that anxious visitation'. He has, somehow, the sense that he is an intruder, disturbing the peace of nature, a lawless marauder, a predatory prowler. After he has done the deed he knows to be wrong, this trouble in his mind is suddenly enormously magnified. What an adult might regard indulgently, even humorously, as a relatively minor schoolboy offence becomes exaggerated in the imagination of the boy himself into a crime committed, a fell deed – 'and when the deed was done' – engendering a Macbeth-like sense of guilt. The obscure sense that he has violated an order of things outside himself finally – as expressed in the growing momentum of the poetry – produces that haunted sense of menacing presences and powers pursuing the guilty one.

A sense of guilt is absent from the rock-climbing birdnesting episode. Instead, the danger here intensifies the exhilaration, heightening the senses and consciousness. The details of the boy's physical situation and mental state are recollected and re-created in the poetry, again with remarkable distinctness and coherence.

Oh! when I have hung
Above the raven's nest, by knots of grass
And half-inch fissures in the slippery rock

[1] Book 1. 306–25.

But ill sustained, and almost (so it seemed)
Suspended by the blast that blew amain,
Shouldering the naked crag, oh, at that time
While on the perilous ridge I hung alone,
With what strange utterance did the loud dry wind
Blow through my ear! the sky seemed not a sky
Of earth – and with what motion moved the clouds![1]

To the boy, suspended alone between earth and sky, the familiar
has again suddenly become unfamiliar. Looked at from this un-
accustomed angle, the universe has become 'strange' – 'with
what strange utterance' . . . 'the sky seemed not a sky . . .' 'The
lethargy of custom' has been broken, 'the film of familiarity' has
fallen away to present a revelation of the world as unknown and
new. The experience is a liberating and, this time, a joyous one,
the fear overcome by the joy.

The most massive of these experiences arises from the boy's
rowing across the lake by himself in a boat that is not his own, a
stolen pleasure. This is another of those frightening imaginative
experiences connected with the boy's having yielded to an over-
powering impulse and done what he knows to be wrong. The
passage begins not much above the level of ordinary matter-of-
fact narrative, statement of circumstances and events in their
historic sequence. But the pleasurable sense of adventuring, as
with the gliding motion of the boat, into a faerie realm of moon-
light and enchantment soon begins to lift the rhythm and to take
us, sharing the boy's imagination, out of our ordinary everyday-
ness. The boy's pleasure, however, has from the beginning been a
'troubled pleasure'.

It was an act of stealth
And troubled pleasure.

Almost before we are aware of what is happening, the poetry of
the huge imaginative experience that develops has taken hold of
us. By an easily explainable accident of changing perspective (cf.
Strange fits of passion, 1799), as the boy rows farther and farther
from the shore, a huge peak – 'black and huge' . . ., 'as if with
voluntary power instinct' – rises into the night-sky from behind
the 'craggy steep', which had hitherto formed the horizon on

[1] Book I. 330–9.

which his eye had been fixed, and interposes itself between him
and the stars.

> When from behind that craggy steep till then
> The horizon's bound, a huge peak, black and huge,
> As if with voluntary power instinct,
> Upreared its head. I struck and struck again,
> And growing still in stature the grim shape
> Towered up between me and the stars, and still,
> For so it seemed, with purpose of its own
> And measured motion like a living thing,
> Strode after me. With trembling oars I turned,
> And through the silent water stole my way
> Back to the covert of the willow tree;
> There in her mooring-place I left my bark, –
> And through the meadows homeward went, in grave
> And serious mood; but after I had seen
> That spectacle, for many days, my brain
> Worked with a dim and undetermined sense
> Of unknown modes of being; o'er my thoughts
> There hung a darkness, call it solitude
> Or blank desertion. No familiar shapes
> Remained, no pleasant images of trees,
> Of sea or sky, no colours of green fields;
> But huge and mighty forms, that do not live
> Like living men, moved slowly through the mind
> By day, and were a trouble to my dreams.[1]

The disturbed conscience has again set the imagination working
on shapes of the external world, changing them into gigantic
images of pursuing presences. There supervenes, in the boy's
troubled experience, the sense of a life not our life, the 'dim and
undetermined sense of unknown modes of being'. The familiar
and accustomed again suddenly becomes unfamiliar, unaccus-
tomed; the homely earth seems alienated, no longer homely.
Imagery that has moved in from the external world, a shadowy
procession of superhuman forms

that do not live
Like living men

[1] Book I. 377–400.

continues, days after, to move slowly through the mind, a Dantean pageantry, but more shadowy, less anthropomorphic.

That the universe is other than the self and that, nevertheless, the self is intimately connected with it, in ever-changing relationship, is again the discovery borne in upon the boy in the skating episode. The scene on the ice has the clarity and exactitude of 17th century Dutch painting. But, though based on simple observation, an imaginative experience develops. The poetry conveys the exhilaration, the animation, the movement of the skaters, the concord of clear sounds through the frosty air and, as day changes into night, the magnificent luminous spectacle of the surrounding earth and sky. There is the sense of individual freedom with, at the same time, domestic and social attachment – 'The cottage windows blazed' . . . 'The village clock tolled six' – and in the end the discovery or rediscovery of another attachment, the profound attachment with nature.

On this occasion the boy is one of a crowd. But even in 'the pack', 'the games confederate', 'the tumultuous throng' the boy is still essentially solitary, less conscious, it seems in the end, of his fellow human beings in his immediate vicinity than of the surrounding universe, a vast other entity, also in apparent motion along with himself. It is indeed when he withdraws into his own solitude that he becomes most conscious of the universe. He enters into a kind of conscious relationship with it, experimenting, playing games with it, a vast accompanying other presence, the one seeming to respond to the other, the two remaining two yet interrelated.

> When we had given our bodies to the wind,
> And all the shadowy banks on either side
> Came sweeping through the darkness, spinning still
> The rapid line of motion, then at once
> Have I, reclining back upon my heels,
> Stopped short; yet still the solitary cliffs
> Wheeled by me – even as if the earth had rolled
> With visible motion her diurnal round!
> Behind me did they stretch in solemn train,
> Feebler and feebler, and I stood and watched
> Till all was tranquil . . .[1]

[1] Book 1. 453–63.

The experience has awakened in the boy a sense of the whole revolving world (cf. 'Rolled round in earth's diurnal course').

In some of the poetry of Book 1 the sense of recovering in all its original freshness a world of boyhood, an early world, a lost Eden –

> I held unconscious intercourse with beauty
> Old as creation . . .

seems to invest with enchantment particular remembered haunts, places of natural beauty associated with boyhood activities, nutting, fishing, kite-flying.

> The woods of autumn, and their hazel bowers
> With milk-white clusters hung; the rod and line,
> True symbol of hope's foolishness, whose strong
> And unreproved enchantment led us on
> By rocks and pools shut out from every star,
> All the green summer, to forlorn cascades
> Among the windings hid of mountain brooks . . .
> The paper kite high among fleecy clouds
> Pull at her rein like an impetuous courser;
> Or, from the meadows sent on gusty days,
> Beheld her breast the wind, then suddenly
> Dashed headlong, and rejected by the storm.[1]

After having been

> doomed to sleep
> Until maturer seasons called them forth

these memories have acquired a visionary quality, sometimes a luminousness which does not blur the outlines but, on the contrary, renders particular features of remembered scenes and episodes preternaturally distinct:

> Those recollected hours that have the charm
> Of visionary things . . .
> And almost make remotest infancy
> A visible scene, on which the sun is shining

as in Vaughan (e.g. *The Retreate*)

---

[1] Book 1. 484–98.

Gleams like the flashing of a shield; – the earth
And common face of Nature spake to me
Rememberable things.

But, for Wordsworth, the significance of this recollected world of boyhood is that in it he discovers the origins and sources of the man the boy has become. There is in Wordsworth's *Prelude* no wish to be a child again, no idealizing or sentimentalizing of childhood. (Some of his recollected experiences are in any case largely painful or disturbing.) The interest is in the development of the human being to maturity.

NOTE

Nutting (1799) and *Yew Trees* (1803) look like parts of *The Prelude*, though left outside it as independent poems. But they associate naturally with the boyhood experiences of Book 1. Each communicates the spirit of a particular place – or the spirit of the hazels, the spirit of the yews, as the life of those places where they seem to haunt. *Nutting* recaptures the boy's sense of finding himself alone in an enchanted place, a silent paradise of hazels with their wealth of nuts ('tempting clusters') where no one had ever been before. The virginal magical place ('a virgin scene') is violently, brutally ravaged and desecrated by the boy himself, such he feels his natural boyish act of possessing himself of the nuts to have been. He experiences in consequence a sense of guilt, as if he had committed a sacrilegious crime.

Perhaps it was a bower beneath whose leaves
The violets of five seasons re-appear
And fade, unseen by any human eye;
Where fairy water-breaks do murmur on
For ever; and I saw the sparkling foam,
And – with my cheek on one of those green stones
That, fleeced with moss, under the shady trees . . .
I heard the murmur . . .
            Then up I rose,
And dragged to earth both branch and bough, with crash
And merciless ravage: and the shady nook
Of hazels, and the green and mossy bower,
Deformed and sullied, patiently gave up

> Their quiet being; and, unless I now
> Confound my present feelings with the past;
> Ere from the mutilated bower I turned
> Exulting, rich beyond the wealth of kings,
> I felt a sense of pain when I beheld
> The silent trees, and saw the intruding sky –
> Then, dearest Maiden, move along these shades
> In gentleness of heart; with gentle hand
> Touch – for there is a spirit in the woods.

Hopkins's *Binsey Poplars* comes to mind as one of the few comparable poems because of its sensitive, delicate feeling for growing things ('hack and wrack the growing green' . . . 'since Nature is so tender . . . to touch') and for the individuality (the selfhood) of a particular place ('sweet especial scene').

Yew Trees also communicates a sense of a particular place with a spirit and mood of its own which a group of yew-trees ('the fraternal four') combine to make. The tough yews ('huge trunks') are solid and substantial objects, yet in combination they make a place that, to the imagination, is ghostly and haunted.

>   – a pillared shade,
> Upon whose grassless floor of red-brown hue,
> By sheddings from the pining umbrage tinged
> Perennially – beneath whose sable roof
> Of boughs, as if for festal purpose, decked
> With unrejoicing berries – ghostly Shapes
> May meet at noontide; Fear and trembling Hope,
> Silence and Foresight; Death the Skeleton
> And Time the Shadow; – there to celebrate,
> As in a natural temple scattered o'er
> With altars undisturbed of mossy stone,
> United worship.

The personifications here have become in the imagination experienced realities, associated with the contorted shapes of the yews as closely as the shadows of the yews might be, unlike the conventional personifications of minor 18th-century verse. The suggestion of a Gothic cathedral ('pillared shades') is subsumed in the sense of the place as a 'natural temple' with altars of stones, 'holy' in a pre-Christian sense, like some temple of an ancient or prehistoric worship.

III

The note of enchantment in the poetry of the experience of places in Book 2[1] appears to have had its origin in the awakenings of adolescence, the adolescent's moments of an intense sense of a magical beauty in earthly places. There is, at this stage of development, more of a conscious feeling for places as places, and for their beauty. The islands of Windermere, though the boy arrives there in a crowd of other boys boat-racing, have each for his imagination a beauty like a spell (cf. the islands of *The Faerie Queene*), a beauty that remains in the memory. The third island, because of its solitude and its ruined shrine, is haunted also by a sense of the past.

> now an Island musical with birds
> That sang and ceased not; now a Sister Isle
> Beneath the oaks' umbrageous covert, sown
> With lilies of the valley like a field;
> And now a third small Island, where survived
> In solitude the ruins of a shrine
> Once to Our Lady dedicate, and served
> Daily with chaunted rites.[2]

The presence of the past has again to do with the character of another visited place, the ruin of St. Mary's Abbey, in the Vale of Nightshade.

> yet a mouldering pile with fractured arch,
> Belfry, and images, and living trees;
> A holy scene! – Along the smooth green turf
> Our horses grazed . . .[3]
> the summons given,
> With whip and spur we through the chauntry flew
> In uncouth race, and left the cross-legged knight,
> And the stone-abbot, and that single wren
> Which one day sang so sweetly in the nave
> Of the old church, that – though from recent showers

---

[1] Cf. *Nutting* (1799) and *Yew Trees* (1803). [2] Book 2. 58–65.
[3] Book 2. 105–8.

The earth was comfortless, and, touched by faint
Internal breezes, sobbings of the place
And respirations, from the roofless walls
The shuddering ivy dripped large drops – yet still
So sweetly 'mid the gloom the invisible bird
Sang to herself, that there I could have made
My dwelling-place, and lived for ever there
To hear such music.[1]

'The cross legged knight' and 'the stone abbot' contribute an
essential element (with the 'living trees', the horses and the single
wren) to the individuality of the place, its unique features and
character (cf. the effect of the metaphor for bare branches in Shake-
speare's sonnet 'Bare ruined choirs where late the sweet birds
sang'). But the poetry conveys something more, a haunting
sense that the place has a life and moods of its own. On that
particular remembered day the mood of the place is cheerless
('comfortless'). But the song of the bird, 'that single wren' so
self-contained, not only resists the mournful mood but magically
transforms it. It is almost as if the bird, 'the invisible bird', were a
spirit in the place, a spirit of gladness. The place is felt both to be
holy (because of the ruined abbey) and ghostly ('sobbings',
'respirations'). Its solitude, with its still stone images, has been
disturbed, its sanctity violated, by the rush of the horses and
riders through it. But the song of 'the invisible bird' finally pre-
vails and remains most vividly in the memory. It has given the
place at a particular moment its particular value, its magical life.
But this living magic is, as it were, a natural magic, the magic of
the fact of life itself, distinguished in Wordsworth's poetry from
the sensationalism of the then fashionable interest in melancholy
ruins, picturesqueness and the supernatural of the Gothic revival.

There is again a note of enchantment, a 'faerie' and even a
mythological quality about the remembered occasion when 'the
Minstral of the troop' is marooned by himself on an island in the
lake – 'like some god o' the isle'.

> while he blew his flute
> Alone upon the rock – oh, then, the calm
> And dead still water lay upon my mind

[1] Book 2. 115–28.

> Even with a weight of pleasure, and the sky,
> Never before so beautiful, sank down
> Into my heart, and held me like a dream![1]

But if there is the beautiful in nature there is also the sublime, in the consciousness of which there is an element of fear or awe. To the imagination of the growing boy there come moments of consciousness of sublimities in nature. There is the remembered occasion from which the poetry – without the aid of the Miltonic grand manner – takes a note of sublimity, when the boy standing alone listening to the sounds of a night storm among the mountains grows conscious of the earth as 'ancient' and as having a 'ghostly language' of its own.

> and I would stand,
> If the night blackened with a coming storm,
> Beneath some rock, listening to notes that are
> The ghostly language of the ancient earth,
> Or make their dim abode in distant winds.[2]

The sense of a living connection between the human being and the natural universe is one of the profoundest intuitions in Wordsworth's poetry.

> No outcast he, bewildered and depressed:
> Along his infant veins are interfused
> The gravitation and the filial bond
> Of nature that connect him with the world.[3]

The lines come in the passage in Book 2 (analysed by Mr. Leavis in his essay) in which the origins of this sense of a connection are traced back to the connection between mother and infant, the tenderness and, indeed, holiness of which are so delicately felt and apprehended in the poetry. Through his mother already the infant human being begins to enter into an intimate relationship

---

[1] Book 2. 169–74.

[2] Book 2. 306–10. This is a passage which originally came in an early poem called *The Pedlar* (composed in 1798 at the time when he had been working on *The Ruined Cottage*). Most of it was later incorporated in various parts of *The Prelude* and *The Excursion*. The experience is there attributed to the Pedlar.

[3] Book 2. 241–4.

with what is not himself, ultimately with what is neither himself
nor his mother, the world beyond either.

> blest the Babe,
> Nursed in his Mother's arms, who sinks to sleep
> Rocked on his Mother's breast; who with his soul
> Drinks in the feelings of his Mother's eye!
> For him, in one dear Presence, there exists
> A virtue which irradiates and exalts
> Objects through widest intercourse of sense . . .[1]
>
> . . .
>
> Is there a flower, to which he points with hand
> Too weak to gather it, already love
> Drawn from love's purest earthly fount for him
> Hath beautified that flower; already shades
> Of pity cast from inward tenderness
> Do fall around him upon aught that bears
> Unsightly marks of violence or harm.[2]

(Cf. the passage about the mother and child in Rilke's *Third
Duino Elegy*.) The human being's earliest connection with what
is outside himself, his connection with his mother, can thus
develop and extend into the mature human being's sense of a
connection between him and the whole of what is outside himself.
Mr. Leavis points to the parallel here between the Wordsworthian
and the Lawrentian intuitions. (Cf. Lawrence's 'Thank God I am
not free any more than a tree is free'. 'We must plant ourselves
again in the universe.') Wordsworth, too, feels the human being
not to be a detached and isolated unit in a mechanical or neutral
universe but to draw his life through a living connection with
what is outside himself.

IV

The special interest of the recollected impressions of Cambridge
in Book 3 is that they are Wordsworth's, a particular northerner's
impressions, the effect on him of the change of place.

[1] Book 2. 234–40.
[2] Book 2. 245–51. In this passage there are a number of truly creative changes
made later than the 1805 version.

Migration strange for a stripling of the hills,
A northern villager.

Certain of these impressions are in themselves vivid and accurate
– for example the individual quality of the bell in the ghostly
atmosphere of the peculiarly Cambridge winter night –

Albeit long after the importunate bell
Had stopped, with wearisome Cassandra voice
No longer haunting the dark winter night.[1]

But the place is felt to have remained to some extent strange to
Wordsworth; it never became completely familiar, even when

the dazzling show no longer new
Had ceased to dazzle.

The northern hill country, which had made him, continues to be
more essentially a part of his life than the immediate Cambridge
scene. 'The motley spectacle' flowing through the streets, courts
and cloisters is observed with 'a strange half-absence' and acquires
in consequence a dream-like quality.

I was the Dreamer, they the Dream.

We discover the youthful Wordsworth withdrawing at intervals
from the social crowd into solitary communings with nature, as
had been his habit among the hills. He had brought with him his
sense of the mystery of things and of the depths of human souls,
deepening his own life, preserving him from shallowness.

O Heavens! how awful is the might of souls . . .
Caverns there were within my mind.

The marble face of Newton seen in the moonlight strikes Words-
worth's imagination characteristically.

The antechapel where the statue stood
Of Newton with his prism and silent face,
The marble index of a mind for ever
Voyaging through strange seas of Thought, alone.[2]

---

[1] Book 3. 306–8.
[2] Book 3. 60–3. The last two lines are a late addition, one of the rare truly
creative additions.

The face has become for Wordsworth an image, virtually a vision, of the mind in solitude exploring a limitless unknown. In contrast, Pope's couplet about Newton has all the confidence of the Augustan Enlightenment.

> Nature and Nature's Laws lay hid in night.
> God said, Let Newton be and all was light.

A confidence the consequence of which Byron, in his turn, with his gift for handling ideas lightly, could relish the absurdity of.

> When Newton saw an apple fall, he found
>   In that slight startle from his contemplation –
> 'Tis *said* (for I'll not answer above ground
>   For any sage's creed or calculation) –
> A mode of proving that the earth turn'd round
>   In a most natural whirl, called 'gravitation';
> And this is the sole mortal who could grapple,
> Since Adam, with a fall, or with an apple.
>
> Men fell with apples, and with apples rose,
>   If this be true; for we must deem the mode
> In which Sir Isaac Newton could disclose
>   Through the then unpaved stars the turnpike road,
> A thing to counterbalance human woes:
>   For ever since immortal man hath glow'd
> With all kinds of mechanics, and full soon
> Steam-engines will conduct him to the moon![1]

Books appear to have always seemed to Wordsworth subordinate to nature as a source of wisdom. But it is clear from some sensitive and delicate lines that he read the pre-18th century English poets with a feeling for them, an imaginative critical grasp of their essential qualities, which our academic studies now seem often to have lost.

> Beside the pleasant Mill of Trompington
> I laughed with Chaucer in the hawthorn shade . . .
> Sweet Spenser, moving through his clouded heaven
> With the moon's beauty and the moon's soft pace.[2]

[1] *Don Juan*. Canto 10, stanzas 1–2.
[2] Book 3. 275 etc.

The vision of the young Milton is perfectly in accord with the effect of Milton's early poetry.

> Angelical, keen eye, courageous look,
> And conscious step of purity and pride.[1]

The 'grave Elders' of the place, 'men unscoured, grotesque in character' – 'a different aspect of old age' from the shepherds of his native hills – persist as remembered figures in the human comedy,[2] the passing show, like puppets at a wake or fair. As such, they have acquired a phantom aspect –

> Old humorists, who have been long in their graves,
> And having almost in my mind put off
> Their human names, have into phantoms passed
> Of texture midway between life and books[3]

– lines which again have something of a Shakespearian quality ('These our actors, as you do see, have vanished . . .').

V

Book 4 begins with the effect on Wordsworth of his return after his first absence, an absence in a strange place (Cambridge), to his native hills and dales. There is the experience of the familiar recovered, the things among which he had grown up, even minute sights, sounds, movements, recaptured but noted in a new way. Things look the same yet not quite so. He has become conscious of aspects of things he had not been conscious of before. In the interval there have been developments in his own consciousness both of nature and of man. He can now make comparisons between the people of two different places. He has become more aware in some respects of people and, in particular, the kind of people those of his native region are,

[1] Book 3, 275 etc.
[2] Cf. Pope's passage about the academic procession in *The Dunciad*, Book 4.

> Prompt at the call, around the Goddess roll
> Broad hats, and hoods, and caps, a sable shoal;
> Thick and more thick the black blockade extends
> A hundred head of Aristotle's friends.

[3] Book 3. 575–8.

those plain-living people now observed
With clearer knowledge.

For the first time in *The Prelude* we have a portrait of a human character other than himself, one who had always been close to him, but perhaps for that reason never before realized as a distinct person, 'my grey haired Dame'.[1]

> Saw her go forth to church or other work
> Of state equipped in monumental trim;
> Short velvet cloak, (her bonnet of the like),
> A mantle such as Spanish Cavaliers
> Wore in old times. Her smooth domestic life,
> Affectionate without disquietude,
> Her talk, her business, pleased me; and no less
> Her clear though shallow stream of piety
> That ran on Sabbath days a fresher course;
> With thoughts unfelt till now I saw her read
> Her Bible on hot Sunday afternoons,
> And loved the book, when she had dropped asleep
> And made of it a pillow for her head.[2]

A humanizing change has also come about in his feelings for the objects of the visible world.

> A human-heartedness about my love
> For objects hitherto the absolute wealth
> Of my own private being.[3]

At this point the poetry expresses a sense of the complexity of experience and, in particular, of one's past life as viewed in recollection.

> As one who hangs down-bending from the side
> Of a slow-moving boat ...
>   and cannot part
> The shadow from the substance, rocks and sky,
> Mountains and clouds, reflected in the depth
> Of the clear flood, from things which there abide

---

[1] Wordsworth, we need to remember, was deprived of his mother when a child by her death. This certainly had something to do with his feelings about nature.
[2] Book 4. 218–30.   [3] Book 4. 233–5.

In their true dwelling; now is crossed by gleam
Of his own image, by a sunbeam now,
And wavering motions sent he knows not whence.[1]

Two experiences stand out from the recollections in this Book
as having deepened his life. The first of these is the conversion
and dedication of his whole being (as he feels it to have been)
brought about by his witnessing the morning spectacle of nature
on his way home after a village dance.

> Magnificent
> The morning rose, in memorable pomp,
> Glorious as e'er I had beheld – in front,
> The sea lay laughing at a distance; near
> The solid mountains shone, bright as the clouds,
> Grain-tinctured, drenched in empyrean light
> And in the meadows and the lower grounds
> Was all the sweetness of a common dawn –
> Dews, vapours, and the melody of birds,
> And labourers going forth to till the fields.[2]

It is characteristic of Wordsworth that the dawn is seen in its
splendour of light as in a vision and yet remains 'a common
dawn' – splendid and yet homely and intimate (cf. 'A sight so
touching in its majesty'). The experience breaks through his
surface life (the social gaiety of the night passed in dancing in a
crowded room) and reaches down to the depths of his being,
effecting (as he feels) a permanent change in him.

The second of those experiences (the hugest imaginative ex-
perience of Book 4) is the meeting with the old soldier.[3] So far,
in the tracing of his development, the primary fact in Words-
worth's consciousness has been the fact of nature. But in this
experience he is, as if for the first time, brought up against
another primary fact, the fact of another man, a human existence
other than his own. This seems, so far as I can make out, the
earliest of those recollected meetings with a man in a desolate
place, as well as the earliest to be made into poetry before being
incorporated in *The Prelude*. (It seems to have happened earlier

---

[1] Book 4. 256 etc.   [2] Book 4. 323–32.
[3] This is one of the earliest passages to have been composed – early in 1798.

than the comparable meeting with the Leechgatherer.) He now takes in the full force, magnitude and mystery of the fact of a Man. When he had supposed himself to be alone, a solitary traveller, the shock of this impact with another life, another consciousness existent in the universe, gives rise to one of those imaginative experiences in Wordsworth's poetry 'analogous to the super-natural' (cf. the Ancient Mariner).[1]

Again he had withdrawn from a crowd – an evening spent in 'a flower-decked room', with all that this implies of social pleasure – and had taken his solitary way homeward by one of those long roads, shining in the moonlight and extending to the horizon, across a bare expanse of moorland, a journey which might be that of the human soul in its naked simplicity.

> No living thing appeared in earth or air.

Suddenly, at a turning of the road, he is confronted by an unex-pected presence – the other. At first visible simply as 'an uncouth shape' without motion, it is recognizably a man's shape, though unusually tall.

> He was of stature tall,
> A span above man's common measure, tall,
> Stiff, lank, and upright; a more meagre man
> Was never seen before by night or day.
> Long were his arms, pallid his hands; his mouth
> Looked ghastly in the moonlight.

The sense – aided by the accident of moonlight – of a ghostly presence does not grow less with the observing of each detail of his appearance. Yet the presence becomes identifiable as that of a man, specifically a military man.

> clothed in military garb,
> Though faded, yet entire. Companionless,
> No dog attending, by no staff sustained,
> He stood.

For all his faded 'military garb' he is in essence a naked soul in the universe, almost indeed as if he had no body – 'a more meagre

---

[1] The whole passage will be found in Book 4, 374 to the end.

man' (cf. the old man in *The Pardoner's Tale*). In stark contrast
to 'the flower-decked room' and to 'the trappings of a gaudy
world', he is –

> A desolation, a simplicity

– stripped also of the social conventions and habitual attitudes
which would in more ordinary circumstances have cushioned the
shock of the collision with him. Thus it comes as another surprise
when sounds issue from his lips. The sense of the supernatural,
the man's ghostliness, is further augmented by the fact of his
persisting motionlessness (cf. the Leechgatherer).

> yet still his form
> Kept the same awful steadiness – at his feet
> His shadow lay, and moved not.

Thus it is yet again a surprise that when 'hailed', as a soul en-
countered among the shadows of the underworld might be, he
responds with a slow and 'measured gesture' (the salute of a
military man that, in this context, might be that of a sentinel ghost
in empty space or the realms of the dead).

> Slowly from his resting-place
> He rose, and with a lean and wasted arm
> In measured gesture lifted to his head
> Returned my salutation; then resumed
> His station as before.

He tells his story, provides (like the Leechgatherer and the Blind
Beggar) his explanation, which is no explanation of the mystery
of what he is.

> He told in few plain words a soldier's tale ...
> And now was travelling towards his native home.

The word 'travelling', in the context of the whole passage, re-
introduces a suggestion of the soul's mysterious journey (cf.
Stepping Westward). The fact of his motionlessness had at first
much to do with the feeling of the supernatural. The fact that he
now unexpectedly begins to move – and appears 'to travel
without pain' – seems equally supernatural.

> he appeared
> To travel without pain, and I beheld
> With an astonishment but ill suppressed,
> His ghostly figure moving at my side.

As he moves, he continues to answer questions about 'his past'. But the mystery of his existence remains. It is not non-existence, it is existence which is inexplicable. To the man himself his earthly career, now nearing its end, is no longer a matter about which he is capable of feeling.

> in all he said
> There was a strange half-absence, as of one
> Knowing too well the importance of his theme,
> But feeling it no longer.

But the Biblical solemnity of his final words –

> With the same ghastly mildness in his look,
> He said, 'My trust is in the God of Heaven,
> And in the eye of him who passes me!'

expresses a sublime trustfulness and dignity (cf. again the Leech-gatherer).

The exactitude with which the experience is conveyed, an experience analogous to the supernatural – we may note, for example, the subtle association of 'ghostly' and 'ghastly' in the passage – might suggest to the modern reader a comparison with the uncanny experience of the meeting with the 'compound ghost' in *Little Gidding*. One difference is that the latter is consciously Dantean and depends for its effect of detachment on the Dantean verse-form combined with what the reader feels to be the more consciously controlled precision of the word-selection (e.g. in deliberately inhibiting any one single meaning from imposing itself). The language of the Wordsworthian narration is again characteristic of his best poetry. We begin from what appears to be (not unlike the great Eliot passage) basically a bare, matter-of-fact, almost prosaic recording of what happened exactly as it is recollected, and yet, before we are aware of the change, the language is working on us creatively, developing the

experience.[1] It is the developing imaginative experience itself
which is again the poetry. The words draw no attention to them-
selves away from the experience they create or re-create, with no
added decoration, no idle 'trappings'. It is as if we were viewing
an object in a medium so purely transparent that we are aware
only of the object, not the medium. Yet, though revealed with
such clarity, without distortion, the object or subject – the recol-
lected experience – is in itself a mystery, the mystery of an un-
known other soul pressing out from the unknown. Wordsworth
is again entirely free from the sensationalism of the then fashion-
able Gothicism. Simply to encounter a man is to encounter a soul,
a being, a life; the earlier or original sense of the word 'ghost' has
once again, in Wordsworth's poetry, been recovered and renewed.

The comparable experience inside *The Prelude* is the meeting
with the Blind Beggar (unexpectedly in the London crowd) and
outside *The Prelude* the meeting with the Leechgatherer. These
particular experiences are central in the whole Wordsworthian
experience. The passage about the Old Soldier inevitably recalls
the parallel passage in *The Leechgatherer* (1802). As the poet
wanders across the moorland, the sudden meeting with a man
lifts that poem too into great imaginative poetry.

> Beside a pool bare to the eye of heaven
> I saw a Man before me unawares:
> The oldest man he seemed that ever wore grey hairs.
>
> As a huge stone is sometimes seen to lie
> Couched on the bald top of an eminence;
> Wonder to all who do the same espy,
> By what means it could thither come, and whence;
> So that it seems a thing endued with sense:
> Like a sea-beast crawled forth, that on a shelf
> Of rock or sand reposeth, there to sun itself;
>
> Such seemed this Man, not all alive nor dead,
> Nor all asleep – in his extreme old age.

[1] There remains in Wordsworth's poetry a solid basis of prose matter-of-
factness – a conviction, for example, of the external world as being tangible and
solid fact – inherited from the 18th century out of which his poetry broke. But
equally his new sense of the mystery of things and of human life gives rise to
those notes of wonder and reverence that are characteristic of Wordsworth.

The images of the huge stone and the sea-beast imaginatively enlarge the impression. There is the feeling that there is something huge about the old man, as if he were more or other than human, and that he is a mystery in that place. ('By what means it could thither come, and whence'.) 'What is he?' we ask. ('not all alive nor dead, nor all asleep'.) For all his motionlessness and his feebleness of 'extreme old age' he affects the imagination as a latent power, both a potentiality and a reality. The image of the sea-beast crawled forth upon a ledge, together with the image of the huge stone couched on the bald top of an eminence, subtly associates him in that waste with other and earlier forms of life and shapes of things and with a prehistoric or primeval world (cf. some passages in Hardy).

> Upon the margin of that moorish flood
> Motionless as a cloud the old Man stood,
> That heareth not the loud winds when they call
> And moveth all together, if it move at all.

We are thus prepared for him to move, if he moves at all, with the kind of shape-changing motion a cloud-shape has. Nevertheless (as at the moment in its creation when the heart of Blake's Tiger begins to beat, the creature to come alive) it comes as a shock of surprise and wonder that he moves –

> At length, himself unsettling, he the pond
> Stirred with his staff, and fixedly did look
> Upon the muddy water.

– and that he speaks, in answer to questions put to him, in the language of men, his speech the solemn Biblical speech of the northern people.

> What occupation do you there pursue?
> This is a lonesome place for one like you? . . .
> His words came feebly, from a feeble chest,
> But each in solemn order followed each,
> With something of a lofty utterance drest –
> Choice word and measured phrase, above the reach
> Of ordinary men a stately speech;
> Such as grave Livers do in Scotland use,

Religious men, who give to God and man their dues.

> He told, that to these waters he had come
> To gather leeches, being old and poor:
> Employment hazardous and wearisome!
> And he had many hardships to endure:
> From pond to pond he roamed, from moor to moor
> Housing, with God's good help, by choice or chance,
> And in this way he gained an honest maintenance.

The explanation of what he is doing there is no explanation or who or what he – or any man – is. His occupation is in fact a very mundane one. He gathers leeches that, as he stands motionless in a pool, fasten themselves to his legs and are then picked off and gathered for sale to the medical profession. There could not be, we might suppose, a more degrading way of earning a bare subsistence, forced on an old man by the injustices of society. Yet the spiritual power of endurance of the old man, his strength of character, his moral dignity and, something more, the mystery of his being, press at us out of the poem. The supernatural effect of the initial impression – 'a feeling analogous to the supernatural' – persists and expands as he is talking, apart from the meaning of the words he utters.

> The old Man still stood talking by my side
> But now his voice to me was like a stream
> Scarce heard nor word from word could I divide;
> And the whole body of the Man did seem
> Like one whom I had met with in a dream . . .
> While he was talking thus, the lonely place,
> The old Man's shape, and speech – all troubled me:
> In my mind's eye I seemed to see him pace
> About the weary moors continually,
> Wandering about alone and silently.

The whole imaginative experience is something bigger, we feel, than the moral drawn, the 'apt admonishment' to the moody poet (whose dejection is now recognized by himself as being by comparison with the old man's fortitude the merest moral weakness).

I could have laughed myself to scorn to find
In that decrepit Man so firm a mind.[1]

VI

The influence of books, though the declared subject of Book 5, is still in the poetry subordinate to the influence of nature, although associated with it. The education of nature is, as Wordsworth believes from experience, the best. The boy Wordsworth (of Book 1) was not, it seems, exceptional among the boys of those parts. Book 5 is memorable – and has been chiefly remembered – for the boy who 'blew mimic hootings to the silent owls that they might answer him'. The boy (though he died) is much like the boy Wordsworth in his responsiveness to the influences of nature, a solitary boy who enjoyed a strange companionship, a mutual responsiveness through sounds and echoes with the owls and distant mountain torrents, as well as with the visible scene both immediate and as reflected in the lake. The poetry recaptures the boy's wonder and the extraordinariness of the things of the natural world. The influences of nature impregnate the growing mind consciously and unconsciously and work on the imagination. In the silences between the 'concourse wild' of the hootings of the owls which the boy has deliberately awakened

> a gentle shock of mild surprise
> Has carried far into his heart the voice
> Of mountain torrents; or the visible scene
> Would enter unawares into his mind,
> With all its solemn imagery.[2]

But almost equally striking and profound in its psychological insight is a passage in Book 5 which illustrates the imagination of a child (the child Wordsworth himself) nourished by imaginative or fanciful literature, and the influence of such literature on his capacity for dealing or not dealing with an event in the actual world. This is the episode of the child's discovery of a heap of clothes by the lakeside and its sequel, the next day, a drowned man brought to the surface. The episode again depends for its powerful effect in the poetry on the exactitude and particularity with which it is recollected and re-created.

[1] Contrast Ignaro in *The Faerie Queene*.   [2] Book 5. 382–6.

Twilight was coming on, yet through the gloom
Appeared distinctly on the opposite shore
A heap of garments, as if left by one
Who might have there been bathing. Long I watched,
But no one owned them; meanwhile the calm lake
Grew dark with all the shadows on its breast,
And, now and then, a fish up-leaping snapped
The breathless stillness. The succeeding day,
Those unclaimed garments telling a plain tale
Drew to the spot an anxious crowd; some looked
In passive expectation from the shore,
While from a boat others hung o'er the deep,
Sounding with grappling irons and long poles.
At last, the dead man, 'mid that beauteous scene
Of trees and hills and water, bolt upright
Rose, with his ghastly face, a spectre shape
Of terror; yet no soul-debasing fear,
Young as I was, a child not nine years old,
Possessed me, for my inner eye had seen
Such sights before, among the shining streams
Of faery land, the forest of romance.[1]

The Wordsworthian interest is in the fact that the imaginative
child does not himself feel the 'terror' – feels 'no soul-debasing
fear' at the 'ghastly face' of death that emerges in the tranquil
and beautiful place. He has seen such sights before – in imagin-
ation

---

[1] Book 5. 435–55. The Styx-like scene of the boatmen searching the black
stream for the drowned Zenobia in Hawthorne's *Blithedale Romance* offers a com-
parison which brings out the distinct qualities of each author. One difference is
that we care for Zenobia, such has been her effect throughout the novel. There-
fore, the cruelty of 'the hooked pole' with which Hollingsworth, 'the Iron Man'
(the modern Puritan), is probing the dark depths, as if he would savagely destroy
the body of the beautiful woman he seeks to find, makes the horror grimly
symbolical.

'. . . with a nervous and jerky movement he began to plunge it into the black-
   ness, that upbore us, setting his teeth and making precisely such thrusts, me-
   thought, as if he were stabbing at a deadly enemy . . . And there, perhaps, she
   lay, with her face upward, while the shadow of the boat and my own pale face
   peering downward, passed slowly betwixt her and the sky.'

There is no such element of 'symbolism' in the Wordsworth passage as there is in
the American novel.

among the shining streams
Of faery land, the forest of romance.

Furthermore, as the passage goes on, these sights he has been familiar with in the realm of the imagination lend 'ideal grace' and 'dignity' to the actual 'sad spectacle'. The reader notes also (perhaps with amusement) that, at this stage in his development, the child had seen no reason to infer, or to do, anything about the heap of clothes. Within the imagination of the child the spectacle is as detached from practicality as a work of 'Grecian art' or 'purest poesy'.

What the *Arabian Nights* did for the imagination of the child, the poetry of Spenser did for the imagination of the youth at Cambridge. This is apparent in the passage about the ash-tree in the next book (Book 6). The poetry of Spenser evidently appealed to the young poet at the age of the youthful awakening of wonder, when a quality of enchantment proceeding from his imagination, aided at times by the accident of moonlight, invested his observations of nature.

Often have I stood
Foot-bound uplooking at this lovely tree
Beneath a frosty moon. The hemisphere
Of magic fiction, verse of mine perchance
May never tread; but scarcely Spenser's self
Could have more tranquil visions in his youth,
Or could more bright appearances create
Of human forms with superhuman powers,
Than I beheld, loitering on calm clear nights
Alone, beneath this fairy work of earth.[1]

But Wordsworth's main discovery at Cambridge seems – or seemed to the poet himself in retrospect – to have been that nature provided him with a truer education than books.

I was a better judge of thoughts than words,
Misled in estimating words, not only
By common inexperience of youth,
But by the trade in classic niceties.[2]

---

[1] Book 6. 85–94.
[2] Book 6. 106–9. (Cf. Pope on verbal education in *Dunciad*, Book 4.)

VII

The best poetry of Book 6 takes its origin in the recollected effect on Wordsworth's imagination of his first sight of the Alps, mountains more enormous in scale than his native hills, presenting almost a new dimension of nature. These experiences among the sublimities of the Alps come at the end of his journey through a jubilant and festive France in what were still the early hopeful days of the Revolution.

> France standing on the top of golden hours,
> And human nature seeming born again.

One effect of the Alpine sublimities and glooms seems to have been – judging from this poetry of a later time – to cast moderating shadows over Wordsworth's own youthful sanguineness.

Though there is no question of any imitation of Dante, whereas there are Miltonic echoes to be allowed for, there is a Dantean quality in some of Wordsworth's lines about the Convent of the Chartreuse. The poetry here has a solidity that Arnold's more gently elegiac *Stanzas from the Grande Chartreuse*, sad with his uncertainties, lack. Wordsworth comes to the place at a moment when the Revolutionaries have threatened the inmates of the Convent with violent expulsion.

> Beheld the Convent of Chartreuse, and there
> Rested within an awful solitude . . .
> . . . riotous men commissioned to expel
> The blameless inmates, and belike subvert
> That frame of social being, which so long
> Had bodied forth the ghostliness of things
> In silence visible and perpetual calm.
> – 'Stay, stay your sacrilegious hands!' – The voice
> Was Nature's, uttered from her Alpine throne.
> . . . She ceased to speak, but while St. Bruno's pines
> Waved their dark tops, not silent as they waved,
> And while below, along their several beds,
> Murmured the sister streams of Life and Death.[1]

---

[1] Book 6. 418 et seq. This whole passage was added later than the 1805 version and is one of the most impressive additions to the poem (c. 1807–8).

He himself was at that time in general sympathy with the Revo-
lution's purging the new world of the dead things of the past. But
(as he creatively recollects it years later) his 'heart responded' to
the voice of Nature when it said

> 'Spare
> These courts of mystery, where a step advanced
> Between the portals of the shadowy rocks
> Leaves far behind life's treacherous vanities,
> For penitential tears and trembling hopes
> Exchanged – to equalise in God's pure sight
> Monarch and peasant: be the house redeemed
> With its unworldly votaries, for the sake
> Of conquest over sense, hourly achieved
> Through faith and meditative reason.'[1]

There are, too, the 'imaginative impulses' of nature in this place,
the Alpine sublimities surrounding the monastery.

> '. . . that imaginative impulse sent
> From these majestic floods, yon shining cliffs,
> The untransmuted shapes of many worlds,
> Cerulean ether's pure inhabitants,
> These forests unapproachable by death,
> That shall endure as long as man endures . . .'
> In sympathetic reverence we trod
> The floors of those dim cloisters, till that hour,
> From their foundation, strangers to the presence
> Of unrestricted and unthinking man.
>   Vallombre's groves
> Entering, we fed the soul with darkness.[1]

The narrative of the crossing of the Alps culminates in the
poetry of the Simplon Pass experience, one of the passages of
great poetry in *The Prelude*. The Wordsworthian psychological
interest in the preceding narrative is in his noting of the fact that
when he and his fellow-travellers were forced to recognize that
what the peasant told them was true – that they *had* 'crossed the
Alps', that they must now follow the course of the stream down-

---

[1] Book 6, 418 et seq. This whole passage was added later than the 1805 ver-
sion and is one of the most impressive additions to the poem (c. 1807–8).

wards – they experienced not a joyful sense of triumph but a shock of disappointment. On first coming to the downward-flowing stream they had instinctively followed a track leading up a mountain-side.

> Conspicuous invitation to ascend
> A lofty mountain.[1]

But a peasant, accidentally met with, directed them back.

> Loth to believe what we so grieved to hear,
> For still we had hopes that pointed to the clouds,
> We questioned him again, and yet again;
> But every word that from the peasant's lips
> Came in reply, translated by our feelings,
> Ended in this, – *that we had crossed the Alps*.[1]

The disappointment, however, as recollected, is followed by the inference, the triumphant recognition of the nature and greatness of the mind of man that reaches out towards infinity.

> Imagination ...
> That awful Power rose from the mind's abyss
> Like an unfathered vapour that enwraps,
> At once, some lonely traveller. I was lost;
> Halted without an effort to break through;
> But to my conscious soul I now can say –
> 'I recognise thy glory:' in such strength
> Of usurpation, when the light of sense
> Goes out, but with a flash that has revealed
> The invisible world ...
> Our destiny, our being's heart and home,
> Is with infinitude, and only there;
> With hope it is, hope that can never die,
> Effort, and expectation, and desire,
> And something evermore about to be.[1]

This, however, remains assertion. It is in the Simplon Pass experience immediately after this ('The melancholy slackening soon dislodged' ... 'entering a narrow chasm ...') that suddenly

---

[1] Book 6, 572 et seq. – The phrases recollecting the disappointment are not in the 1805 version, an instance of a recollection being further developed in the poetry.

we find the creative imagination of the poet working directly and powerfully as poetry. The physical landscape, such is the effect on the imagination of the sublimities of this Alpine place, assumes in the poetry the character of a symbolic landscape seen in a vision.

> The immeasurable height
> Of woods decaying, never to be decayed,
> The stationary blasts of waterfalls,
> And in the narrow rent at every turn
> Winds thwarting winds, bewildered and forlorn,
> The torrents shooting from the clear blue sky,
> The rocks that muttered close upon our ears,
> Black drizzling crags that spake by the way-side
> As if a voice were in them, the sick sight
> And giddy prospect of the raving stream,
> The unfettered clouds and region of the Heavens,
> Tumult and peace, the darkness and the light –
> Were all like workings of one mind, the features
> Of the same face, blossoms upon one tree.[1]

There is an Inferno-like vision of discord – 'winds thwarting winds, bewildered and forlorn' – conflict on a universal scale, spatial and temporal. In addition to a sense of infinities of height and depth, there is a sense of an infinity of time (not of timelessness but of time going on and on).

> The immeasurable height
> Of woods decaying, never to be decayed.

The actual narrow place seems to expand into a vision of a universe of constructed contrasts, the 'clear blue sky' and the 'black drizzling crags', Heaven and Earth (even Hell). There is an experience of forces broken loose, yet struggling and thwarted in a constricted space, 'the narrow rent'; imprisoned, yet overhead there are the 'unfettered clouds and region of the Heavens'. The 'woods decaying' are yet 'never to be decayed'.[2] The 'blasts of

---

[1] Book 6. 624–37.

[2] Cf. in *Yew Trees* (1803) that single yew tree, standing alone in its own darkness, its strength and durability, its ancientness

> a living thing
> Produced too slowly ever to decay.

waterfalls' are yet 'stationary'. We have here a vision of the contrarities of existence comparable with Blake's, the universe or (perhaps we should say) in its essence human experience itself as a structure of opposing opposites.

> Tumult and peace, the darkness and the light.

Suddenly, in the concluding lines, as in a flash of illumination, the tragic vision culminates and is resolved in an intuition of unity in diversity, harmony in discordance, order in disorder, an inclusive wholeness and oneness of infinitely varied, complex being.

> . . . all like workings of one mind, the features
> Of the same face, blossoms upon one tree.

This is not merely philosophy ('the One and the Many') but poetic insight or vision.

Book 6 reminds us incidentally that Wordsworth did make the acquaintance of nature in regions other than that of Westmorland and Cumberland, though he is and remains, wherever he is, essentially what his native region made him.

VIII

We do not usually associate Wordsworth with London. Yet Book 7, *Residence in London*, is one of the most interesting books of *The Prelude*. It contains a great deal of freshly experienced observation of the London spectacle in its amazing diversity, while at least one passage of great Wordsworthian poetry gives depth to the observation. Wordsworth's London is 'the great city' as viewed for the first time by a northerner wandering through its crowded streets in his own solitude, full of innocent wonderment and fresh and alert interest in what he sees, yet brooding and thoughtful, bringing with him his vision of nature and of man. Wherever he is, the external world – 'nature' in that sense – continues to be essentially that region of it where he grew up. It enters as imagery into his poetry as it had entered from his earliest

years into his mind – 'become a portion of his mind and life.' He
is accompanied in the London streets by his own creative memor-
ies of his native hills and dales, a consciousness of nature as a
surrounding immensity and mystery and, at the same time,
pressing out from individuals in the London crowd, the mystery
of man. The stream of passers-by in the London streets is to
Wordsworth made up of individual souls, each of whom is
potentially realizable as such, a reality and a mystery, as much so
as the Old Soldier or Leechgatherer met with among moorland
wastes and mountain solitudes.

Wordsworth and Byron have been conventionally grouped
together as 'Romantics' as well as contemporaries. Yet it would
be hard to find anywhere in literature more of a contrast than that
between Wordsworth's London in Book 7 of *The Prelude* and
Byron's London in Canto XI of *Don Juan*.[1] The different
qualities of each poet, at his best, could not be better brought out
than by this comparison. The comparison could be extended to
include Shelley's London in *Peter Bell the Third* ('Hell is a city
much like London . . .').

The passage of great Wordsworthian poetry in Book 7 that
gives depth to the observation is that in which the stream of
people flowing through the London streets takes on the quality
of 'a second-sight procession', a vision of human life passing from
the unknown into the unknown, in which

> The face of every one
> That passes by me is a mystery.

and in which he is arrested by the sight of a blind beggar.

---

[1] Byron's London is that of the aristocratic 'society' of the Regency he had
once moved in, looked back upon by a Byron now detached from it by time, place
and experience, with the gay disenchantment and freedom of his maturer years in
Italy. It was possible for him to do so in *Don Juan*, of course, because he had
luckily discovered a mode of expression in verse that freed him from his youthful
Romantic rhetoric, as well as gloom, and allowed him, as it were, to talk easily
and familiarly in the idiom he was accustomed to convivially among his friends
(as some of his letters also show). The 'great world', its shams and conventions,
is now viewed critically, humorously (in some moods sadly) in retrospect as 'the
little world' of the aristocratic society of the Regency period in which he himself
in his brief time, had cut such an extraordinary dash, a transient bright surface
world that has already evaporated (with his own youth).

As the black storm upon the mountain top
Sets off the sunbeam in the valley, so
That huge fermenting mass of human-kind
Serves as a solemn back-ground, or relief,
To single forms and objects, whence they draw,
For feeling and contemplative regard,
More than inherent liveliness and power.
How oft, amid those overflowing streets,
Have I gone forward with the crowd, and said
Unto myself, 'The face of every one
That passes by me is a mystery!'
Thus have I looked, nor ceased to look, oppressed
By thoughts of what and whither, when and how,
Until the shapes before my eyes became
A second-sight procession, such as glides
Over still mountains, or appears in dreams;
And once, far-travelled in such mood, beyond
The reach of common indication, lost
Amid the moving pageant, I was smitten
Abruptly, with the view (a sight not rare)
Of a blind Beggar, who, with upright face,
Stood, propped against a wall, upon his chest
Wearing a written paper, to explain
His story, whence he came, and who he was.
Caught by the spectacle my mind turned round
As with the might of waters; and apt type
This label seemed of the utmost we can know,
Both of ourselves and of the universe;
And, on the shape of that unmoving man,
His steadfast face and sightless eyes, I gazed,
As if admonished from another world.[1]

The imagery from Wordsworth's native hills enters into his vision of the London crowd enlarging the vision to include a consciousness of the universe. There is a dream-like sensation, to which the slow solemnity of the verse movement contributes, of being borne along in the stream of people, the flow of life, from which however 'single forms and objects' abruptly stand out.

[1] Book 7. 619–49.

Suddenly the attention is arrested by the face of the blind beggar with all that he so strangely and powerfully expresses of the mystery of human existence. As in the cases of the Old Soldier and the Leechgatherer, 'his story', the explanation that he wears, is no explanation of his mystery. He also, as they at first are, is an 'unmoving man' and seems, as they do, to have his source in, and draw his power from, 'another world'.

There is as much the quality of vision here in Wordsworth's poetry as in Dante's, the more authentically so because of the absence from the Wordsworth passage of any conscious or unconscious imitation of Dante. The passages in *The Waste Land* ('A crowd flowed over London Bridge . . .') and in *Little Gidding* (the meeting with the 'compound ghost' in the early hours in the London street) and Shelley's *Triumph of Life* are, of course, consciously related in form as well as substance to these poets' reading of Dante, whereas Wordsworth's personal vision simply happens, in this passage, to be in itself of a similar kind to Dante's.

But, unlike Eliot, Wordsworth could not have said 'Unreal City'. On the contrary, each individual in the flowing crowd is, for Wordsworth's imagination, a reality and not less so for being also a mystery ('the mystery, the depth of human souls'). Each is potentially an Old Soldier, a Leechgatherer, a Blind Beggar. In so far as they are 'ghostly' they are so once again in the sense that they are 'souls', each a life, a being. Hence the solemnity and reverence with which Wordsworth can speak of their mysterious depths of being, as he can speak of the mysterious depths of the universe. They are unknowns but not the less realities.

The comparison between Wordsworth's visions of human life and Shelley's in *The Triumph of Life* makes the difference between the two poets unusually clear. The Shelleyan enchantments and disenchantments, aspirations and sinkings, ardours and despairs have given way (in this, his fragmentary last long poem) to a maturer disenchantment than is to be found earlier in Shelley's poetry, a sense that life is a hollow dream. The poem, in its more lucid and ordered passages, has certainly the authentic note of great poetry.

'Let them pass,'
I cried, 'the world and its mysterious doom

'Is not so much more glorious than it was,
That I desire to worship those who drew
New figures on its false and fragile glass

'As the old faded.' – 'Figures ever new
Rise on the bubble, paint them as you may;
We have but thrown, as those before us threw,

'Our shadows on it as it passed away.'

. . .

'Whence camest thou? and whither goest thou?
How did thy course begin?' I said, 'and why?

'Mine eyes are sick of this perpetual flow
Of people, and my heart sick of one sad thought –
Speak!' . . .

'If, as it doth seem,
Thou comest from the realm without a name

'Into this valley of perpetual dream,
Show whence I came, and where I am, and why –
Pass not away upon the passing stream.'

The 'dome of many coloured glass'[1] which in *Adonais* 'stains the
white radiance of eternity' (in the sense not simply of smudges
but dyes with varied colours) has become in *The Triumph of Life*
'false and fragile glass'. There is no such note of disenchantment
in Wordsworth. On the contrary, there is, as I said, the sense of a
reality pressing out from individual lives in 'the moving pageant',
which is thus not an empty spectacle.[2]

In particular, for Wordsworth's imagination, the pause in the
life of the great city that comes with night allows the conscious-
ness of the calm of outer nature to break in (cf. the sonnet *Upon
Westminster Bridge*).

the peace
That comes with night; the deep solemnity
Of nature's intermediate hours of rest,

[1] Cf. the dome in *Kubla Khan* and in Yeats's *Byzantium*.

[2] Keats's vision of the stairs of the temple and of Moneta in the great fragment
for a revised *Hyperion* (he too had been reading Dante) has in this respect more
in common with Wordsworth, as well as with Shakespearian tragedy, than with
Shelley. It is a vision of reality – tragic reality – rather than of life as an unreal
dream or nightmare.

When the great tide of human life stands still:
The business of the day to come, unborn,
Of that gone by, locked up, as in the grave;[1]
The blended calmness of the heavens and earth,
Moonlight and stars, and empty streets, and sounds
Unfrequent as in deserts.[2]

The life of the city has its ebbs and flows, its sudden outbreaks,
sometimes violent – a theme that recurs later in *The Prelude* in
Wordsworth's recollections of his experience of revolutionary
Paris.

                                    at late hours
Of winter evenings, when unwholesome rains
Are falling hard, with people yet astir,
The feeble salutation from the voice
Of some unhappy woman, now and then
Heard as we pass, when no one looks about,
Nothing is listened to. But these, I fear,
Are falsely catalogued; things that are, are not,
As the mind answers to them, or the heart
Is prompt, or slow, to feel. What say you, then,
To times, when half the city shall break out
Full of one passion, vengeance, rage, or fear?
To executions, to a street on fire,
Mobs, riots, or rejoicings?[3]

The resemblances here in the subject-matter to that of Johnson's
London make the differences of attitude as well as of form the
more striking – the mordant Hogarthian realism and satiric edge
of Johnson's imitation of Juvenal and the profound awed solem-
nity of Wordsworth.

One of the occasions when the city 'breaks out' is the Bar-
tholomew Fair. Wordsworth describes 'the anarchy' of the Fair
with a relish for the bizarre, the grotesque, the odd, which we do
not usually associate with him.

All out-o'-the-way, far-fetched, perverted things
All freaks of nature.

[1] Cf. Hopkins's 'womb-of-all, home-of-all, hearse-of-all night'.
[2] Book 7. 654–62.   [3] Book 7. 662–75.

He sees the Fair as an epitome of the City ('O blank con-
fusion . . .') to too many, at least, of her inhabitants

> Living amid the same perpetual whirl
> Of trivial objects.[1]

But characteristically Wordsworth goes on

> It is not wholly so to him who looks
> In steadiness, who hath among least things
> An under-sense of greatest; sees the parts
> As parts, but with a feeling of the whole . . .
> And comprehensiveness and memory flow,
> From early converse with the works of God . . .
> This did I feel in London's vast domain.
> The Spirit of Nature was upon me there . . .
> Through meagre lines and colours, and the press
> Of self-destroying, transitory things.[1]

The spectacle of London has its place and meaning in the greater
whole which, for Wordsworth, includes always the memory of
his native region with its stable enduring hills.[2] Unlike Byron
Wordsworth never was or would have wished to become 'a man
of the World' and consequently never had to free himself from
it; in that sense he was 'born free'. The force of Byron is in the
effort of liberation – liberation of the individual from conventions
etc.

I have singled out the passage of great poetry – as it singles
itself out – both for its own sake and because it gives depth to the
whole London book of *The Prelude*. But throughout the book,
forming as it were its more prosaic basis, there is the freshly
personal observation of the comedy (and grotesqueries) of the
London scene, as it was not lost on the young Wordsworth and
persists in his recollections, though of course he is never measur-
able with Chaucer or Shakespeare as one of the great observers of

[1] Book 7. 725 et seq.
[2] Cf. *Upon Westminster Bridge* (1802). In the early morning, when the air is
still 'smokeless', the city wears 'like a garment . . . the beauty of the morning'.
'Domes, theatres, and temples' bring in a majestic and serene classical note, as in a
painting by Claude, associating London with Athens, Rome and Carthage, and
perhaps Jerusalem. But domes, theatres and temples are also associated in this
poem with 'valley, rock, or hill' steeped in the first splendour of the sun as on the
first morning of the newly created world.

the human comedy. The huge Vanity Fair of London, the motley
spectacle of its multitudinous life, is viewed by Wordsworth in
recollection, as he must have first viewed it, with innocent enjoy-
ment and wonderment, with occasionally a slow ponderous
humour, but also again with something of the 'strange half-
absence' of one whose essential life was elsewhere, conscious of
having reserves of inner strength, sources he had drawn on from
earliest childhood.

There is certainly another influence, if an influence subordinate
to that of 'nature', which affects Wordsworth's way of viewing
the London spectacle – the influence of Shakespeare ('All the
world's a stage...' 'These our actors...'). He refers to the
influence on his imagination of his earliest readings of Shakes-
peare.

> made me recognise
> As at a glance, the things which I had shaped
> And yet not shaped, had seen and scarcely seen.

Among the recollections of the London entertainments are
Wordsworth's youthful impressions of the theatre, the popular
Shakespearian theatre of the period, the theatre of Mrs. Siddons;
its mimicry of the shifting human scene or its fairy land – the
theatre that was at a not so much later period to have a formative
effect on the imagination of Dickens.

> Yet was the theatre my dear delight;
> The very gilding, lamps and painted scrolls
> Wanted not animation...
> the ever-shifting figures of the scene,
> Solemn or gay: whether some beauteous dame
> Advanced in radiance through a deep recess
> Of thick entangled forest, like the moon
> Opening the clouds; or sovereign king, announced
> With flourishing trumpet, came in full-blown state
> Of the world's greatness, winding round with train
> Of courtiers, banners, and a length of guards...
> or mumbling sire,
> A scare-crow pattern of old age dressed up
> In all the tatters of infirmity
> All loosely put together, hobbled in,

Stumping upon a cane with which he smites,
From time to time, the solid boards, and makes them
Prate somewhat loudly of the whereabout
Of one so overloaded with his years.[1]

IX

In Book 8 – Love of Nature leading to Love of Man – a book
which has its special relevances both to his recollected London
experiences in the preceding book and to his recollected experi-
ences in France in the succeeding three books, Wordsworth
enlarges on how his view of man was formed during his early
years through the association of man with nature in his native
region.[2] There were tragedies among the hills – and tales told of
tragedies (the material of *The Brothers*, cf. the great passage in
that poem about changes and tragic accidents among the hills).

Man suffering among awful Powers and Forms;
Of this I heard, and saw enough to make
Imagination restless; nor was free
Myself from frequent perils; nor were tales
Wanting, – the tragedies of former times,
Hazards and strange escapes, of which the rocks
Immutable, and everflowing streams,
Where'er I roamed, were speaking monuments.[3]

Inevitably, in a region where the principal occupation was that of
sheep-farming, the image of man which earliest possessed Words-
worth's imagination was that of the Shepherd, a heroic figure
amidst the perils of the mountains ('Powers of my native region').
Thus, though Wordsworth distinguishes between the real shep-
herds of his native region and those of literary convention, a
visionary idealizing quality invests the figure of the shepherd of
his childhood recollections. (It may be that those recollections
are influenced also by his later recollections of the Alps.)

[1] Book 7. 400 et seq.
[2] There is a passage here in which nature in England is preferred to an Oriental
paradise which is remarkably like an unmagical version of *Kubla Khan* – 'dream
of flowery lawns, with domes of pleasure . . . rocks, dens and groves . . . in no
discordant opposition . . . the landscape endlessly enriched with waters running,
falling or asleep.' – a place not, however, unlike some of the English landscape
gardens of the period.
[3] Book 8. 165–72.

> Your snows and streams
> Ungovernable, and your terrifying winds,
> That howl so dismally for him who treads
> Companionless your awful solitudes!
> There, 'tis the shepherd's task the winter long
> To wait upon the storms ...
>   And when the spring
> Looks out, and all the pastures dance with lambs,
> And when the flock, with warmer weather, climbs
> Higher and higher, him his office leads
> To watch their goings ...
>   For this he quits his home
> At day-spring, and no sooner doth the sun
> Begin to strike him with a fire-like heat,
> Than he lies down upon some shining rock,
> And breakfasts with his dog ...
>   the lingering dews of morn
> Smoke round him, as from hill to hill he hies,
> His staff protending like a hunter's spear,
> Or by its aid leaping from crag to crag,
> And o'er the brawling beds of unbridged streams ...
> A freeman ...[1]

The shepherd, larger than life to the eye of the schoolboy through the magnifying effects of the mists or glorified by the light of the setting sun, is seen also by the inner eye, the visionary power of the imagination, as having a Biblical nobility – as indeed his life of perils entitles him to be seen.

> A rambling schoolboy, thus,
> I felt his presence in his own domain,
> As of a lord and master, or a power,
> Or genius, under Nature, under God ...
> By mists bewildered, suddenly mine eyes
> Have glanced upon him distant a few steps,
> In size a giant, stalking through thick fog,
> His sheep like Greenland bears; or, as he stepped
> Beyond the boundary line of some hill-shadow,

[1] Book 8. 219 et seq.

His form hath flashed upon me, glorified
By the deep radiance of the setting sun.[1]

Yet it is equally characteristic of Wordsworth that this figure of
heroic dimensions is recognized as a man in common with other
men, 'husband, father'. This then is the origin and source of that
reverence for, and faith in, the nature of man that is with the poet
still in the London streets, that he took with him to revolutionary
France, and that he finally recovered through a renewed associa-
tion with nature in the years when his best poetry began.

> were it otherwise,
> And we found evil fast as we find good
> In our first years, or think that it is found,
> How could the innocent heart bear up and live![2]

Something corresponding to that early faith had to be not only
recovered but re-established on a more stable basis of truth, if life
for him was to be endurable, tranquillity and joy restored.

X

The three books (Books 9, 10, 11) of Wordsworth's recollections
of his experiences in revolutionary France show how his faith in
human nature, the basis of his liberal sympathies and of his early
hopes for the Revolution, causing him to suppose that the simple
overthrow of age-old tyranny would inaugurate the reign of
natural goodness and love among men, suffered a severe assault
and radical test. The best poetry in these three books (the passages
in Book 10) comes from a tragic sense of things going wrong, his
early over-sanguine view of human nature as naturally good pro-
foundly shaken by brutal events. The shock of this discovery of
evil is so great that his faith in human nature could scarcely have
survived, he recognizes in retrospect, had it not been anchored in
his earliest associations of man and nature and capable of being
recovered by the recovery of these associations.

The first of the three books (Book 9) is interesting chiefly for
its record of Wordsworth's friendship with the revolutionary
idealist Beaupuis. Particularly memorable is the episode of the
meeting with the 'hunger-bitten girl' and Beaupuis' words.

[1] Book 8. 256–70.   [2] Book 8. 308–11.

"'Tis against *that*
That we are fighting.'

But it is in the poetry of Book 10 that we come closest to the
great human tragedy then (in that recollected time) being
publicly enacted in France. There is first the passage expressing
his overwrought state of mind, sitting at night in his room in the
Paris where there had recently been the September Massacres.
The proximity and actuality of tragedy become almost palpable.
The sense of menace, not only the sense of what has so recently
happened but also the foreboding of something as terrible about
to happen again, that what has occurred can and indeed will
inevitably (as do natural forces) recur, the dreadful past and the
dreadful future pressing on the present, work together on his
imagination till they produce Macbeth-like hallucinations and
voices.

> But that night
> I felt most deeply in what world I was,
> What ground I trod on, and what air I breathed.
> High was my room and lonely, near the roof
> Of a large mansion or hotel, a lodge
> That would have pleased me in more quiet times;
> Nor was it wholly without pleasure then.
> With unextinguished taper I kept watch,
> Reading at intervals; the fear gone by
> Pressed on me almost like a fear to come.
> I thought of those September massacres,
> Divided from me by one little month,
> Saw them and touched: the rest was conjured up
> From tragic fictions or true history,
> Remembrances and dim admonishments.
> The horse is taught his manage, and no star
> Of wildest course but treads back his own steps;
> For the spent hurricane the air provides
> As fierce a successor; the tide retreats
> But to return out of its hiding-place
> In the great deep; all things have second birth;
> The earthquake is not satisfied at once;
> And in this way I wrought upon myself,

Until I seemed to hear a voice that cried,
To the whole city, 'Sleep no more.' The trance
Fled with the voice to which it had given birth;
But vainly comments of a calmer mind
Promised soft peace and sweet forgetfulness.
The place, all hushed and silent as it was,
Appeared unfit for the repose of night,
Defenceless as a wood where tigers roam.[1]

Human nature has its hurricanes, its tides that ebb and flow dangerously, its earthquakes, its jungle. This is the authentic note of tragedy. The effect of these experiences – of having been so near physically to these terrible events – persists long afterwards, disturbing his mind and life, working on his imagination.

my nights were miserable;
Through months, through years, long after the last beat
Of those atrocities, the hour of sleep
To me came rarely charged with natural gifts,
Such ghastly visions had I of despair
And tyranny, and implements of death;
And innocent victims sinking under fear,
And momentary hope, and worn-out prayer,
Each in his separate cell, or penned in crowds
For sacrifice, and struggling with fond mirth
And levity in dungeons, where the dust
Was laid with tears. Then suddenly the scene
Changed, and the unbroken dream entangled me
In long orations, which I strove to plead
Before unjust tribunals, – with a voice
Labouring, a brain confounded, and a sense,
Death-like, of treacherous desertion, felt
In the last place of refuge – my own soul.[2]

This poetry, composed years later, is unmistakably in accord with Wordsworth's earliest poetry (*Guilt and Sorrow, The Borderers*).

In Book 11 there are the famous lines in which Wordsworth gives memorable expression to those earlier hopes that had been so shaken, the feelings of young men of liberal idealism at the

[1] Book 10. 63–93.
[2] Book 10. 398–415. A passage considerably developed after the 1805 version.

time of the beginning of the Revolution, the fall of the prison of
the Bastille –

> Bliss was it in that dawn to be alive,
> But to be young was very Heaven!
>   ... the whole Earth
> The beauty wore of promise – that which sets ...
> The budding rose above the rose full blown.

– the dream that in this world, human nature being naturally
good, a reign of goodness might be attainable. The disappoint-
ment of these hopes, as described in Book 11, produced that
crisis of the mind from which he is painfully emerging in his
earliest original poetry.

XI

In Books 12 and 13 – both entitled 'Imagination and Taste, how
impaired and restored' – Wordsworth turns from these matters
of the previous three books ('human ignorance and guilt',
'spectacles of woe', 'disappointment, vexing thoughts, confusion
of the judgment', 'utter loss of hope itself and things to hope for'),
turns with relief and gratitude back to his theme of the restorative
and re-creative influence of nature.

> I saw the spring return ...

But these influences depend for their workings on the imagination
working creatively back on them and can be impaired by the
despotism of the corporal eye. Here is one of the differences
between Wordsworth and the 18th century (e.g. the 18th-century
descriptive poets) that associate him with Blake.

> I speak in recollection of a time
> When the bodily eye, in every stage of life
> The most despotic of our senses, gained
> Such strength in me as often held my mind
> In absolute dominion ...[1]
>
>   I had known
> Too forcibly, too early in my life,
> Visitings of imaginative power

[1] Book 12. 127–31.

For this to last: I shook the habit off
Entirely and for ever, and again
In Nature's presence stood, as now I stand,
A sensitive being, a creative soul.
   There are in our existence spots of time,
That with distinct pre-eminence retain
A renovating virtue . . .
This efficacious spirit chiefly lurks
Among those passages of life that give
Profoundest knowledge to what point, and how,
The mind is lord and master — outward sense
The obedient servant of her will. Such moments
Are scattered everywhere, taking their date
From our first childhood.[1]

I have quoted a lengthy amount of this passage from Book 12 because it introduces some of the truly remarkable poetry of Wordsworth's recollected childhood and boyhood experiences – a return towards the end of *The Prelude* to the subject-matter of the origins and sources of his imaginative development from which in Book 1 he began – 'visitings of imaginative power'.

The earliest of these is again one of those experiences in his childhood which arose from a shock of fear, the consequent heightening of the consciousness causing it to stand out with exceptional distinctness long afterwards in the memory of the mature man. The child is lost, and suddenly knows he is lost, in a waste of moorland, his fright intensified when he comes upon the place of a gibbet where in former times a murderer had been hanged. The recording of the experience, though the tone is throughout solemn and elevated, begins characteristically as a plain, almost matter-of-fact, narrative of exactly what happened. The poetry is again in the imaginative experience which develops and which it re-creates.

        I remember well
That once, while yet my inexperienced hand
Could scarcely hold a bridle, with proud hopes
I mounted, and we journeyed towards the hills:
An ancient servant of my father's house

[1] Book 12. 201 et seq.

Was with me, my encourager and guide:
We had not travelled long, ere some mischance
Disjoined me from my comrade; and, through fear
Dismounting, down the rough and stony moor
I led my horse, and, stumbling on, at length
Came to a bottom, where in former times
A murderer had been hung in iron chains.
The gibbet-mast had mouldered down, the bones
And iron case were gone; but on the turf,
Hard by, soon after that fell deed was wrought,
Some unknown hand had carved the murderer's name.
The monumental letters were inscribed
In times long past; but still, from year to year
By superstition of the neighbourhood,
The grass is cleared away, and to this hour
The characters are fresh and visible:
A casual glance had shown them, and I fled,
Faltering and faint, and ignorant of the road:
Then, reascending the bare common, saw
A naked pool that lay beneath the hills,
The beacon on the summit, and, more near,
A girl, who bore a pitcher on her head,
And seemed with difficult steps to force her way
Against the blowing wind. It was, in truth,
An ordinary sight; but I should need
Colours and words that are unknown to man,
To paint the visionary dreariness
Which, while I looked all round for my lost guide,
Invested moorland waste and naked pool,
The beacon crowning the lone eminence,
The female and her garments vexed and tossed
By the strong wind.[1]

The imaginative impact of the solitary girl who 'seemed with difficult steps to force her way . . .' is the recurrent Wordsworthian experience of the unexpected intrusion of another life where it had seemed there was no life other than his own, an energy of life forcing its way through a resistant element, an

[1] Book 12. 225–61.

individual soul seen as an image crossing his field of vision, traversing with purposeful effort the wide space in the universe. 'It was, in truth, an ordinary sight'. But it assumes the quality of an imaginative vision. The dreariness is a 'visionary dreariness' because it proceeds, in part, from the child's own imagination. The dreary place is made the more dreary because of his own sense of being lost. His inner desolation intensifies the external desolation; he has, in part, imaginatively created the desolation.

After an interval of some years he revisits the same place, but in an entirely different mood. Though it is in fact a desolate place, and furthermore a place where he had as a child experienced the shock of discovering himself to be lost, his mood is now one of a young lover's happiness – 'the loved one at my side' – a happiness that invests the revisited place with its 'golden gleam'.

> When, in the blessed hours
> Of early love, the loved one at my side,
> I roamed, in daily presence of this scene,
> Upon the naked pool and dreary crags,
> And on the melancholy beacon, fell
> A spirit of pleasure and youth's golden gleam;
> And think ye not with radiance more sublime
> For these remembrances, and for the power
> They had left behind? So feeling comes in aid
> Of feeling, and diversity of strength
> Attends us, if but once we have been strong.
> Oh! mystery of man, from what depth
> Proceed thy honours.[1]

The comparison of this passage with Crabbe's *The Lover's Journey* again brings out the differences between the two contemporary poets. Crabbe's tale opens with the general proposition:

> It is the soul that sees; the outward eyes
> Present the object; but the mind descries.

But his tale is a comedy which depends partly on the humorous recognition, chastening to our human pride, of the extent to which our perceptions are at the mercy of our subjective moods.

[1] Book 12. 261–73.

Wordsworth, on the other hand, in his experiences recognizes with a kind of religious reverence the mysterious working of the imagination, the creative power of the mind and also, in this particular instance, a holiness in love – 'the blessed hours'.[1]

But Wordsworth at his conclusion of the passage develops a further recognition, that of the cumulative power, in the mind, of successive experiences, however diverse, promoting a kind of organic growth or development. The earlier painful disturbance experienced by the child in that same place gives increased depth and power to the later, totally different feelings of the youthful lover's joy, adds 'radiance more sublime' to the new vision of the revisited place. Experience builds on experience, successive experiences re-enforcing, deepening and being deepened by their predecessors. Experiences accumulate and merge into one another, interweaving into a single strengthening texture. The feelings Wordsworth had experienced as a child and later as a youth in that same place have thus become 'a portion of his life and mind'.

Book 12 concludes with another moment of heightened consciousness that becomes in Wordsworth's life a creative memory. The boy away at school looks forward eagerly to the Christmas holidays. He walks to the intersection of the two moorland roads by one of which he knows the horses will come in a few days to fetch him and his brothers home for Christmas. The mood of the boy is thus one of hopefulness despite the outward dreariness of the moorland scene on a bleak day. But in these Christmas holidays his father dies, changing his boyish life suddenly to tragedy. Then, ever after, that bleak day, which had been at the time a day of hope, that dreary spectacle when he had looked with 'such anxiety of hope' – in retrospect it now seems, all the more, to have been an 'anxiety of hope' – remains imprinted on the memory, permanently associated with the ensuing tragedy. That is the bare outline. But the poetry recreates the whole experience in all its power and complexity with characteristic exactitude and a Biblical simplicity and dignity of phrase (e.g. 'sojourners in my father's house').

---

[1] As Keats, too, was to declare, 'I am certain of nothing but of the Holiness of the Heart's Affections and of the Truth of the Imagination', and as Blake had earlier declared 'Everything that lives is holy'.

One Christmas-time,
On the glad eve of its dear holidays,
Feverish, and tired, and restless, I went forth
Into the fields, impatient for the sight
Of those led palfreys that should bear us home;
My brothers and myself. There rose a crag,
That, from the meeting-point of two high-ways
Ascending, overlooked them both, far stretched;
Thither, uncertain on which road to fix
My expectation, thither I repaired,
Scout-like, and gained the summit; 'twas a day
Tempestuous, dark, and wild, and on the grass
I sate half-sheltered by a naked wall;
Upon my right hand couched a single sheep,
Upon my left a blasted hawthorn stood;
With those companions at my side, I watched,
Straining my eyes intensely, as the mist
Gave intermitting prospect of the copse
And plain beneath. Ere we to school returned, –
That dreary time, – ere we had been ten days
Sojourners in my father's house, he died;
And I and my three brothers, orphans then,
Followed his body to the grave. The event,
With all the sorrow that it brought, appeared
A chastisement; and when I called to mind
That day so lately past, when from the crag
I looked in such anxiety of hope;
With trite reflections of morality,
Yet in the deepest passion, I bowed low
To God, Who thus corrected my desires;
And, afterwards, the wind and sleety rain,
And all the business of the elements,
The single sheep, and the one blasted tree,
And the bleak music from that old stone wall,
The noise of wood and water, and the mist
That on the line of each of those two roads
Advanced in such indisputable shapes;
All these were kindred spectacles and sounds
To which I oft repaired, and thence would drink,

As at a fountain; and on winter nights,
Down to this very time, when storm and rain
Beat on my roof, or, haply, at noon-day,
While in a grove I walk, whose lofty trees,
Laden with summer's thickest foliage, rock
In a strong wind, some working of the spirit,
Some inward agitations thence are brought.[1]

This memory, which could have been merely a melancholy or bitter one, has thus been converted in Wordsworth's life to a permanent source of inner strength.[2]

Between these two passages of recollected experiences in Book 12, at the point of the characteristically Wordsworthian recognition of the mind's greatness ('Oh mystery of man from what a depth . . .') there comes the tragic, and prophetic, further recognition that such sources of life and inspiration, and with them the power of the imagination itself, can decline and fail.

I am lost, but see
In simple childhood something of the base
On which thy greatness stands; but this I feel,
That from thyself it comes, that thou must give,
Else never canst receive. The days gone by
Return upon me almost from the dawn

[1] Book 12. 287–332.

[2] This is one of the characteristic differences between the passage and, for example, Hardy's *Neutral Tones* in which the psychological interest is again both similar and dissimilar to Wordsworth's, but in which there is a nakedness or absence of any consolation. Certain aspects or features of the place where there has been a painful emotional crisis (a lovers' parting), a crisis producing a heightening of the consciousness, stand out and remain distinct in the memory. Particular images (especially, for example, the suggestion of 'gray ashes' in 'fallen from an ash and were gray') –

We stood by a pond that winter day
And the sun was white as though chidden of God
And a few leaves lay on the starving sod
They had fallen from an ash and were gray

– these particular images persist starkly in the memory permanently associated with the feelings once experienced there.

Your mouth and the God-curst sun and a tree
And a pond edged with grayish leaves.

They symbolically define those feelings by giving them substance, shape and body, 'the solidity of objects'. The outer landscape has formed an inner landscape corresponding to and recalling exactly, in sharp outline, the original state of mind.

Of life: the hiding-places of man's power
Open; I would approach them, but they close.
I see by glimpses now; when age comes on,
May scarcely see at all.[1]

XII

The most significant Wordsworthian passage in Book 13 is that
on the symbolical value for him of lonely roads – roads that seem
to extend beyond the horizon's limit into eternity – and on chance
meetings on such roads with wayfarers.

> Converse with men, where if we meet a face
> We almost meet a friend, on naked heaths
> With long long ways before, by cottage bench,
> Or well-spring where the weary traveller rests.
> Who doth not love to follow with his eye
> The windings of a public way? the sight,
> Familiar object as it is, hath wrought
> On my imagination since the morn
> Of childhood, when a disappearing line,
> One daily present to my eyes, that crossed
> The naked summit of a far-off hill
> Beyond the limits that my feet had trod,
> Was like an invitation into space
> Boundless, or guide into eternity.[2]

Hence, from an early age, his reverence for the wayfarers – 'the
wanderers of the earth' – and even fear of them (not without
cause, perhaps).

> Awed have I been by strolling Bedlamites;
> From many other uncouth vagrants (passed
> In fear) have walked with quicker step.[3]

---

[1] Book 12. 273–82. Wordsworth's apprehension and concern about this is
discernible also in the *Intimations Ode* (composed 1803–6). But the nearest
parallel is, of course, Coleridge's great *Dejection Ode* (1802)

> Oh Lady! we receive but what we give
> And in our life alone doth nature live . . .

though whereas Coleridge says we receive only what we give, Wordsworth says
we must give else we can never receive, a significant difference.

[2] Book 13. 138–51.   [3] Book 13. 157–9.

Something of the England of Shakespeare seems to have been
perceived by Wordsworth (recalling in particular certain passages
in *Lear*) to have still lingered in these remoter regions.

> When I began to enquire,
> To watch and question those I met, and speak
> Without reserve to them, the lonely roads
> Were open schools in which I daily read
> With most delight the passions of mankind,
> Whether by words, looks, sighs, or tears, revealed;
> There saw into the depths of human souls,
> Souls that appear to have no depth at all
> To careless eyes.[1]

In this discovery about man he discovers his subject.

> Of these, said I, shall be my song;
> ... my theme
> No other than the very heart of man.[2]

The conclusion of Book 13 brings us back to the Wordsworth
of *Guilt and Sorrow* and *The Borderers* – the period of his life
when 'on Sarum's Plain' (the 'Sarum's Plain' also of *Lear*) he had
himself

> paced the bare white roads
> Lengthening in solitude their dreary line
> ... and I remember well
> That in life's every-day appearances
> I seemed about this time to gain clear sight
> Of a new world.[3]

This is the period, he recognizes, when he began to have a new or
renewed vision or way of seeing things, when his original poetry
began to come.

The final large-scale recollected experience in *The Prelude* is
that of the effect on the imagination of climbing Snowdon (Book
14) when, at a certain elevation, the moon is discovered shining
down on the mist below. Thus by a sudden accident of light, the
external world sublime and mysterious in itself, with its abysses
and expanses, becomes, again as in an imaginative vision, a

---

[1] Book 13. 160–8.   [2] Book 13. 232, 240–1.   [3] Book 13. 316–17, 367–70.

symbol of the mind and its relationships with the visible and
invisible world.

> There I beheld the emblem of a mind
> That feeds upon infinity ...
> To hold fit converse with the spiritual world,
> And with the generations of mankind
> Spread over time, past, present, and to come,
> Age after age, till Time shall be no more.[1]

XIII

It appears, therefore, that Wordsworth's original poetry begins
from a period of disturbance in his life, from experience of
suffering, from contemplation of tragic events and facts. But the
deep sources of his poetry lie earlier still, as he discovered, in
experiences of his childhood, boyhood and youth. The need to
recover equilibrium – to find 'tranquillity' – appears to be what
caused him to begin to work back in and through his poetry to
those earlier experiences, to trace his development from his
origins to his maturity, seeking to discover and recover the
foundations of life, the bases of stability, the reservoir of imagin-
ative power and joy in nature and man.

The evidence that Wordsworth must have undergone a
radical disturbance of mind between the year 1791, when he left
Cambridge to reside in France, and the years 1794–6, when his
earliest original poetry began to come, is that poetry itself. The
need and the effort to come to terms with the disturbing facts of
experience, to discover consolations for human tragedies, to find
a cure for the disordered soul, to recover the natural human
capacity for joy, faith and hope, to establish some true and stable
basis of life are what give Wordsworth's poetry both its initial
and its prolonged impulsion and direction.

> Must hear Humanity in fields and groves
> Pipe solitary anguish; or must hang
> Brooding above the fierce confederate storm
> Of sorrow barricaded evermore
> Within the walls of cities.

[1] Book 14. 70–1, 108–11.

As the poetry goes on, however, it seems in time to be at an increasing remove from the human tragedies to which it continues to allude. There is in the end some justice in the stricture that Wordsworth 'averts his gaze from half of human fate'. The Lake District made him; the Lake District unmade him, perhaps, in the end. It had become too much a place of retirement. The 'tranquillity', achieved at first with difficulty and because Wordsworth desperately needed to achieve it, gradually becomes more apparent than 'the emotion' from which the poetry 'takes its origin'.

The famous statement, 'Poetry takes its origin from emotion recollected in tranquillity', which in itself contains a great deal of sense, very well describes a large part of Wordsworth's own poetry – the quality of 'coolness', for example, which distinguishes it from Lawrence. But the experiences of his best poetry are 'recollected' with remarkable distinctness and power, as if they were happening again. They are relived, however, with a new contemplative insight into them in the now mature mind of the poet, the 'philosophic mind' which the years have brought and which has nothing necessarily to do with having found 'a philosophy'. Wordsworth's 'recollections' were, at least to some extent, deliberate and purposeful, a searching re-examination of his past experience in order to get to know his own nature and life. These experiences, many of which had originally occurred in early life, have gained in depth and power, in having become part of his developing life, and gained in meaning and relevance for his mature mind which now ponders over them. It is in and through these experiences that his mind and life have been, as he discovered, a single organic development from his beginnings. As these recollected experiences have been transmuted into his poetry they are now, because of his new insight into them, illuminated and illuminating beyond anything they were for the child or youth who originally experienced them. Growing up or maturing from childhood to manhood or womanhood becomes one of the main subjects explored in depth by the greater novelists. A succession of 19th-century novels (e.g. *Great Expectations*[1])

---

[1] The opening episode in *Great Expectations* is, of course, as characteristically Dickensian as the boyhood experiences in *The Prelude* are Wordsworthian. Pip and Pip's consciousness of what is happening, with its controlled combination of

prove to be essential autobiography in much the kind of way that Wordsworth's *The Prelude* can now be recognized as having originated.

---

humour and horror, could not be mistaken for anything else than a Dickensian imaginative creation. Yet here it is also very specifically a child's experience, reproduced by the novelist exactly as it would have seemed at the time to the imaginative child, Pip, beginning with his groping for clues to his identity among the tombstones surrounded by the waste of marshland extending level to the horizon.

CHAPTER FOUR

WORDSWORTH: POEMS CONTEMPORARY WITH *THE PRELUDE* AND LATER

I

Poems Contemporary with *The Prelude*

Wordsworth's best poems – they are among his very best – composed during the years when he was at work on the original version of *The Prelude* show particularly the new (or recovered) interest in the psychology of the individual which is greatly developed in the 19th-century novels.

Strange fits of passion (1799) is one of these, though a poetic success on the edge, precariously balanced between the sublime and the ridiculous or at least the banal, such is its extreme reduction to simplicity of expression. But it does work, as an imaginative experience, for the reader who is in the right frame of mind to receive it, who takes in fact the hint in the opening lines –

> I will dare to tell
> But in the lover's ear alone –

to accept it, as a very private and personal communication, at least with respect. After the attention has been caught by the startling first line, the poem quietly unfolds as an authentic and psychologically illuminating event plainly and barely recorded. The reader becomes convinced that this recollected experience happened exactly as described.

The situation, both external and psychological, is similar to that of Crabbe's *Lover's Journey* – but there could not be a contrast more characteristic of the two poets than that between Wordsworth's strange experience, discovering the extraordinary in the ordinary, and Crabbe's comedy. In Wordsworth's poem the lover rides towards his sweetheart's cottage in a 'sweet dream' (cf. 'A slumber did my spirit seal') intensified by the mesmeric effect of the moon on which his eyes are unconsciously fixed. When he is suddenly deprived of that bright object – the moon being obscured by the cottage roof at a particular point of his approach – the shock of that deprivation produces a sharp, irrational impulse of panic: 'If Lucy should be dead'. The natural anxieties and fears about the loved one, submerged by the mood of joyful anticipation, rise suddenly to the surface.[1] His mood is abruptly changed, a 'strange fit of passion', a change precipitated by an ordinary, explainable alteration in the external world, an accident of perspective.

To suspend his sense of humour, to check what Johnson calls his 'risibility', is a small price to pay if the reader is not to lose the experience which is this not-so-simple poem.

> hoof after hoof
> He raised, and never stopped.

The words (not unlike some of the awkward exactitudes in Hardy's poetry) reproduce the sense of mechanical regularity, seemingly automatic motion onwards of the horse, as the rider in his trance-like state is borne along to the moment when the spell is abruptly broken.

There is no such risk of absurdity in the great brief tragic poem *A slumber did my spirit seal* (also 1799). There is here no averting of the mind, no taking refuge, no evasion and no consolation. There is the naked recognition nakedly presented of the fact that she who was alive is dead. The living, breathing being has become a 'thing'. It is this elementary fact, simply confronted, that is tragic.

> A slumber did my spirit seal;
> I had no human fears:
> She seemed a thing that could not feel
> The touch of earthly years.

[1] Cf. at the moment of his reunion with Desdemona after the storm, Othello's sense that that maximum happiness cannot in the nature of things last.

> If it were now to die
> 'Twere now to be most happy; for, I fear
> My soul hath her content so absolute,
> That not another comfort like to this
> Succeeds an unknown fate.

No motion has she now, no force;
She neither hears nor sees;
Rolled round in earth's diurnal course,
With rocks, and stones, and trees.

Each word counts, not a word is wasted in the classic economy of this poem. The word 'human', one of the words which have a particular force here, implies that the fears are such as would be natural for one human being to have about another, fears of mortality. The slumber that seals his spirit seems not so much 'the film of familiarity', 'the lethargy of custom' (of which Coleridge speaks in *Biographia Literaria*, Chapter 14), as something like the 'sweet dream' of *Strange fits of passion* which, nevertheless, is proved to have been a kind of unconsciousness that wrapped him round, 'sealing' him, as in a tomb, from reality. She 'seemed', in his dream, a 'thing' – another word which has particular force in this context – not subject to death as ordinary mortals are, beyond its reach, outside the earthly condition, for whom he need not have human (or mortal) fears. The word 'touch' makes of the abstraction 'time' ('earthly years') a tangible and intimate reality.

In the second of the two stanzas of the poem she has indeed become a 'thing' in the sense of a lifeless object. The shock of recognition of her present inertia, her having now no force, is registered. The imagination suddenly expands in the third line to take in the universe ('earth's diurnal course'). The turning globe suggests, as occasionally in Hardy, a fateful and irresistible inevitability, felt also in the measured, unrelenting movement of the rhythm (cf. Hardy's *A Broken Appointment*). The earth rolls round carrying her round with it, now a lifeless object with the other objects on its surface. This is one of the very few unmitigatedly tragic moments of recognition in Wordsworth's poetry.

II
The Excursion

Though *The Excursion* remains nearly all much more on a prose level than *The Prelude*, there are some striking things that can be dug out of it, at intervals, throughout its great length, if we have

the patience to disengage these from the increasing Words-
worthian wordiness. Furthermore, though Wordsworth the poet
has now subsided too much into Wordsworth the sage, a great
deal of pondering on human experience has preceded and gone
into *The Excursion*.

The Excursion largely takes the form of a dialogue between two
characters met with by Wordsworth among the hills, the Wan-
derer and the Solitary. It is to some extent also an interior
dialogue, because the two characters represent an opposition
between the kind of man Wordsworth himself conceived he
might have become, a disillusioned man still imprisoned in
sceptical rationalist attitudes (the Solitary), and the kind of man
he would wish ideally to be like (the Wanderer). There is also
significantly present in *The Excursion* yet another character, the
Pastor, who explicitly represents and expresses the traditional
Anglicanism which the more and more conservative Wordsworth
has come back to – the church spire a conspicuous landmark
visible in the dale from the hills. The traditional pieties are felt as
a sustaining and consoling strength associated with the enduring
hills.

The despondency of the Solitary (which gives its title to Book
3) is such as Wordsworth himself had been through until re-
stored by the influences of nature. The history of the Solitary
is in part Wordsworth's own. It is from the recollection of his
own state of mind that the poetry comes and has the note of
authenticity.

> Then my soul
> Turned inward, – to examine of what stuff
> Time's fetters are composed; and life was put
> To inquisition, long and profitless!
> By pain of heart – now checked – and now impelled –
> The intellectual power, through words and things,
> Went sounding on, a dim and perilous way![1]

Even the joyless philosophic Solitary can however extract some
consolation from nature, though his poetry has an elegiac note,
a haunting sense of mortality, an echo of Virgilian sadness
(cf. Wordsworth's *Dion* and *Laodameia*, Arnold and some of

---

[1] Book 3. 695–701.

Tennyson). We can at least enjoy the sun, live for the present hour, cultivate self-sufficiency, etc.

> . . . nor did e'er,
> From me, those dark impervious shades, that hang
> Upon the region whither we are bound,
> Exclude a power to enjoy the vital beams
> Of present sunshine.[1]
>   Such a stream
> Is human Life . . .
> And such is mine, – save only for a hope
> That my particular current soon will reach
> The unfathomable gulf, where all is still.[2]

The Wanderer describes the Solitary's way of speaking thus (Book 4) –

>   Your discourse this day,
> That, like the fabled Lethe, wished to flow
> In creeping sadness, through oblivious shades
> Of death and night, has caught at every turn
> The colours of the sun.[3]

In Book 4 the vision of the generations of mankind following one another, a continuous succession, among the hills, sustained in their lives by a traditional piety, brings back the note of Wordsworth's greater poetry.

>   a thought arose
> Of Life continuous, Being unimpaired;
> That hath been, is, and where it was and is
> There shall endure, – existence unexposed
> To the blind walk of mortal accident;
> From diminution safe and weakening age;
> While man grows old, and dwindles, and decays;
> And countless generations of mankind
> Depart; and leave no vestige where they trod.
> We live by Admiration, Hope and Love . . .[4]
>   A consciousness is yours
> How feelingly religion may be learned

---

[1] Book 3. 295–9.   [2] Book 3. 986–91.   [3] Book 4. 1122–6.   [4] Book 4. 754–63.

In smoky cabins, from a mother's tongue –
Heard where the dwelling vibrates to the din
Of the contiguous torrent, gathering strength
At every moment – and, with strength, increase
Of fury; or, while snow is at the door,
Assaulting and defending, and the wind,
A sightless labourer, whistles at his work –
Fearful; but resignation tempers fear,
And piety is sweet . . .
And they had hopes that overstepped the Grave.[1]

On the whole the Wanderer's answer to the philosophers warms into eloquence rather than poetry. But there is poetry in an occasional image:

That one, poor, finite object, in the abyss
Of infinite Being, twinkling restlessly! . . .[2]
And central peace, subsisting at the heart
Of endless agitation . . .[3]
Within the circuit of this fabric huge,
One voice – the solitary raven, flying
Athwart the concave of the dark blue dome,
Unseen, perchance above all power of sight –
An iron knell![4]

The note of Wordsworth's greater poetry has momentarily entered.

Book 5 (The Pastor) and Books 6 and 7 (The Churchyard among the Mountains), in which the Pastor gives 'some portraits of the dead from his own observation of life among the mountains' including 'his account of persons interred in the churchyard', introduce subject-matter which will remind readers of resemblances as well as the differences between Wordsworth and Crabbe.

The Wanderer, the Solitary and the Poet have descended from the mountains towards 'a grey church tower' in the dale. The sceptical Solitary speaks, with respect, of

[1] Book 4. 789 et seq.   [2] Book 4. 993–4.   [3] Book 4. 1146–7.
[4] Book 4. 1177–81.

> The cross itself, at whose unconscious feet
> The generations of mankind have knelt.[1]

They pass through the churchyard with its reminders of mortality. There is in *The Excursion* a relationship again still with the pensive, meditative elegiac poetry of the 18th century (another elegy in a country churchyard) despite the absence of the 18th-century formality and neatness. The echoes, however, are from Shakespeare (the Histories, e.g. *Richard II*) rather than from Milton.

> Here standing, with the unvoyageable sky
> In faint reflection of infinitude
> Stretched overhead, and at my pensive feet
> A subterraneous magazine of bones,
> In whose dark vaults my own shall soon be laid.[2]

The Solitary rejects (as Johnson and Crabbe had done) the idealized or enchanted view of 'humble life' in rural places. 'The simple race of mountaineers'

> partake man's general lot
> With little mitigation. They escape,
> Perchance, the heavier woes of guilt; feel not
> The tedium of fantastic idleness:
> Yet life, as with the multitude, with them
> Is fashioned like an ill-constructed tale.[3]

But what is unmistakably a more radical, indignant dissatisfaction is uttered in the personal voice of the poet himself, speaking in the age that followed the French Revolution.

> Who can reflect, unmoved, upon the round
> Of smooth and solemnized complacencies,
> By which, in Christian lands, from age to age
> Profession mocks performance. Earth is sick,
> And Heaven is weary, of the hollow words
> Which States and Kingdoms utter when they talk
> Of truth and justice.[4]

The Pastor meets them. The Wanderer appeals to him to dispel the melancholy and the disquieting questionings voiced by

---

[1] Book 5. 337–8.   [2] Book 5. 342–6.   [3] Book 5. 427–32.   [4] Book 5. 375–81.

the Solitary. It is indeed as much from his experience and obser-
vation of people as from doctrine that the representative of the
Church of England 'dispels the gloom'. He dispels it partly by
being the kind of character he himself is and partly from his
reminiscences and anecdotes of characters who had lived and died
in his parish.[1] The Solitary expresses what is certainly also
Wordsworth's recognition that the subjects of Tragedy are as
much to be found in humble life as in the lives of kings and
heroes.

> Exchange the shepherd's frock of native grey
> For robes with regal purple tinged; convert
> The crook into a sceptre; give the pomp
> Of circumstance; and here the tragic Muse
> Shall find apt subjects for her highest art.
> Amid the groves, under the shadowy hills,
> The generations are prepared; the pangs,
> The internal pangs, are ready; the dread strife
> Of poor humanity's afflicted will
> Struggling in vain with ruthless destiny.[2]

Most of the tales the Pastor relates of humble lives among the hills
are tragedies.

> These Dalesmen trust
> The lingering gleam of their departed lives
> To oral record, and the silent heart;
> Depositories faithful and more kind
> Than fondest epitaph: for, if those fail,
> What boots the sculptured tomb?[3]

There is the tale of Ellen, the cottage girl who

> once had moved
> In virgin fearlessness, with step that seemed
> Caught from the pressure of elastic turf
> Upon the mountains gemmed with morning dew.[4]

(Cf. 'O so light a foot, Will ne'er wear out the everlasting flint.'
Romeo and Juliet.) Though this tale in *The Excursion* is not the

---

[1] His narratives are largely the substance of Books 6 and 7 (both books
entitled 'The Churchyard among the Mountains').
[2] Book 6. 548–57.   [3] Book 6. 610–15.   [4] Book 6. 819–22.

equal of Crabbe's (or Wordsworth's own) best, there are one or
two moments of memorable poetry in it.

> It was the season of unfolding leaves,
> Of days advancing toward their utmost length,
> And small birds singing happily to mates
> Happy as they. With spirit-saddening power
> Winds pipe through fading woods; but those blithe notes
> Strike the deserted to the heart; I speak
> Of what I know, and what we feel within.[1]

Tragic as they are, these tales of actual people 'dispel the
gloom' emanating from the sceptical philosopher, a gloom that is
further dispelled by the characters of old individuals met with
among the hills.

> Haunting with rod and line the craggy brooks . . .
> A man of hope and forward-looking mind
> Even to the last.[2]

> A Man he seems of cheerful yesterdays
> And confident to-morrows.[3]

Book 8 of *The Excursion*, though not notable for any remark-
able poetry, has a special interest as registering Wordsworth's
attitude towards the changes produced even in the life of the
remote communities among the hills by the intrusion of manu-
facturing industry (the Industrial Revolution) – changes the
causes and effects of which in human nature Blake had already
been so profoundly and imaginatively conscious of. The Wan-
derer indignantly deplores not only the disfigurement of nature
but also the disruption of the traditional life of the people. A
village becomes Dickens's Coketown. The picture of a child
employed in a cotton-mill associates Wordsworth with Blake,
Dickens and Lawrence – shows once again the affinity there is
between these four great authors. Yet the failure of anything in
Book 8 to become fully poetry surely indicates that compared
with Blake, Dickens and Lawrence, Wordsworth is no longer
fully engaged here with his subject. The Solitary corrects the
Wanderer's tendency, in condemning these present things, to
idealize the past. He reminds him of the poverty there always was

---

[1] Book 6. 855–60.   [2] Book 7. 276–7.   [3] Book 7. 557–8.

– crazy huts, tottering hovels, ragged offspring, families of beggars and vagrants on darksome heaths and furze-clad commons – in a way that recalls Crabbe. But Wordsworth, speaking in his own person with his own voice, had earlier in this same dialogue associated himself specifically with the feeling and attitude of the Wanderer.[1]

III

Late Poems

The two sonnets which seem to me Wordsworth's best are unexpectedly late – *Surprised by joy* (1812? published 1815) and *Why art thou silent!* (1835). These poems evidently come from exceptional moments, brief visitations of intense feeling. Their immediacy is such that they appear to have escaped from the formula 'emotion recollected in tranquillity'. The livingness of their rhythms and imagery is the index of their authenticity. They have chiefly to do with time and absence. Wordsworth is sharing the common human experience of growing old, severance from dear ones, deaths of friends (the material of some of the best poems also of Hardy and Yeats).[2]

---

[1] It cannot be accidental that in the same year as *The Excursion* the two Wordsworthian exercises in the Hellenism of the period, *Laodameia* and *Dion*, were also published. They belong to the elegiac 19th-century romantic dream of a serene Ancient Greek world – like Greek sculptures in moonlight – which continued to appeal and to calm such vexed spirits as that of Arnold. (The origins of the dream can be traced back, of course, much earlier than Winckelmann and the Germans of the romantic period. It is there in Milton. Its association with boyhood and youth must have to do with Education in the Classics, the memory of the appeal of Classical mythology and poetry to the imagination early in life.)

[2] The *Extempore Effusion upon the Death of James Hogg* (also 1835) is another late poem which shows that Wordsworth was still, at moments, capable of intensity of feeling. The deaths of friends and brother poets – the comparison with Dunbar's *Lament for the Makars* comes to mind – have evidently affected Wordsworth deeply. Through the simple directness of its expression of this personal feeling the poem becomes an expression of universal and elemental human feeling, a man speaking to men in that sense, expressing what all men feel and experience in common about the fundamental things that happen to all. The poem includes at least one striking image – 'London with its own black wreath'.

> Nor has the rolling year twice measured,
> From sign to sign, its steadfast course,
> Since every mortal power of Coleridge
> Was frozen at its marvellous source . . .

Surprised by joy – impatient as the Wind
I turned to share the transport – Oh! with whom
But Thee, deep buried in the silent tomb,
That spot which no vicissitude can find?
Love, faithful love, recalled thee to my mind –
But how could I forget thee? through what power,
Even for the least division of an hour,
Have I been so beguiled as to be blind
To my most grievous loss? – That thought's return
Was the worst pang that sorrow ever bore,
Save one, one only, when I stood forlorn,
Knowing my heart's best treasure was no more;
That neither present time, nor years unborn
Could to my sight that heavenly face restore.

The abrupt opening reproduces the sudden impulse of joy which takes him by surprise and which he instinctively turns to share with the dear one at his side. But it is checked almost at once by 'Oh! with whom . . .?' – the pang of the realization that she to whom he turns is not there, that she is dead. There is again a change of direction with 'But how could I forget thee?' and yet again a final change with 'Save one, one only,' as he recalls the first moment of bereavement, the realization of irremedial and permanent loss.

Thus a few moments of intense and fluctuating experience, sudden sharp recognitions, flows and ebbs of feeling, joy, pain, are lived through – the poem is exactly that. It moves through an evolution, in its few lines, which corresponds to the turnings and recoils of the experiencing mind of a man caught unawares, carried along by shifting currents of feeling in unexpected directions, checked by sudden thoughts, recovering balance and stability. In reading we go through a living, changing process, as

Like clouds that rake the mountain-summits,
Or waves that own no curbing hand,
How fast has brother followed brother
From sunshine to the sunless land! . . .

Our haughty life is crowned with darkness,
Like London with its own black wreath,
On which with thee, O Crabbe! forth-looking,
I gazed from Hampstead's breezy heath.

varied as it is intense. The rhythmical irregularities of this sonnet are those of life – the 'strange, irregular rhythm of life'[1] itself – like the rhythmical subtleties of Donne or Shakespeare.

Why art thou silent! is addressed to someone who is again not there. Addressed in the present tense; the emotion is again not recollected, certainly not in tranquillity.

> Why art thou silent! Is thy love a plant
> Of such weak fibre that the treacherous air
> Of absence withers what was once so fair?
> Is there no debt to pay, no boon to grant?
> Yet have my thoughts for thee been vigilant –
> Bound to thy service with unceasing care,
> The mind's least generous wish a mendicant
> For naught but what thy happiness could spare.
> Speak – though this soft warm heart, once free to hold
> A thousand tender pleasures, thine and mine,
> Be left more desolate, more dreary cold
> Than a forsaken bird's-nest filled with snow
> 'Mid its own bush of leafless eglantine –
> Speak, that my torturing doubts their end may know!

These moments of personal grief become actual and immediate, assume shape and substance in the poem through the combination of exactly that rhythm and these images. Love is a plant – the rhythmical emphasis rests momentarily at the end of the line on 'plant' – of weak fibre, if it can be withered by absence; the heart is 'soft' and 'warm' and – if his torturing doubts should be ended by some desolating certainty – the desolation the heart would then experience is brought home through the image of the 'forsaken bird's-nest filled with snow'. We hear, too, as we read, the changing intonations of the voice. 'Speak', particularly so in this context, is high-pitched, an agonized cry of appeal. Its repetition doubles its effect.

To find the near equivalents in poetry of these two sonnets of Wordsworth – essentially dramatic presentations of an individual's experiencing mind in a verse movement that, though they are sonnets, is very nearly that of dramatic verse – we should again have to look back across the 18th century to Shakespeare and

---

[1] Henry James, *The Art of Fiction*.

to the Shakespearian poetry of the 17th century, notably the
Songs and Sonets of Donne. But when we turn to the greater
novels of the 19th century, we find again, in whole passages,
such essentially dramatic poetic presentations of complex states
of mind.

CHAPTER FIVE

CRABBE: *TALES IN VERSE*

I

In the succession from Pope and Johnson, Crabbe is the last of the three great poets in the English Augustan line:[1] there is a fitness in the fact that Pope himself read and approved Johnson's *London* (1738), and that Johnson himself read and approved Crabbe's *Village* (1783). But Crabbe, the successor of Johnson, is also a contemporary of Wordsworth, as well as of Jane Austen.

At a first glance Crabbe's poetry seems to have everything in common with Pope's and Johnson's, the poetry of his two great 18th-century predecessors in the moral observation of life. Yet his poetry proves, on closer acquaintance, to be as individual and original as each of theirs is.

In some ways Crabbe may be felt in his poetry to have closer affinities with Johnson than with their great original, Pope, and this may be as much a matter of temperament as of nearer proximity in period. But Crabbe has the gifts of a novelist (or dramatist), as Johnson has not, gifts that associate him with Jane Austen. Johnson's power is in his generalizations from experience, the generalizations of a man who has observed life and felt and thought about it deeply. Crabbe's criticism of life, at its fullest and most concentrated in *Tales* (1812), is, on the other hand, developed through and by means of characters, scenes and dialogues presented in verse. These, although in the more formal Popean verse and in the characteristically 18th-century Augustan idiom of wit, recall Chaucer as much as Pope.

Crabbe and Jane Austen may be associated further – with Wordsworth and, later, George Eliot, at least in her earlier works – as great English provincials. Pope and Johnson are metropolitan (qualified in Pope's case by his particular kind of Horatianism and pleasure in landscape-gardening, and in Johnson's case by his being a great individual), though from that centre they survey human life as a whole. Crabbe and Jane Austen, like Pope and

[1] See *Revaluation*, Ch. 4.

Johnson, observe human nature in society, the great 18th-century subject, but in their case it is observed in provincial society in their different parts of England. That provincial life had never been mirrored so fully and accurately as by Crabbe and Jane Austen. Yet these authors are not simply recorders of manners. They are observers of human nature in depth and successors of Pope and Johnson as moral observers.

But Crabbe and Jane Austen are not simply the 18th century going on throughout what is called the Romantic Period. Both are highly original authors, doing new things – Jane Austen in the novel, Crabbe in the verse tale – things that had not been done exactly in their way in literature before. In particular, both express in their art the developing psychological interest in the individual and the complexities of relationships between individuals. As Jane Austen re-creates and develops the novel, as inherited from the 18th-century novelists, into a supremely important modern art, Crabbe re-creates the verse tale, partly with the aid of a few hints from Pope (e.g. the tale of Balaam in the third of the *Moral Essays*), but above all from the inspiration of Chaucer and of Shakespeare, to express developing insights into the individual life. It is certainly not an accident that the quotations with which Crabbe heads each of his tales are all from Shakespeare; like Jane Austen and Scott, he was well grounded in Shakespeare, particularly in the 'moral observation' with which the plays (in the often-quoted phrase) are 'saturated'. The fact that Crabbe's verse and idiom are firmly in the tradition of Pope and Johnson should not obscure the respects in which he is not like Pope and not like Johnson and the respects in which, in the essence of his poetry itself, he is recognizably contemporary with Wordsworth – just as Wordsworth's originality should not obscure the fact of his 18th-century roots – and a predecessor of the 19th-century novelists.

In many ways Crabbe, working as he does in the tradition of Pope, is as different from Pope – the 'brilliant' Pope – as he is from Wordsworth. His poetry seldom, if ever, in any single passage matches the range and diversity of Pope, when Pope's wit and imagination are working fully and intensely as one. Nor has he Pope's controlled, imaginative exuberance, fanciful and witty fertility held in place, given direction and point by the strict formality of the verse, the formal neatness and balance. Nor has he Pope's degree of delicacy and subtlety, his sensitiveness of touch and quick flexibility, his changing lights and shades, his gaiety of wit shadowed by depths of sadness. But, of course, Pope again and again transcends his own Augustanism, a successor of Marvell as much as of Dryden, reminding us at times even of Keats rather than of Dryden.

Nor do we find in Crabbe the 'visionary' quality and insight of Wordsworth, Wordsworth's sense of the mystery of the human mind and of its living connections with the non-human mystery of nature. Crabbe and Wordsworth have, however, more in common than this might suggest, more in common in some respects than either has with Pope. Wordsworth's community of Cumberland and Westmorland sheep farmers and villagers, with its traditional life, religion and morality, has largely made Wordsworth what he is, even when a solitary wanderer brooding among the moors, and is a stabilizing presence in his poetry, as Crabbe's community is in his.

But Crabbe's achievement, though different from Pope's and Wordsworth's, is also a great and original one; and there are the respects in which it may rather be compared (and contrasted) with Jane Austen's.

Both Crabbe and Jane Austen are, of course, necessarily selective in their art. Jane Austen's provincial society in her part of England and in her particular milieu in that society seems, from her novels, relatively more 'polite' and materially comfortable than Crabbe's. The poverty some of her characters suffer from is rather of the genteel kind. Jane Austen rightly concentrates her novelist's art not only on the life she knows at first hand but on what most intensely interests her as a subject or problem for each of her novels in turn. When she wrote the words (unfairly quoted against her) 'let other pens dwell on guilt and misery', she may well have been thinking of Crabbe, whose work she admired as she admired Johnson's *Rasselas*.

Crabbe (as we see already in *The Village*) was deeply concerned about poverty and its effects as he observed them all round him in his particular parish in his particular part of England. But the wretchedness of the poor, though an important part of his total subject, is not his exclusive subject. His range takes in all social, as well as moral, levels. In the *Tales* he portrays the lives of the squires, the parsons, the merchants and the relatively well-to-do as authentically as the struggles of the poor. With the same clarity and stringency as he portrays harsh material circumstances, he portrays moral failures, the weaknesses and perversities of our common human nature in all social ranks and conditions. One of the reasons, indeed, why Crabbe has been only grudgingly accorded his rightful place in the great English tradition is, perhaps, what has seemed to many readers the bleakness of his view of life, not only his portrayal of the harsh struggle for existence in his part of England, but his unenchanted view of human nature and the neutral tones of his art, his austere presentation of home truths, facts about human nature that are often not palatable. This, for many readers, has scarcely been compensated for by the high professional standards of workmanship, of skilled craftsmanship in language and verse, which he has inherited from Pope and Johnson and maintained in his work, a precision, exactitude and economy in the choice and arrangement of words that compares favourably with some of the poetic effusions of Crabbe's contemporaries, who frequently rely too much on inspiration and spontaneity to carry their poetry through.

Further, though Crabbe has, like Johnson (and Hogarth), basically a sombre or grim, indeed a tragic (rather than a comic) sense of life, his idiom is still the idiom of wit, and he is often at his characteristic best in a kind of astringent comedy presented with a dry humour. The reader gradually discovers that Crabbe's unenchanted view of life, seen often as simultaneously tragic and comic, is qualified by a deep unobtrusive humanity, his moralism by a charitableness that comes from deeply felt experience and an understanding knowledge of human nature.

The way in which the poet Crabbe uses his gifts as a novelist is, of course, more exactly, as a master of the art of the short story in verse. In this art of selection, concentration and compression, each tale develops from its idiom, which is still in Crabbe the idiom of 18th century Augustan wit. The formal couplet verse and the neatness and balance of phrase in each line or couplet have much to do with the effect of wit – the rational and moral intelligence exposing human nature and human life to conscious appraisal and judgement in concise, lucid, sharp-edged or pointed expression. The wit is in the detail or texture of the tales; but each of the best tales, as a unified whole, is itself a compact structure of ironic wit composed of contrasts and antitheses of characters and episodes, morals and manners, attitudes and values.

II

Crabbe begins as a poet – *The Village* (1783) shows – from Johnson, thus taking his place in the direct line from Pope, the central line of 18th-century poetry. That Crabbe is nearer not only in time but in character and sensibility to Johnson than to Pope, the reader feels in the weightier movement of the verse, though we have to allow for the youthful poet's imitation of the older poet and for the fact that Johnson himself not only read but corrected *The Village.*

> Say ye, oppress'd by some fantastic woes,
> Some jarring nerve that baffles your repose . . .
> Who with sad prayers the weary doctor tease
> To name the nameless ever new disease;
> Who with mock patience dire complaints endure,
> Which real pain, and that alone, can cure;
> How would ye bear in real pain to lie,
> Despised, neglected, left alone to die?[1]

Here is no pleasing pensiveness but a manlier realism, controlling a heavier gloom, a tragic sense of life that suggests an affinity with Johnson. Crabbe's 'potent quack' might have come straight out of Hogarth's art.

> A potent quack, long versed in human ills,
> Who first insults the victim whom he kills;
> Whose murd'rous hand a drowsy bench protect,
> And whose most tender mercy is neglect.[2]

At the same time these lines recall some of the effects in Johnson's own youthful *London.*

> Some frolick drunkard, reeling from a feast,
> Provokes a broil and stabs you for a jest . . .
> Invades the sacred hour of silent rest
> And leaves unseen a dagger in your breast.

[1] 250–9.   [2] 282–5.

We can appreciate why Juvenal was more congenial to Johnson than Horace, whom Pope 'imitated', and why Johnson himself was in some ways more congenial for Crabbe to begin from than Pope.

The Village (Crabbe's response to Goldsmith's Deserted Village) is already a most notable poetic rejection of the poetical pastoralism that Johnson, too (for example in his criticism of Lycidas), had rejected with similar force. It is equally a rejection of the kind of literary Horatianism that was fashionable or that in Cowper's case was, perhaps, a necessity. For Crabbe, as an authentic provincial, the country is not a place of quiet retirement. The small borough town or village affords no refuge from life. He recognizes that human nature and manners and morals may be studied in the provinces as in the metropolis. What gives his poetry its note of authority, beginning already in The Village, which has, however, its special intensity, is the exactitude of his portrayal of life in his particular part of England, where for most people life was a hard struggle of poverty and toil, where the sea and the land were not distinctly differentiated, where the sea invaded the land and the soil was poor and barren, where moral failures and crime, as well as physical defeat, were as likely and frequent as, on the other hand, 'the sad splendour' of hard-won moral and human triumphs. The grim horrors of the workhouse, the last receptacle before death of the poverty-stricken and defeated, are portrayed a generation before Dickens with Hogarthian-Dickensian imaginative force.

III

The Village was composed in what was still the age of Johnson; The Parish Register, The Borough and Tales (1812) were published in what was by then the age of Wordsworth.

In The Parish Register the matter and manner of the Crabbe of Tales is beginning to take shape, particularly in Burials, the last of the three sections of the poem. Reminiscences of characters of the parish and the lives they lived are formed into sharply distinct character sketches together with brief life-histories that could be the germs of tales. There has begun to be recognizable another influence, in addition to Pope and Johnson, that of an earlier and greater English master, Chaucer. Dryden had 'translated' Chaucer into what became the English Augustan verse and idiom, and had at least made good Dryden out of Chaucer. There was, after all, that link between Chaucer and the 18th-century poets. But clearly Crabbe was reading Chaucer for himself, frequenting the original source. (See Crabbe's own Preface to *Tales*, 1812.) There begin to appear such Chaucerian (as well as Popean) characters as Footman Daniel in *Marriages*:

> Blue was his coat, unsoil'd by spot or stain;
> His hose were silk, his shoes of Spanish grain . . .
> And thus, with clouded cane, a fop complete,
> He stalk'd the jest and glory of the street.
> Join'd with these powers, he could so sweetly sing,
> Talk with such toss, and saunter with such swing;[1]

and (reminiscent also of Dryden) Andrew Collett in *Burials*:

> Big as his butt, and, for the selfsame use,
> To take in stores of strong fermenting juice . . .
> His own exploits with boastful glee he told,
> What ponds he emptied and what pikes he sold . . .
> He sang the praises of those times, when all
> 'For cards and dice, as for their drink, might call;
> When justice wink'd on every jovial crew,
> And ten-pins tumbled in the parson's view.'[2]

If *The Parish Register* and its much more considerable successor, *The Borough*, did no more than provide an authentic record, as they do, of what provincial life and manners were actually like in England about 1800, they would be interesting for that alone. In this respect Crabbe was doing something similar to what Scott was doing for the Scotland of the recent past. But Crabbe's right to a place with the greater English novelists depends, of course, much more on the acute psychological and moral understanding and observation of human nature he has begun to show.

In the grim little tale of Catherine, in whom the love of objects has replaced the love of persons, Catherine is in some respects an early sketch for Dinah in *Procrastination*. The precious and (some of them) bizarre objects and animal pets that have come to fill her rooms and her heart express the proud, cold possessiveness and

---

[1] 328–9, 335–8.   [2] 77–8, 99–100, 103–6.

luxurious and weird tastes she has developed in the withering and
deadening of her natural human sympathies:

> A parrot next, but dead and stuff'd with art
> (For Poll, when living, lost the lady's heart,
> And then his life; for he was heard to speak
> Such frightful words as tinged his lady's cheek) . . .
> A grey old cat his whiskers lick'd beside;
> A type of sadness in the house of pride.
> The polish'd surface of an India chest,
> A glassy globe, in frame of ivory, press'd;
> Where swam two finny creatures; one of gold . . .[1]

When her death approaches she cannot bring herself to renounce
those glittering possessions that have taken possession of her.

There is also occasionally a Dickensian imaginative energy that
moves the descriptive realism beyond descriptive realism, as in
his description of deserted, neglected, crumbling rooms that
anticipate those of the funereal houses in *Dombey and Son, Little
Dorrit* and other novels, rooms that have a ghostly, nightmarish,
Gothic life of their own, as has Dickens's whole smoky, foggy,
labyrinthine London (teeming, however, with living people,
swarming with individual 'characters').

Another note in Crabbe distinct from Pope or Chaucer is his
particular sense of place in his particular region, the fens, the
frowning coast and, occasionally, the savage, untamed, wolfish,
criminal propensities in human nature that find such wild and
lonely places congenial:

> His, a lone house, by Deadman's Dyke-way stood;
> And his a nightly haunt, in Lonely-wood.[2]

IV

Half a century earlier than *Middlemarch, The Borough* portrays a
provincial town community – in Crabbe's poem a community
influenced and coloured by its geographical setting as that of a
small seaport on a tidal estuary surrounded by fen-land and heath.
There is also a further development of Crabbe's art in this poem
(towards the greater art of the *Tales*) in the portrayal of individual

---

[1] *Burials*, 354–7, 360–4.   [2] *Baptisms*, 791–2.

characters; for example, the old sinners, Blaney, Clelia and Benbow who at the penniless ends of their lives have condescended to inhabit the almshouse.

The tidal estuary, the sea, the fen-land, which have largely determined and shaped the character of the borough and the characters and lives of its inhabitants, are presences in the poem, described in some of the most unforgettable poetry with exact particularity and immediacy – and contrasted with the rich farm- and meadow-land by an inland river. Yet the flora of fen and heath provide a wealth of their own, a wealth of botanical interest and, for a poet's imagination, the curious fascination of organic forms and varying colours on what is, as farm-land, an unproductive wilderness. Crabbe has a feeling for wild nature in his particular region as Wordsworth has in his, though it is a different feeling for a different kind of wild nature. Nature in Crabbe's poetry can subtly reflect an individual's moods and feelings. But nature for Crabbe is not necessarily either a source of spritual strength or physical sustenance for the human creature.

The juiceless foliage and the tasteless fruit.

Crabbe is nearer Cobbett with his practical farmer's sense. Though fen-land, heath and seashore fascinate and arouse his curiosity as botanist and poet, they are as farm-land poor or un-cultivable. Crabbe's special strength as a landscapist is his sobriety of style (not unlike Wordsworth's in this respect – in contrast to the Miltonic grand manner and diction of the 18th-century poetic landscapists), his cool exactitude of observation, his botanist's eye and, occasionally, something more intense, an almost Lawrentian feeling for plant life as another kind of life from human. There is a felt connection between the hostile luxuriance of the weeds and the poverty of the poor in their hovels (Letter 18) – the tropical profusion, the jungle of hostile and menacing weeds.

> Here the strong mallow strikes her slimy root,
> Here the dull nightshade hangs her deadly fruit:
> On hills of dust the henbane's faded green,
> And pencill'd flower of sickly scent is seen;
> At the wall's base the fiery nettle springs,

With fruit globose and fierce with poison's stings.[1]

But the strength of *The Borough* – or that side of it which is
developing towards the art of the *Tales* – is in the portraiture.
There is, for example, the character of the Vicar (Letter 3)
portrayed with a subtlety of wit and humour that recalls Chaucer
as much as Pope, an effect of wit in which insight into human
nature has found a happy neatness and pointedness of expression.

> His constant care, was no man to offend.[2]

In his youthful days the Vicar pays frequent visits to a mother and
daughter, causing the girl – fortunately for herself a sensible girl
– to wonder what his intentions might be.

> She, with her widow'd mother, heard him speak,
> And sought awhile to find what he would seek:
> Smiling he came, he smiled when he withdrew,
> And paid the same attention to the two:
> Meeting and parting without joy or pain,
> He seem'd to come that he might go again.[3]

This little tragi-comic episode of his youth is consistent with his
character to the end. He takes refuge more and more in the
blameless habits of a settled retiring life, paying visits and pre-
senting flowers from his garden to 'his fair friends' (with compli-
ments reminiscent of the poetry of George Herbert).

> Not without moral compliment; how they
> 'Like flowers were sweet, and must like flowers decay.'[4]

There are, different again, the Hogarthian lawyers (Letter 6)
in the tradition from Swift (or earlier still from Ben Jonson), as
well as from Pope.

> All bring employment, all augment his bills:
> As feels the surgeon for the mangled limb,
> The mangled mind is but a job for him.[5]

There is the contrast between the successful lawyer's spacious and
sumptuous mansion and the small office where, spider-like, he
draws in his prey. There is the strategy of lawyer Swallow in
possessing himself of the fortunes of 'simple heirs', youthful

_____

[1] 292–7.   [2] 16.   [3] 25–30.   [4] 89–90.   [5] 125–7.

wastrels of the types portrayed in *The Rake's Progress* or Johnson's 'Long expected one and twenty'.

There is again that Dickensian imaginative power which occasionally breaks through Crabbe's on the whole much more sober and evenly regulated art, as when the smoke-filled room of the Smokers Club seems to change from unpleasant actuality to nightmarish fantasy at midnight and relapses to a sordid anticlimax. The way the conversation lamentably fails to flow is convincingly imitated in the succeeding verse dialogue.

But it is, above all, in the characters and life-histories of three inhabitants of the almshouse, Blaney, Clelia, Benbow (Letters 14, 15, 16), that the Crabbe of the verse *Tales* is already showing more fully his mastery of his art. Their downfalls are, of course, the consequence of their own recklessness, weakness and follies. This moral fact is clearly marked and pointed in the verse. But what is also expressed is the sense that they are flesh and blood. The moralistic intention (as stated in Crabbe's own footnote to Letter 14) proves to be only one element in the total effect produced by the poetry. Blaney and Clelia, as their characters and careers are portrayed and presented, come to life in the creative art of a poet with a novelist's sense of life. The poetry and the wit open out into a larger, more genial, more charitable view, with humour and pathos.

> 'With all her faults,' he said, 'the woman knew
> How to distinguish – had a manner too.'[1]

There is a magnanimity in Sir Denys's words about poor Clelia with which the poetry has brought us fully into accord – even though Sir Denys himself is comically in the habit of overvaluing what he calls 'manner'.

The portrayal of Blaney's *Rake's Progress* (Letter 14) has indeed a comic zest that, in the poetry, transcends the moralistic intention so that we are impelled, as we contemplate his career, not so much merely to censure Blaney as to exclaim with wonder, 'What a life was Blaney's!' And so to his downfall and degradation:

> Lo! now the hero shuffling through the town,
> To hunt a dinner and to beg a crown.[2]

[1] Letter 15, 204–5.   [2] Letter 14, 142–3.

But the most sparkling and high-spirited of these characters, whose bright, evanescent, deplorable career we witness with wonder and dismay, is certainly Clelia. She meets 'the Lovelace of his day' and that proves her undoing. The middle-aged Clelia is discovered in an austerer setting, but essentially the same Clelia with plenty of spirit still.

> Then as a matron Clelia taught a school.

She is next discovered – another surprising transition – the mistress of the Griffin and of the Griffin's landlord till another disaster:

> Th' insolvent Griffin struck his wings sublime; –
> Forth from her palace walk'd th' ejected queen,
> And show'd to frowning Fate a look serene;
> Gay, spite of time, though poor, yet well attired,
> Kind without love, and vain if not admired.[1]

We follow Clelia's progress and decline through to its final stage before her admission to the almshouse. There is here something of the note of Pope's 'in the worst inn's worst room . . .' – lines that evidently haunted Crabbe.

> Now friendless, sick, and old and wanting bread,
> The first-born tears of fallen pride were shed –
> True, bitter tears; and yet that wounded pride,
> Among the poor, for poor distinctions sigh'd.
> Though now her tales were to her audience fit;
> Though loud her tones, and vulgar grown her wit,
> Though now her dress – (but let me not explain
> The piteous patchwork of the needy-vain,
> The flirtish form to coarse materials lent,
> And one poor robe through fifty fashions sent);
> Though all within was sad, without was mean, –
> Still 'twas her wish, her comfort to be seen:
> She would to plays on lowest terms resort,
> Where once her box was to the beaux a court;
> And, strange delight! to that same house where she
> Join'd in the dance, all gaiety and glee,

[1] Letter 15, 155–9.

Now with the menials crowding to the wall
She'd see, not share, the pleasures of the ball.[1]

The presence of old Benbow, with his complexion that recalls
Bardolph's, an old soaker and drinking companion, is the one
which is most incongruous with the propriety of the almshouse,
such is his unending flow of unsuitable anecdotes and reminis-
cences of the 'good old days' disturbing the peace of the sober
house. From old Benbow's reminiscences comes one of Crabbe's
portrayals of a type of English squire of the 18th century, his
manner of life already, it seems, regarded as old-fashioned.

Then lived the good Squire Asgill – what a change
Has death and fashion shown us at the Grange!
He bravely thought it best became his rank
That all his tenants and his tradesmen drank:
He was delighted from his favourite room
To see them 'cross the park go daily home
Praising aloud the liquor and the host.[2]

'Bounds of all kinds he hated', and would have felt 'choked and
imprison'd' by his grounds being enclosed about

The good old house, to keep old neighbours out.
Along his valleys, in the evening hours,
The borough damsels stray'd to gather flowers;
Or by the brakes and brushwood of the park,
To take their pleasant rambles in the dark.
Some prudes, of rigid kind, forbore to call
On the kind females – favourites at the hall;
But better nature saw, with much delight,
The different orders of mankind unite.
'Twas schooling pride to see the footman wait,
Smile on his sister, and receive her plate.[3]

The present state of things at the Grange is seen (by old Benbow)
as a melancholy contrast, a fallen world.

Oh! could the ghost of our good squire arise,
And see such change, – would it believe its eyes?[4]

[1] Letter 15, 174–91. [2] Letter 16, 65–71. [3] Letter 16, 85–95.
[4] Letter 16, 126–7.

Finally, there are Crabbe's darker, more sombre studies of characters of the Borough who fall into crime. There is the Parish Clerk, Jachin, a case of Pharisaical pride, the strict Puritan who falls from the state of spiritual superiority he imagines himself to be in, begins to help himself from the church-box, justifying his practice to his own conscience, until he is found out.

And there is, above all, the tale of Peter Grimes, a grim study of crime and remorse, the unappeased sense of guilt, within the man himself, producing retribution. This is a subject which had occupied Wordsworth, too, in his early works, *Guilt and Sorrow* and *The Borderers*, and Coleridge in *The Ancient Mariner*. The source for all three poets, apart from their own experience, is recognizably *Macbeth* in each case. But Crabbe is again at his own characteristic best in his descriptions of the fen-land estuary as reflecting the states of mind of Peter, the solitary criminal outcast, who has become almost the wild spirit of the place.[1]

V

It is in virtue of his *Tales* (1812) that Crabbe takes his place as Chaucer does, as much with the English novelists as with the poets. I shall glance at a number of these to suggest in particular that their range and variety are more considerable than at first they may seem to be or that we may have remembered them to have been.

The tale of *The Gentleman Farmer* develops from the character, more especially the psychological and moral weaknesses, of this particular gentleman farmer. His taste is reflected in the surprisingly showy, yet elegant, furnishings of his rooms.

> His rooms were stately, rather fine than neat,
> And guests politely call'd his house a Seat;
> At much expense was each apartment graced,
> His taste was gorgeous, but it still was taste;
> In full festoons the crimson curtains fell,
> The sofas rose in bold elastic swell;
> Mirrors in gilded frames display'd the tints
> Of glowing carpets, and of colour'd prints.[2]

[1] Cf. the marshland episodes in *Great Expectations*.   [2] 55–62.

Sceptical about doctors, lawyers and priests, he declares he will dispense with their services and be guided solely by Reason, Truth and Nature.

But how free he proves to be the tale will show. There enters 'the neat Rebecca'. The basic cause of Gwyn's ultimate breakdown and surrender is that fear of life which originally caused him to withdraw into the Horatian retirement of being 'a gentleman farmer'. He affects to despise forms and conventions and the notions of simple people. But to a greater extent than he knows he is 'social man' and influenced by the attitudes of his neighbours. He begins to suffer from inexplicable fears and anxieties and imaginary illnesses, a developing hypochondria.

On the advice of the neat Rebecca he consents after all to call in a doctor, her cousin Mollet, who once installed in the household makes himself indispensable to his patient. But still the nervous fears increase – 'these inward griefs and troubles of the soul'. On the advice of Mollet and Rebecca, Gwyn next consents to call in a spiritual adviser, the evangelical Wisp, and as a convert goes through the form of marriage with Rebecca. Finally we see poor Gwyn, the free-thinking 'gentleman farmer', enlightened 'improver', of the beginning of the tale, helplessly enslaved by those sinister Hogarthian figures, Mollet, Wisp and Rebecca.

> Mollet his body orders, Wisp his soul,
> And o'er his purse the Lady takes control . . .
> And fair Rebecca leads a virtuous life –
> She rules a mistress, and she reigns a wife.[1]

Procrastination, one of the best of Crabbe's tales, is an exposure of what can happen in a human soul, the gradual death of feeling over the years, the hardening of the heart that finally makes possible inhumanity to a fellow-creature.

First we see the prudent Dinah and her Rupert as two young lovers prevented from marrying by lack of means and at the mercy of a rich and jealous aunt, Dinah's guardian. The aunt's sinister influence, and how she exerts it, a few concentrated lines convey. A prospect opens for Rupert across the sea, a delusive prospect as it proves. The years pass. The love of the precious

---

[1] 513 et seq.

objects displayed in her wealthy aunt's house consoles Dinah and
gradually supplants the love of Rupert.

> Saw clean'd the plate, arranged the china-show,
> And felt her passion for a shilling grow.[1]

Avarice occupies Dinah's heart; then, after she has at last inherited
her aunt's wealth, a love also of splendour and luxury.

> Around the room an Indian paper blazed,
> With lively tint and figures boldly raised;
> Silky and soft upon the floor below,
> Th' elastic carpet rose with crimson glow.[2]

An ensnaring, entrapping power, catlike in its splendour, is
subtly suggested. The clock in particular – Time passing, dis-
guised behind a luxurious façade – assumes in the poetry a
symbolical import. Its metallic, mechanical action, essentially a
hard, steely mechanism at work, behind its external ornamental
glitter, is the kind of thing the heart of the outwardly pious Dinah
herself has changed into.

> Above her head, all gorgeous to behold,
> A time-piece stood on feet of burnish'd gold;
> A stag's-head crest adorn'd the pictured case,
> Through the pure crystal shone the enamell'd face;
> And while on brilliants moved the hands of steel,
> It click'd from prayer to prayer, from meal to meal.[3]

There is an element of hypocrisy creeping in, too, a hypocritical
piety. Dinah with her visitors has become one of the Pharisaical
strait-laced.

> They then related how the young and gay
> Were thoughtless wandering in the broad highway:
> How tender damsels sail'd in tilted boats,
> And laugh'd with wicked men in scarlet coats.[4]

On this scene, there is the sudden entry of the maidservant, the
'tall Susannah, maiden starch'.

> 'I think the devil's in the man!' she cried.[5]

[1] 94–5.   [2] 160–3.   [3] 174–9.   [4] 182–5.   [5] 107.

The importunate sailor-man at the door is none other than Rupert returned, after years of vain struggle, as poor as when he left. The hypocrisy and inhumanity of the changed Dinah come out in the dialogues, conventional platitudes and pious clichés (like those in Swift's lines on the reception of the news of his own death). So the tale moves to the stroke of inhumanity with which, with terrible finality, it ends:

> One way remain'd – the way the Levite took . . .
> She cross'd and pass'd him on the other side.[1]

The Patron is not only an exposure of aristocratic patronage that recalls Johnson on patrons, but a tale of disenchantment. A fanciful, sensitive youth with poetic gifts and ambitions is taken up by a lordly patron and is destroyed by his contact with the aristocratic world. He indulges the delusive dreams it fosters. The dreams get shattered and, with the dreams, himself.

The tale opens, as is often Crabbe's way, with a portrayal of the young man's origins and background, his father's decent middle-class household with its prudential virtues and frugalities. This prepares for the sudden contrast with the great and splendid aristocratic world into which John is received.

The more John's fancy flourishes, the more painfully conscious does he become of the frugal and prudential constrictions of his father's household. The question that perplexes his father, on the other hand, is whether his son has enough sense to counter-balance his poetic fancy. The young poet has developed the not so useless 18th century gift of satire, the usefulness of which has introduced him to the aristocratic world of lordly patronage.

> 'John, thou'rt a genius; thou hast some pretence,
> I think, to wit, – but hast thou sterling sense?'[2]

The father, a borough bailiff, has plenty of that commodity; and his advice to his son, which would doubtless seem to the recipient in actual life too long and is perhaps too long also for the art of the short tale, provides at least a counterbalance, in the tale, of 18th century good sense against the youth's romantic dreams and delusions.

The summer at the great house soon passes. With the description of the autumnal scene an elegiac note enters the tale.

Cold grew the foggy morn, the day was brief,
Loose on the cherry hung the crimson leaf;
The dew dwelt ever on the herb; the woods
Roar'd with strong blasts, with mighty showers the floods:
All green was vanish'd, save of pine and yew,
That still display'd their melancholy hue;
Save the green holly with its berries red,
And the green moss that o'er the gravel spread.[1]

My Lord and Lady and the Lady Emma herself depart for town.
John is left behind, abruptly and coldly.

Yes he must speak; – he speaks, 'My good young friend,
You know my views; upon my care depend;
My hearty thanks to your good father pay,
And be a student. – Harry, drive away.'[2]

In the stillness and gloom of the great empty house, John (like
Chaucer's Troilus left desolate after Criseyde's departure) wanders
from deserted room to deserted room recalling past happiness.
Summoned to town at last by a cool letter, he is kept vainly
waiting for an audience with Lord Frederick in the chilly splen-
dour of the great town house, as many a struggling young author
had done before.

'Be pleased to wait; my lord has company' ...
Cold was the day; in days so cold as these
There needs a fire where minds and bodies freeze.
The vast and echoing room, the polish'd grate,
The crimson chairs, the sideboard with its plate ...
'Was he forgotten?' Thrice upon his ear
Struck the loud clock, yet no relief was near.
Each rattling carriage, and each thundering stroke
On the loud door, the dream of fancy broke;
Oft as the servant chanced the way to come,
'Brings he a message?' no! he pass'd the room:
At length 'tis certain; 'Sir, you will attend
At twelve on Thursday!' Thus the day had end.[3]

But John is not tough. From his sense of humiliation and broken
dreams there follow, in fatal sequence, madness, sickness and

[1] 426-33.   [2] 460-3.   [3] 523-43.

premature death (and his father's heartbreak). There is one final
glimpse of the Lord Frederick and the Lady Emma when the
news of the young man's death reaches their august ears. The tone
of aristocratic insolence is accurately caught.

> 'But is he dead – and am I to suppose
> The power of poison in such looks as those?'
> She spoke, and pointing to the mirror, cast
> A pleased gay glance, and curtsied as she pass'd.
> My lord, to whom the poet's fate was told,
> Was much affected, for a man so cold:
> 'Dead!' said his lordship, 'run distracted – mad!
> Upon my soul I'm sorry for the lad;
> And now no doubt th' obliging world will say
> That my harsh usage help'd him on his way.'[1]

The Frank Courtship is a masterpiece of wit in its structure as
well as in its texture. There is a beautiful compactness and balance
in the arrangement of the tale as a whole, as well as in the detail.
The whole lucid, yet genial, comedy composes and forms itself
into a single piece of 'wit' – in the important Augustan sense. The
effect of wit comes out particularly in the concise, pointed
dialogues.

In a distinct, sharply focused light, as concentrated comedy, the
tale shows the influence of different upbringings, social back-
grounds, and traditional manners and morals on individual
characters; and it shows two high-spirited young people working
their way through a clash of attitudes and temperaments to a new
kind of marriage, unfamiliar in the society of their elders, a more
intelligent kind of human relationship: a marriage of equals.

Every part of this classic verse tale is relevant to every other
part, the beginning to the end. The portrayal, at the beginning, of
the strict Puritan household of Jonas, the Cromwellian husband
and father, a stern, patriarchal Old Testament character, a domes-
tic dictator, whose word is law in his house, will be discovered to
have the most exact relevance to all that follows in the tale. *His*
marriage is of a very different kind from the one formed by the
young couple in the tale, in a wooing very different from the one
prescribed for them by his paternal authority.

[1] 700–9.

For Jonas is a member of a Puritan remnant, descendants of the Cromwellian 'saints'. Not that they are so other-worldly. Crabbe neatly indicates the combination in the Puritan trading-class of godliness and moral strictness with the pursuit of lawful gain, almost the moral obligation to 'do well', to thrive and prosper with the aid of sobriety, frugality and strictness of life.

The old man innocently consents that his daughter, Sybil, should for a time live as a companion with her aunt in another town, 'a lively place'. This introduces a contrast into Sybil's life and into the tale. The household of the comparatively un-puritanical aunt, who is not averse to such worldly pleasures as playing whist, opens out a new scene of life for Sybil, different from home. It enables her to make comparisons between the two households, two different ways of life. In consequence, the annual visit to her stern father's house imposes on the lively girl temporarily a degree of constraint, demure looks and behaviour, even a degree of connivance with her aunt at dissembling.

> 'Yes! we must go, my child, and by our dress
> A grave conformity of mind express;
> Must sing at meeting, and from cards refrain,
> The more t' enjoy when we return again.'
> Thus spake the aunt, and the discerning child
> Was pleased to learn how fathers are beguiled.
> Her artful part the young dissembler took,
> And from the matron caught th' approving look ...
> He gazed admiring; she, with visage prim,
> Glanced an arch look of gravity on him;
> For she was gay at heart, but wore disguise,
> And stood a vestal in her father's eyes.[1]

But Sybil is an essentially frank nature and such behaviour goes against the grain.

> For Sybil, fond of pleasure, gay and light,
> Had still a secret bias to the right.[2]

Nevertheless Sybil's stay in her aunt's house is, as it proves, an essential stage in her education as an individual. She soon enough outgrows her aunt's genteel worldliness; it begins to bore her,

[1] 105–30.   [2] 133–4.

and she welcomes the change implied in a summons from her
father to return home.

Meanwhile the autocratic father has been arranging Sybil's
future for her. This has necessitated some hard bargaining between
himself and a well-to-do widow of the same sect for a suitable
marriage between his daughter and her son. The preliminaries of
the marriage of Sybil and Josiah having, unknown to Sybil her-
self, been settled, she is summoned at last from her aunt's. The
father is disconcerted, even shocked by the change in manners he
now for the first time observes in his daughter.

> 'The maid is virtuous,' said the dame – Quoth he,
> 'Let her give proof, by acting virtuously:
> Is it in gaping when the elders pray?
> In reading nonsense half a summer's day?
> In those mock forms that she delights to trace,
> Or her loud laughs in Hezekiah's face?
> She, O Susannah, to the world belongs;
> She loves the follies of its idle throngs.'[1]

That Sybil has a very different conception of love and marriage
is amusingly manifested in her high-spirited outbreak to her
mother on what she regards as the behaviour of a true lover and
on what she regards as her due.

> 'I must be loved,' said Sybil; 'I must see
> The man in terrors who aspires to me;
> At my forbidding frown his heart must ache,
> His tongue must falter, and his frame must shake:
> And if I grant him at my feet to kneel,
> What trembling, fearful pleasure must he feel;
> Nay, such the raptures that my smiles inspire,
> That reason's self must for a time retire.'
> 'Alas! for good Josiah,' said the dame,
> 'These wicked thoughts would fill his soul with shame;
> He kneel and tremble at a thing of dust!
> He cannot, child:' – the child replied, 'He must.'[2]

From his first entrance and appearance Sybil quickly forms her
own estimate of the young man, weighing up his qualities, good

[1] 234–41.   [2] 294–305.

and bad. In the encounter the two prove to be equally and well
matched.

> He saw a foe with treacherous purpose fraught –
> Captive the heart to take, and to reject it, caught.
> Silent they sat; – thought Sybil, 'That he seeks
> Something, no doubt; I wonder if he speaks:'
> Scarcely she wonder'd, when these accents fell
> Slow in her ear, 'Fair maiden, art thou well?'
> 'Art thou physician?' she replied; 'my hand,
> My pulse, at least, shall be at thy command.'[1]

With the greatest candour each tells the other's faults – the frank
courtship. The effect of the dialogue is, in some respects, in its
substance as well as in its formal neatness and concision, beauti-
fully similar to the gravely witty, moral dialogue poems of
Marvell.

> Then sternness she assumed, and – 'Doctor, tell;
> Thy words cannot alarm me – am I well?'
> 'Thou art,' said he, 'and yet thy dress so light,
> I do conceive, some danger must excite:'
> 'In whom?' said Sybil, with a look demure:
> 'In more,' said he, 'than I expect to cure' . . .
> 'Speak'st thou at meeting?' said the nymph; 'thy speech
> Is that of mortal very prone to teach;
> But wouldst thou, doctor, from the patient learn
> Thine own disease? – the cure is thy concern.'
> 'Yea, with good will.' – 'Then know 'tis thy complaint,
> That, for a sinner, thou'rt too much a saint;
> Hast too much show of the sedate and pure,
> And, without cause, art formal and demure:
> This makes a man unsocial, unpolite;
> Odious when wrong, and insolent if right.
> Thou mayst be good, but why should goodness be
> Wrapt in a garb of such formality?'[2]

The angry father supposes that his rebellious, his perverse
child has so conducted herself that all is lost. On the contrary, out
of the candid encounter, a mutual respect and esteem and, some-

[1] 362–9.   [2] 374–9, 414–25.

thing more, a mutual love have been born. With true judgement they have tested and chosen each other. The choice had to be their own and not their parents'. Though critical of each other's manners, each recognizes the other's intrinsic worth, and a marriage of equals is promised that contrasts with that of Sybil's parents. The unexpected fortunate conclusion to this comedy happens to be fortunate because Sybil's own true choice happens to accord with her father's will. But the tension the reader feels arises partly from the recognition that, if Sybil had found her suitor wanting, she would have felt tragically constrained to oppose her father.

The complications of the little comedy called *The Widow's Tale* arise from the intrusion of urban cultivated refinement on the old coarseness of manners in the country. The tale shows the necessity sometimes, if life is to go on, of reconciling refinement of sensibility and taste with usefulness, and of recognizing intrinsic worth in another, however unrefined (as in Johnson's Dr. Levet) or however genteelly refined (as in the Widow of this tale). This sounds a ponderous account of what is here, on the surface, light comedy. But there is nearly always a weighty moral import in Crabbe's tales, even when the tone is wittily light.

A farmer's daughter comes home from a superior school in town, a refined young lady, and the coarse manners of the farm disgust her.

> To Farmer Moss, in Langar Vale, came down
> His only daughter, from her school in town;
> A tender, timid maid, who knew not how
> To pass a pig-sty, or to face a cow:
> Smiling she came, with petty talents graced,
> A fair complexion, and a slender waist.
> Used to spare meals, disposed in manner pure,
> Her father's kitchen she could ill endure:
> Where by the steaming beef he hungry sat,
> And laid at once a pound upon his plate;
> Hot from the field, her eager brother seized
> An equal part, and hunger's rage appeased;
> The air surcharged with moisture, flagg'd around,
> And the offended damsel sigh'd and frown'd . . .[1]

[1] 1–14.

Her squeamishness angers her father. She must share the work of
the farm-house, learn in time to be a useful farmer's wife. But she
recoils from the idea of ever being a farmer's wife. She frequently
flies to the company of an impoverished but 'refined' widow
regarded by the farming community as 'useless'. To Nancy the
widow seems the fine flower of refinement and taste, and her
cottage on the green a romantically idyllic refuge. But the widow
herself conscientiously dispels Nancy's romantic dream about
her cultured cottage and herself. The refined and 'useless' widow
turns out to have a great deal of good sense and right feeling.
Thus 'the school-bred miss', gently persuaded by the widow's
cautionary tale, becomes a Farmer's Wife and as such proves she
has 'real worth', while at the same time she imparts her 'neat
taste' to the farm.

The Mother is a study of selfish coldness of heart where we
should least expect it, in a mother. The mother of this tale is
shown as, throughout a lifetime of vanity, consistently what she
is from ber beginnings ('By nature, cold . . .'), the spoiled child,
then the spoiled beauty and cold heiress demanding flattery, then
the petulant spoiled wife, whom her mild and over-solicitous
husband pampers in vain.

'Would she some seaport, Weymouth, Scarborough, grace?' –
'He knew she hated every watering-place.'
'The town?' – 'What! now 'twas empty, joyless, dull?'
'In winter?' – 'No; she liked it worse when full.'
She talked of building – 'Would she plan a room?' –
'No! she could live, as he desired, in gloom.'
'Call then our friends and neighbours.' – 'He might call,
And they might come and fill his ugly hall;
A noisy vulgar set, he knew she scorn'd them all.' . . .
'My dear, my gentle Dorothea, say,
Can I oblige you?' – 'You may go away.'[1]

He finally does oblige her by going away effectually; he con-
veniently dies and at last obtains her praise 'graved on a marble
tomb'.

Left with two daughters, one plain, the other a beauty like
herself, the mother graciously allows her plain daughter, Lucy, a

[1] 47–61.

sensible and good girl, to be taken off her hands by a worthy aunt.

> 'Thou art the image of thy pious aunt.'[1]

The beautiful mother and beautiful daughter then form an unhindered alliance, birds of a feather. Meanwhile, a youthful rector, overcoming the opposition of his 'high family' – 'a lofty race' – becomes Lucy's suitor. The mother is capriciously difficult about giving her consent. The other daughter, the beauty, dies, the favoured one for whom 'a high marriage' had been planned by the mother,

> Who grieved indeed, but found a vast relief
> In a cold heart, that ever warr'd with grief.[2]

The plain daughter has now become the heiress. The brilliant mother no longer regards the youthful rector as good enough, materially, to be a match for an heiress, however plain. The girl's feelings are overridden by the mother, whose moment of triumph comes with the news that the youthful rector has 'sacrificed his passion to his pride'.

The tale concludes with a chilling glimpse of the mother, having outlived both her daughters, caring only for herself and her carefully preserved beauty, as egotistic and vain as ever.

> In her tall mirror then she shows her face,
> Still coldly fair with unaffecting grace...[3]

The astringent little comedy of *Arabella* is an ironical exposure of how imperfectly we may understand our own motives and may disguise them from ourselves as being wholly virtuous.

Arabella, the only daughter of the Rector, Dr. Rack, is learned and moral, a model held up to all other daughters in the town by their mammas with no very happy results.

> For, whatsoever wise mammas might say,
> To guide a daughter, this was not the way;
> From such applause disdain and anger rise,
> And envy lives where emulation dies...
> This reasoning maid, above her sex's dread,
> Had dared to read, and dared to say she read;
> Not the last novel, not the new-born play;

Not the mere trash and scandal of the day;
But (though her young companions felt the shock)
She studied Berkeley, Bacon, Hobbes and Locke.[1]

It is not surprising that such a prodigy finds no one good enough,
by her high and severe standards, in a succession of suitors.

'Twelve brilliant years' pass for an Arabella continuing in 'the
single state', which she is encouraged to prefer by 'a virgin
friend' of more advanced years. The mellowing effect which time
may, however, produce, making us more tolerant and even com-
plaisant, is described in one of Crabbe's fine, dry, clear, unsenti-
mental passages.

Time to the yielding mind his change imparts,
He varies notions, and he alters hearts;
'Tis right, 'tis just to feel contempt for vice;
But he that shows it may be over-nice:
There are, who feel, when young, the false sublime,
And proudly love to show disdain for crime;
To whom the future will new thoughts supply,
The pride will soften, and the scorn will die . . .
Why would not Ellen to Belinda speak,
When she had flown to London for a week,
And then return'd, to every friend's surprise,
With twice the spirit, and with half the size?
She spoke not then – but, after years had flown,
A better friend had Ellen never known.
Was it the lady her mistake had seen?
Or had she also such a journey been?
No: 'twas the gradual change in human hearts,
That time, in commerce with the world, imparts;
That on the roughest temper throws disguise,
And steals from virtue her asperities.
The young and ardent, who with glowing zeal
Felt wrath for trifles, and were proud to feel,
Now find those trifles all the mind engage,
To soothe dull hours, and cheat the cares of age;
As young Zelinda, in her quaker dress,
Disdain'd each varying fashion's vile excess,

¹ 15–18, 23–8.

And now her friends on old Zelinda gaze,
Pleased in rich silks and orient gems to blaze.[1]

The 'twelve brilliant years' have not left Arabella herself un-
changed and she is now surprisingly willing to listen to and even
encourage the suit of a certain Merchant. 'The virgin friend',
whose motives are mixed and impure, attempts to save Arabella
from the married state. The kind Friend has made inquiries and
now discloses to Arabella the scandalous background of her
Merchant. But the Arabella of these later years has now sur-
prisingly little difficulty in finding sufficient reasons to convince
herself, if no one else, that it is her religious duty to marry and
redeem him.

The Lover's Journey is one of the finest of Crabbe's *Tales*; it
happens also to offer the reader of Crabbe and Wordsworth an
occasion for a comparison between these two poets. The in-
fluence of the mind on the way we see or experience natural
objects – as well as the influence of natural objects on the mind –
is of course one of the primary interests of Wordsworth's (as of
Coleridge's) poetry. One effect of the experiences with 'nature' in
the great passages of Wordsworth is a religious sense of reverence
and awe in the presence of the mystery of nature and the mystery
of man, and also a sense of the moral dignity of man and of the
dignity of the imagination, the creative power of the mind. The
note of Wordsworth is one of solemnity.

The Lover's Journey is, on the other hand, comedy. It illus-
trates with an irony that is characteristic of Crabbe the influence
our moods can have on the way we see natural objects. The irony
and the humour of Crabbe's tale arise from a sense of the absurd-
ity of its being so, that supposedly rational men should be so at
the mercy of their inward moods and fluctuations of feeling as to
be unable to see external objects as they are. The effect of the
comedy is chastening to our human pride: it takes us down by
showing how absurdly subjective we are. This particular tale
expresses also perhaps something of the indulgent amusement of
middle age, supposedly the age of sense, at the extravagances and
enthusiams of youth looked back upon, as these are here repro-
duced in the romantic young lover, Orlando.

[1] 190–7, 204–23.

The landscapes of Crabbe's tale are very solidly present, exactly observed and described in the poetry. It is the lover's responses to these varied landscapes that are comically at the mercy of his changing moods. The effect depends on the simultaneous presence of a delicately exact sense of the landscapes as objects and, in relation to these landscapes, a delicately exact sense of the young man's moods as these change, at times abruptly, in accordance with the accidents of the day, the expectation of his sweetheart's presence, her unexpected absence, then again her recovered presence, and so on.

Crabbe's language, though his verse continues to be the 18th-century couplet verse, is as free from 'poetic diction' as Wordsworth's – and as is most of the best 18th-century poetry, the poetry of Pope and Johnson. (Johnson's disapproval of 'poetic diction' is expressed in his Life of Gray, for example, very much as Wordsworth was to express his disapproval.) This is as much so in Crabbe's descriptions of nature as of human nature, except when (as Pope does also) he uses poetic diction for some special effect, to burlesque pastoral affectations or the romanticizing poetical moods of his young lover; for John in *The Lover's Journey* is, in his own romantic fancy, Orlando, and his Susan is Laura.

Orlando is riding towards his Laura in a mood of joyful anticipation.

> First o'er a barren heath beside the coast,
> Orlando rode, and joy began to boast.
> 'This neat low gorse,' said he, 'with golden bloom,
> Delights each sense, is beauty, is perfume;
> And this gay ling, with all its purple flowers,
> A man at leisure might admire for hours;
> This green-fringed cup-moss has a scarlet tip,
> That yields to nothing but my Laura's lip;
> And then how fine this herbage! men may say
> A heath is barren; nothing is so gay:
> Barren or bare to call such charming scene
> Argues a mind possess'd by care and spleen.'
> Onward he went, and fiercer grew the heat,
> Dust rose in clouds before the horse's feet;

For now he pass'd through lanes of burning sand,
Bounds to thin crops or yet uncultured land;
Where the dark poppy flourish'd on the dry
And sterile soil, and mock'd the thin-set rye.
'How lovely this!' the wrapt Orlando said;
'With what delight is labouring man repaid!
The very lane has sweets that all admire,
The rambling suckling, and the vigorous brier;
See! wholesome wormwood grows beside the way,
Where dew-press'd yet the dogrose bends the spray;
Fresh herbs the fields, fair shrubs the banks adorn,
And snow-white bloom falls flaky from the thorn;
No fostering hand they need, no sheltering wall,
They spring uncultured, and they bloom for all.'
The lover rode as hasty lovers ride,
And reach'd a common pasture wild and wide;
Small black-legg'd sheep devour with hunger keen
The meagre herbage, fleshless, lank, and lean.[1]

To a Cobbett the barren heath would signify poor farming land
(the sterile soil, the meagre herbage). But Orlando is in a mood to
drink in the vivid beauty, particularly its flora, through all his
senses; to him it is gay.

'Ay, this is Nature,' said the gentle Squire.[2]

The wretched hovels of a moorland hamlet and their impover-
ished inhabitants are transmuted in his enchanted fancy to an
idyllic pastoral scene, children at play in an age of innocence,
joyful rustics in a state of nature, maidens who go to the dance.
Some vicious-looking gipsies are similarly idealized. The fen-land
and the salt-marsh by which in the same mood he continues to
ride are agreeable to sight, hearing and smell, and also filled with
botanical interest.

Like all attracted things, he quicker flies,
The place approaching where th' attraction lies.[3]

The enchantment is broken, the mood abruptly altered by his
discovery on arrival that his Laura is not there, has gone to visit
a friend.

[1] 34–65.   [2] 74.   [3] 100–1.

'What, gone! – "Her friend insisted – forced to go;
Is vex'd, was teased, could not refuse her" – No?
"But you can follow." Yes! "The miles are few,
The way is pleasant; will you come? – Adieu!" '[1]

The way is, in fact, as it happens, pleasant on this additional, or
much extended, journey – or would be but for the changed mood
of the disappointed, vexed Orlando. He now rides through lovely
meadows by a majestic inland river, rich farm-land, smiling
scenes of rural plenty.

' I hate these scenes,' Orlando angry cried,
'And these proud farmers! yes, I hate their pride:
See! that sleek fellow, how he strides along,
Strong as an ox, and ignorant as strong;
Can yon close crops a single eye detain
But his who counts the profits of the grain?
And these vile beans with deleterious smell,
Where is their beauty – can a mortal tell?
These deep fat meadows I detest; it shocks
One's feelings there to see the grazing ox . . .
I hate these long green lanes; there's nothing seen
In this vile country but eternal green;
Woods! waters! meadows! Will they never end?
'Tis a vile prospect: – "Gone to see a friend?" '[2]

He rides past one of the great houses, with its landscape garden,
the noble flower of English Augustan civilization.

Spread o'er the park he saw the grazing steer,
The full-fed steed, and herds of bounding deer.[3]

The elevated diction is here in order, as it is in the poetry of
the conclusion of Pope's Fourth Epistle of the *Moral Essays*. The
children of the great house play in the chequered shade under the
noble elms. Here, if anywhere, the traveller might find enchant-
ment in the prospect. Not so the now disenchanted Orlando. The
poetry here echoes the disenchanted note of some of the poetry
of the 18th century.

'Man is a cheat . . .'

[1] 210–13.   [2] 244–63.   [3] 266–7.

A wedding in a pleasant town, looked down upon from a hill, is contemplated with 'spleen'. But as Orlando again draws nearer his Laura, another change comes over his mood, resentment melts away and, finally, in her actual presence joy is restored. As he accompanies his Laura on the return journey to her house, his attention is now so absorbed that the pleasant landscape passes unseen. And again, on his own journey home alone, by the same fen and moor, absorbed by his inward vision the external scene is now to him a blank.

Edward Shore is a tale of a moral lapse followed by the total break-up of a young man of 'genius', who had conceived himself to be superior to moral lapses, because guided solely by the light of Reason.

> 'Art thou not tempted?' – 'Do I fall?' said Shore.
> 'The pure have fallen.' – 'Then are pure no more.
> While reason guides me, I shall walk aright,
> Nor need a steadier hand, or stronger light.'[1]

The tale opens with Johnsonian lines on the dangers that assail 'genius' (though, by comparison, Crabbe's lines have not the massive force, the solidity of concrete definition, the weight and authority of Johnson's great lines in *The Vanity* about the scholar's lot). The first signs of an inner instability are that he can settle to no employment because unconvinced of the *raison d'être* of each and every profession, not so much from scepticism as from a kind of over-confident idealism. Thus he rejects Law, not only as a profession he himself might usefully follow, but as a necessity for human nature. He thinks Reason a sufficient guide, Reason without Religion. Consequently he lacks what Jane Austen calls 'principle' – to 'firmly fix the vacillating mind'. In this state of mind, his courtship of his Anna remains indecisive, and he forms, instead, a friendship with a middle-aged rationalist and sceptic.

His doubts do not, however, prevent this comfortable middle-aged philosopher from marrying a young beauty.

> Yet, lo! this cautious man, so coolly wise,
> On a young beauty fix'd unguarded eyes.[2]

---

[1] 75–8.   [2] 192–3.

Young Shore continues to spend his evenings in the company of his philosophic friend, though these evenings are complicated now by a third presence, his friend's unphilosophic young wife.

> And when she saw the friends, by reasoning long,
> Confused if right, and positive if wrong,
> With playful speech, and smile that spoke delight,
> She made them careless both of wrong and right . . .
> Their manner this – the friends together read,
> Till books a cause for disputation bred;
> Debate then follow'd, and the vapour'd child
> Declared they argued till her head was wild.[1]

The middle-aged philosopher has middle-aged habits and is not averse to being by himself while his young friend 'improves' his ignorant young wife. The inevitability of the natural consequences is traced with dry irony by a poet who knows human nature, as the middle-aged philosopher unhappily does not. In the evening walk, for example, there is the influence of nature on youthful susceptibilities.

> But oft the husband, to indulgence prone,
> Resumed his book, and bade them walk alone.
> 'Do, my kind Edward – I must take mine ease –
> Name the dear girl the planets and the trees:
> Tell her what warblers pour their evening song,
> What insects flutter, as you walk along;
> Teach her to fix the roving thoughts, to bind
> The wandering sense, and methodise the mind.'
> This was obey'd; and oft when this was done,
> They calmly gazed on the declining sun;
> In silence saw the glowing landscape fade,
> Or, sitting, sang beneath the arbour's shade:
> Till rose the moon, and on each youthful face
> Shed a soft beauty and a dangerous grace.[2]

After his lapse 'the fallen hero' plunges into a reckless course of self-destruction, possessed by remorse and shame, unable to turn as the young wife does to Religion. He descends into those two dreaded conditions, the debtor's prison and, finally, madness.

---

[1] 198–201, 210–13.   [2] 222–35.

From the former he is rescued by 'an anonymous friend', the middle-aged philosopher himself, who in spite of his irreligion behaves decently – one of Crabbe's just touches. But he sinks finally into the latter state, loss of that reason in which in his pride he had placed his sole trust.

Jesse and Colin is not, as the title might suggest, simply a cottage idyll, though that is the frame. Within that frame the central study in the Tale is of the sinister household of an insanely suspicious rich aunt and her three rather terrible dependants (though they have their explanations), a dark prison or labyrinth of suspicion, distrust and deception, from which the innocent vulnerable girl escapes back to her Colin in the village of her childhood. Innocence does triumph in the end. But the rich aunt's mansion and its inmates are as terrible as anything in Hogarthian art or Juvenal's, or as Johnson's lines about rich old age surrounded by greedy heirs.

Jesse, a vicar's daughter, is received into the 'vast mansion' of the rich aunt as an orphan on the death of her father. It proves anything but a haven of refuge. The innocent girl is subjected to her first severe shock, a violence done to her nature, when her aunt, taking her, as it were, into her closest confidence, explains the use she is to be put to in return for her keep, that she should spy on the three other dependants. The aunt reiterates her terrible promise or threat –

> And recollect I have a will to make.[1]

A succession of further shocks are sustained by Jesse when she is approached in turn by each of the three dependants with intimate confidences which reveal the nature of each. Each is, of course, different from the other. Their exposures of one another are at the same time self-exposures.

> It is a labyrinth in which you stray.
> Come, hold my clue, and I will lead the way . . .
> Come, I have drawn the curtain, and you see
> Your fellow-actors . . .[2]

In horror the girl flees from her experience of grandeur and evil to a life of simple goodness in her Colin's cottage. But this tale

[1] 348.   [2] 209–10, 259–60.

is not simple 18th-century Horatianism. It is too penetrating a study of the darker side of human nature to be simply that.

The Struggles of Conscience, as the title and the accompanying quotations from *Macbeth* and *Richard III* indicate, is a study of the fate of a man with a conscience who perversely goes against it more and more, till finally it destroys him. This is, of course, one of the great tragic subjects explored by Shakespeare and explored again in Shakespearian depth, after Crabbe's time, by George Eliot. Pope's Sir Balaam and Dryden's Shimei may have been among Crabbe's literary models for Fulham; but the modern reader might well be reminded also of Bulstrode. The type was evidently common enough in English life. It must often strike the reader of this and other of Crabbe's tales how close his England was to the provincial England of George Eliot's youth as recollected and evoked in her novels.

Fulham has acquired a Puritan conscience through an early conversion. But desire of gain – first lawful, then by degrees more and more unlawful – drives Fulham against his conscience and finally into crime and a nightmarish sense of guilt that is his nemesis.

As is often Crabbe's way, the tale begins with a sketch of the family and social background, the early life and upbringing of his character as these have shaped him and, later, continue to influence his whole life. Fulham is brought up in a particular sect, attends its meetings in an upper room, till at a certain age 'a warm Preacher' breaks through his indifference and awakens his conscience. From that moment he finds he has acquired an uneasy and troublesome conscience with which he has to live. When he has succeeded to his uncle's business (that of a 'serious Toyman') he finds he is troubled also with something else, desire of gain. This necessitates his seeking to make continual adjustments and arrangements with his difficult conscience. The dialogues between Fulham and his Conscience (recalling also similar dialogues in Bunyan) are Crabbe's art of dialogue in verse at its best, and are neat, pointed, ironic exposures of the refuges, subterfuges and evasions of the truth to which human nature is prone.

Never will I to evil deed consent;
Or, if surprised, oh! how will I repent!

Should gain be doubtful, soon would I restore
The dangerous good, or give it to the poor;
Repose for them my growing wealth shall buy,
Or build – who knows? – an hospital like Guy.[1]

Fulham enters on dubious money-making ventures, takes risks.

'Still it may happen.' – 'I the sum must pay.'
'You know you cannot.' – 'I can run away.'
'That is dishonest.' – 'Nay, but you must wink
At a chance hit: it cannot be, I think.
Upon my conduct as a whole decide,
Such trifling errors let my virtues hide.
Fail I at meeting? am I sleepy there?
My purse refuse I with the priest to share?
Do I deny the poor a helping hand?
Or stop the wicked women in the Strand?
Or drink at club beyond a certain pitch?
Which are your charges? Conscience, tell me which?'[2]

The risks come off; he is now a successful man. But each further
deviation from rectitude causes him further acute trouble with his
Conscience.

'Why he was troubled when he kept the laws?'
'My laws?' said Conscience. – 'What,' said he, 'are thine?'[3]

He complains that his worthy neighbours have easier Consciences
than the one he is afflicted with.

'Nay, but,' at length the thoughtful man replied,
'I say not that; I wish you for my guide;
Wish for your checks and your reproofs – but then
Be like a Conscience of my fellow-men:
Worthy I mean, and men of good report,
And not the wretches who with Conscience sport:
There's Bice, my friend, who passes off his grease
Of pigs for bears', in pots a crown apiece;
His conscience never checks him when he swears
The fat he sells is honest fat of bears;
And so it is, for he contrives to give

[1] 84–9.   [2] 120–31.   [3] 170–1.

> A drachm to each – 'tis thus that tradesmen live;
> Now why should you and I be over nice?
> What man is held in more repute than Bice?"[1]

Fulham's plunge into crime, sordid crime, whereby he accumu-
lates wealth, is traced in the latter part of the tale.

> Upon his board, once frugal, press'd a load
> Of viands rich, the appetite to goad;
> The long-protracted meal, the sparkling cup,
> Fought with his gloom, and kept his courage up.[2]

As a consequence his Conscience has become finally his implacable
enemy and 'murders sleep'.

> In every thoughtful moment on she press'd,
> And gave at once her dagger to his breast ...
> The night of horror – when he starting cried,
> To the poor startled sinner at his side,
> 'Is it in law? am I condemn'd to die? ...
> Wilt thou, dread being, thus thy promise keep?
> Day is thy time – and wilt thou murder sleep?"[3]

The conclusion of the tale is frankly reminiscent of Shakespeare.
Yet the language is by comparison basically prosaic, according
to the 18th-century usage, within the formal verse, though
effectively direct. Thus the line

> And gave at once her dagger to his breast

more specifically recalls, not Shakespeare, but Johnson's

> And leaves unseen a dagger in your breast.

Advice; or The Squire and the Priest is one of Crabbe's master-
pieces and also one of the most Chaucerian of his tales. The wit,
the humour, the good sense and balanced judgement, the human-
ity, and also a degree of geniality unusual in the more dry,
astringent Crabbe, are qualities which in this beautifully poised
comedy Crabbe shares with Chaucer.

The portrait of the Squire – a thoroughly English 18th-century
type – with which the tale opens, is not less original, not less

[1] 185–98.   [2] 456–9.   [3] 466–7, 482–9.

characteristic of Crabbe, for reminding the reader of, for example, Chaucer's portrait of the Franklin, not only in the subject of the portrait himself, a self-indulgent country gentleman, but in the gently ironic art in which he is portrayed. The Squire's joys, too, are of 'the grosser kind'.

> A wealthy Lord, of far-extended land,
> Had all that pleased him placed at his command;
> Widow'd of late, but finding much relief
> In the world's comforts, he dismiss'd his grief;
> He was by marriage of his daughters eased,
> And knew his sons could marry if they pleased;
> Meantime in travel he indulged the boys,
> And kept no spy nor partner of his joys.
> These joys, indeed, were of the grosser kind,
> That fed the cravings of an earthly mind;
> A mind that, conscious of its own excess,
> Felt the reproach his neighbours would express.
> Long at th'indulgent board he loved to sit,
> Where joy was laughter, and profaneness wit;
> And such the guest and manners at the Hall,
> No wedded lady on the Squire would call.
> Here reign'd a favourite, and her triumph gain'd
> O'er other favourites who before had reign'd;
> Reserved and modest seem'd the nymph to be,
> Knowing her lord was charm'd with modesty . . .
> Our Squire declared, that from a wife released,
> He would no more give trouble to a priest;
> Seem'd it not, then, ungrateful and unkind
> That he should trouble from the priesthood find?[1]

The cause of his unease is 'the stern old Rector of the place'. What the Squire thinks he needs for the comfort of his mind is 'a gentle pastor, civil and discreet'. He has in fact already selected, as successor to the old Rector, one whom he supposes will be exactly such, his nephew, at present at College. The youth is prepared by his uncle and mother for his part as the right kind of worldly priest and sees no objection to being provided with a comfortable future. But, on leaving College, James comes under

[1] 1–26.

the influence of a 'Preacher' and the whole plan is unexpectedly imperilled.

> His zeal grew active – honest, earnest zeal.[1]

The Squire, unaware of the change in his nephew – the irony depends on this – entertains him the night before he himself is to be present at church for the first time to hear his young nephew preach as the new Rector. James's diffidence, reticence and even abstinence are easily accounted for as the effect of natural nervousness about the morrow.

> 'Cast, my dear lad, that cursed gloom aside:
> There are for all things time and place; appear
> Grave in your pulpit, and be merry here:
> Now take your wine – for woes a sure resource,
> And the best prelude to a long discourse' . . .
> He took his glass, and then address'd the Squire:
> 'I feel not well, permit me to retire.'[2]

The Squire's Advice to his nephew (which gives the Tale the first of its alternative titles) forms the centre-piece of the comedy. The irony again recalls both Chaucer and Pope –

> To sleep the cushion and soft Dean invite
> Who never mentions Hell to ears polite –

but is none the less Crabbe's individual art at its best. The complacent Squire cautions him against unorthodox enthusiasm – 'that gloomy faith' –

> That starving faith, that would our tables clear,
> And make one dreadful Lent of all the year.[3]

The ironic comedy grows richer.

> 'For, James, consider – what your neighbours do
> Is their own business, and concerns not you:
> Shun all resemblance to that forward race
> Who preach of sins before a sinner's face . . .
> Yet of our duties you must something tell,
> And must at times on sin and frailty dwell;

[1] 110.　　　　[2] 149–63.　　　　[3] 198–9.

Here you may preach in easy, flowing style,
How errors cloud us, and how sins defile:
Here bring persuasive tropes and figures forth,
To show the poor that wealth is nothing worth;
That they, in fact, possess an ample share
Of the world's good, and feel not half its care:
Give them this comfort, and, indeed, my gout
In its full vigour causes me some doubt;
And let it always for your zeal suffice
That vice you combat, in the abstract – vice . . .
In general satire, every man perceives
A slight attack, yet neither fears nor grieves;
But name th'offence, and you absolve the rest,
And point the dagger at a single breast.

'Yet are there sinners of a class so low,
That you with safety may the lash bestow:
Poachers, and drunkards, idle rogues, who feed
At others' cost, a mark'd correction need . . .

'Remember well what love and age advise:
A quiet rector is a parish prize;
Who in his learning has a decent pride;
Who to his people is a gentle guide;
Who only hints at failings that he sees;
Who loves his glebe, his patron, and his ease,
And finds the way to fame and profit is to please.'[1]

Next morning, in church, as James's sermon and demeanour
turn out to be shockingly not at all what his uncle had intended,
advised, and expected they should and would be, the Squire's
surprise, alarm, amazement and consternation mount in a comic
crescendo.

But when the text announced the power of grace,
Amazement scowl'd upon his clouded face
At this degenerate son of his illustrious race . . .
For now no crazed fanatic's frantic dreams
Seem'd vile as James's conduct, or as James:
All he had long derided, hated, fear'd,

[1] 216–62.

This, from the chosen youth, the uncle heard; –
The needless pause, the fierce disorder'd air,
The groan for sin, the vehemence of prayer.[1]

The effect of the new unpredicted James on the village and even on the Squire's own cronies develops and accumulates in ways that dismay and painfully unsettle the old Squire.

Matrons of old, with whom he used to joke,
Now pass his honour with a pious look;
Lasses, who met him once with lively airs,
Now cross his way, and gravely walk to prayers.[2]

An old drinking companion now has his confused misgivings and reservations – 'truth is truth' and 'right is right' – and departs after only the third bottle.

The Squire's habitual world begins to break up. His 'lass' herself, for her own ends, hints that the forms of marriage ought to be gone through.

'It was the wretched life his honour led,
And would draw vengeance on his guilty head;
Their loves (Heav'n knew how dreadfully distress'd
The thought had made her!) were as yet unbless'd:
And till the Church had sanction'd –' Here she saw
The wrath that forced her trembling to withdraw.[3]

But though she has enraged the Squire, he himself begins to be deeply shaken.

But must himself the darling sin deny,
Change the whole heart, – but here a heavy sigh
Proclaim'd, 'How vast the toil! and, ah, how weak am I!'[4]

One of Crabbe's finest strokes concludes the tale. James himself has become troubled at some of the effects of his zeal – the parish divided, discord where there had been harmony.

James too has trouble – he divided sees
A parish, once harmonious and at ease . . .
Though zealous still, yet he begins to feel
The heat too fierce that glows in vulgar zeal.[5]

[1] 295–310.   [2] 341–4.   [3] 379–84.   [4] 391–3.   [5] 394–403.

He recognizes the fault is partly his own. His native good sense and, indeed, his sense of humour are engaged by his observations of people and the ways they have been affected, and qualify and correct his moralistic zeal.

> His native sense is hurt by strange complaints
> Of inward motions in these warring saints;
> Who never cast on sinful bait a look,
> But they perceive the devil at the hook:
> Grieved, yet compell'd to smile, he finds it hard
> Against the blunders of conceit to guard.[1]

The Squire and the Priest have both modified and moderated their attitudes. The comedy comes to rest at a balance. Good sense and virtue are reconciled. The Anglican and Augustan poet takes in this tale the larger view.

Resentment is another study of the hardening of the heart and consequent uncharitableness and inhumanity to a fellow-creature, in this case as an effect of resentment at a wrong suffered. Strict insistence on just retribution becomes indistinguishable from personal vindictiveness and revenge (cf. James's Madame de Mauves).

The lady's resentment, which strikes such deep roots and makes her so rigid and obdurate, is not without just cause. She has been grossly deceived and injured by the husband in whom she had placed an absolute trust.

The tale opens with portraits of a sober merchant and a discreet, well-to-do lady whom he persuades to become his second wife with what appear to her sensible and virtuous reasons. Crabbe's grave merchant has some resemblances to Chaucer's ('Ther wiste no wight that he was in dette'). He, too, is keeping up appearances.

> Grave was the man, as we have told before;
> His years were forty – he might pass for more . . .
> Though frugal he, yet sumptuous was his board,
> As if to prove how much he could afford . . .
> Among these friends he sat in solemn style,
> And rarely soften'd to a sober smile:

[1] 408–13.

For this, observant friends their reasons gave –
'Concerns so vast would make the idlest grave.'[1]

The lady, who is to prove capable in the given circumstances of
'making a stone of her heart', is introduced as a gentle lady and
discreet. The grave merchant knows exactly how she must be
wooed, in an appropriately unromantic manner. On her side, she
unromantically assures herself that he is a man of solid means as
well as solid virtues. The note of irony is dramatically borne out
by the sudden event. As the wife now of a great merchant on a
ceremonial public occasion – a banquet for the launching of a
ship – she is led by her husband apart into the privacy of his study
where sits a lawyer.

> Forth from her room, with measured step she came,
> Proud of th'event, and stately look'd the dame;
> The husband met her at his study door –
> 'This way, my love – one moment, and no more:
> A trifling business – you will understand –
> The law requires that you affix your hand;
> But first attend, and you shall learn the cause
> Why forms like these have been prescribed by laws.'
> Then from his chair a man in black arose,
> And with much quickness hurried off his prose –
> That 'Ellen Paul, the wife, and so forth, freed
> From all control, her own the act and deed,
> And Forasmuch ——' said she, 'I've no distrust,
> For he that asks it is discreet and just;
> Our friends are waiting – where am I to sign? –
> There? – Now be ready when we meet to dine.'[2]

The so discreet, now so trustful lady has signed away her fortune.
This act of deception takes the reader himself off his guard, as it
is intended to do, and in a Chaucerian aside Crabbe agrees with
what he imagines would be the shocked reader's comments.

> Now, says the reader, and with much disdain,
> This serious merchant was a rogue in grain;
> A treacherous wretch, an artful, sober knave,
> And ten times worse for manners cool and grave;

[1] 33–50.   [2] 128–43.

And she devoid of sense, to set her hand
To scoundrel deeds she could not understand.
Alas! 'tis true; and I in vain had tried
To soften crime that cannot be denied.[1]

The merchant staves off his impending ruin with his wife's
fortune. But ruin inexorably descends and exposes him. The
deceived and impoverished wife flees from him to a cottage till,
later in life, having inherited another fortune, she is comfortable
again, dispensing charity to the poor. The only exception she
makes, the one sufferer from whom she withholds her charity, is
her husband, now a beggar excluded from her house.

The climax comes during an exceptionally severe winter. It
is her maidservant Susan, and not the gentle Lady, who spontane-
ously feels and expresses natural human kindness and pity ever
more urgently as the old beggar's need for succour grows ever
more urgent. In the dialogues between Susan and the Lady, by
means of a few sharp and distinct contrasts, the old beggar's
suffering condition and hence the extremity of the Lady's in-
humanity are made immediate, the actuality of his distress as an
old man exposed to cold and hunger in the snow outside in the
street as viewed from the windows of the warm and well-pro-
visioned house. But the now ungentle Lady is obdurate.

'He that doth evil, evil shall he dread.'
'The snow,' quoth Susan, 'falls upon his bed –
It blows beside the thatch, it melts upon his head' . . .
'Think on his crime.' – 'Yes sure 'twas very wrong;
But look (God bless him!) how he gropes along.'
'Brought me to shame.' – 'Oh! yes, I know it all –
What cutting blast! and he can scarcely crawl;
He freezes as he moves – he dies if he should fall:
With cruel fierceness drives this icy sleet –
And must a Christian perish in the street,
In sight of Christians? – There! at last, he lies . . .'
'Peace! Susan, peace! pain ever follows sin.'
'Ah! then,' thought Susan, 'when will ours begin?' . . .
'Wilful was rich, and he the storm defied;
Wilful is poor, and must the storm abide,'

[1] 146–53.

Said the stern lady; "tis in vain to feel;
Go and prepare the chicken for our meal.'[1]

She does not relent, that is, until too late, when she yields at last
to Susan's pleading – partly 'seduced', as she says, 'by her maid'
– and sends help to the old man. Susan comes back with the news
that the help has been sent too late.

'Dead!' said the startled lady. – 'Yes, he fell
Close at the door where he was wont to dwell . . .'[2]
'And every day in ease and peace to dine,
And rest in comfort – What a heart is mine!'[3]

The Convert is the moral biography of one John Dighton and,
though in the idiom of wit, comes in its conclusion nearer tragedy
than comedy.

John's origins are obscure. From an early age, penniless and
friendless, he has to fend for himself. He brings himself up, a Jack
of all trades and tricks, a precocious youngster with plenty of
pluck, like certain of Dickens's youngsters of the streets, learns
how to make his own way in the world, against all the odds, by a
diversity of means, honest and dishonest.

With spirit high John learn'd the world to brave,
And in both senses was a ready knave;
Knave as of old, obedient, keen, and quick,
Knave as at present, skill'd to shift and trick;
Some humble part of many trades he caught,
He for the builder and the painter wrought;
For serving-maids on secret errands ran,
The waiter's helper, and the ostler's man;
And when he chanced (oft chanced he) place to lose,
His varying genius shone in blacking shoes . . .[4]

His course is abruptly changed when he falls ill with a fever, is
afraid to die, confesses his sins and is converted by a Teacher.

. . . resolved, should he from sickness rise,
To quit cards, liquors, poaching, oaths, and lies:
His health restored, he yet resolved and grew
True to his masters, to their meeting true . . .

[1] 365–420.   [2] 473–4.   [3] 489–90.   [4] 29–38.

Though terror wrought the mighty change, yet strong
Was the impression, and it lasted long . . .
His manners strict, though form'd on fear alone,
Pleased the grave friends, nor less his solemn tone,
The lengthen'd face of care, the low and inward groan.[1]

Fear, not Reason, is the basis of his Faith, and, indeed, John's trouble throughout his life is that he is ruled by extremes of feeling instead of moderating reason.

John now becomes a thriving stationer and married man, and, by degrees, this brings about a modification in his attitude.

His fear abated – 'What had he to fear –
His profits certain and his conscience clear?'
Above his door a board was placed by John,
And 'Dighton, Stationer', was gilt thereon;
His window next, enlarged to twice the size,
Shone with such trinkets as the simple prize;
While in the shop, with pious works, were seen
The last new play, review, or magazine:
In orders, punctual, he observed – 'The books
He never read, and could he judge their looks?
Readers and critics should their merits try,
He had no office but to sell and buy;
Like other traders, profit was his care;
Of what they print, the authors must beware.'[2]

John not only begins to find it profitable to sell other books than pious ones, he begins himself to look into some of the books he sells – 'liberal' books. The zealots are troubled in mind about what they fear to be a brother's fall, and a deputation of the brethren, headed by the Teacher, waits on John. Something similar to the tone and accent and absurd rhetorical exaggerations of the Friar's discourse to another John in *The Summoner's Tale* reappears in the Teacher's address to John in Crabbe's tale.

'John,' said the teacher, 'John, with great concern
We see thy frailty, and thy fate discern –
Satan with toils thy simple soul beset,
And thou art careless slumbering in the net:

[1] 65–80.   [2] 131–44.

Unmindful art thou of thy early vow;
Who at the morning meeting sees thee now?
Who at the evening? "Where is brother John?"
We ask; – are answer'd, "To the tavern gone."
Thee on the Sabbath seldom we behold;
Thou canst not sing – thou'rt nursing for a cold:
This from the churchmen thou hast learn'd, for they
Have colds and fevers on the Sabbath-day;
When in some snug warm room they sit, and pen
Bills from their ledgers – world-entangled men.
   'See with what pride thou hast enlarged thy shop;
To view thy tempting stores the heedless stop.
By what strange names dost thou these baubles know,
Which wantons wear, to make a sinful show?
Hast thou in view these idle volumes placed
To be the pander of a vicious taste?
What's here! a book of dances! you advance
In goodly knowledge – John, wilt learn to dance?
How! "*Go*," it says, and "*to the Devil go!*
And shake thyself!" I tremble – but 'tis so . . .
Do print the Koran and become a Turk.
   'John, thou art lost; success and worldly pride
O'er all thy thoughts and purposes preside . . .
   'And here thy wife, thy Dorothy behold,
How fashion's wanton robes her form enfold!
Can grace, can goodness with such trappings dwell?
John, thou hast made thy wife a Jezebel.'[1]

So to the climax:

   'Wretch that thou art!' an elder cried, 'and gone
For everlasting!' – 'Go thyself,' said John;
'Depart this instant, let me hear no more;
My house my castle is, and that my door.'[2]

But John is still governed, as in his youth, by his feelings and
reacts (like Silas Marner) from one extreme to another, never
attaining a balance, never coming to rest in the mean of reason-
ableness. John becomes a man of liberal reading and emancipated

<hr />

[1] 189–237.   [2] 304–7.

views but without a centre of stability, without a faith. The brethren pass by the shop. They comment

'The world has won him with its tempting store
Of needless wealth, and that has made him poor.'[1]

John's trouble is that this is much what he himself, the former convert, feels. His wordly prosperity has steadily increased, but he has lost his faith and failed to find happiness.

'But what are all my profits, credit, trade,
And parish honours? – folly and parade.'[2]

Though he has remarried, he has no surviving son, no heir. His last days are cheerless in the extreme, without a faith, with no longer anything to live for. He sums up his barren life in phrases that echo (faintly) those of Macbeth (quoted by Crabbe with the title of the Tale) and dies a disappointed old man.

'And as I more possess'd, and reason'd more,
I lost those comforts, I enjoy'd before . . .
Now sick and sad, no appetite, no ease,
Nor pleasure have I, nor a wish to please;
Nor views, nor hopes, nor plans, nor taste have I;
Yet, sick of life, have no desire to die.'
He said, and died; his trade, his name is gone,
And all that once gave consequence to John.[3]

This is one of the more tragic of the Tales. On the other hand, three of the best of the Tales which I have *not* touched on are the comedies of Justice Bolt (*The Dumb Orators*) and of Counter and Clubb and their wives (*The Wager*) and, more astringent, *The Learned Boy*.

Tales (1812) is the climax of Crabbe's achievement. *Tales of the Hall* and the other later tales contain many fine things. But on the whole they are relaxed and diffuse by comparison, a gentle decline. I am inclined to see Crabbe's *Tales*, Wordsworth's *Prelude* and Byron's *Don Juan* as the most solid of the larger-scale achievements of the English poetry of the 19th century. They are also the poems that come nearest, in their subject-matter and in their art, to the novels.

---

[1] 408–9.   [2] 374–5.   [3] 438–47.

CHAPTER SIX

BYRON: *BEPPO, THE VISION OF JUDGMENT* AND *DON JUAN*

I

Where are we to place Byron's *Don Juan* in relation to the poetry and to the novel of the 19th century? John Galt[1] wrote of *Don Juan* at the time of its appearance, 'It is professedly an epic poem, but it may more properly be described as a poetical novel.' He goes on to describe it further, 'Bold and buoyant throughout, it exhibits a free irreverent knowledge of the world, laughing or mocking as the thought serves, in the most unexpected antithesis to the proprieties.' Certainly, if it were to be called an epic, it would have to be qualified as a comic or satiric epic. But if we then attempt to see it in relation to the burlesque or mock epics among the comic or satiric poems of the 18th century, Pope's *Rape of the Lock* or *The Dunciad*, we see at once that *Don Juan* does not at all conform with these. On the contrary, great as was Byron's admiration for Pope, *Don Juan* (or *Beppo* or *The Vision of Judgment*) could not be more different from Pope or from any poem in the English Augustan line. It is in many ways more different from Pope than from the pre-Popeian *Hudibras*. There are some resemblances with *Tom Jones*, which Byron also admired and which Fielding himself thought of as a comic prose epic of contemporary ordinary life. But when we have noted these resemblances – the character and adventures (or misadventures) of the hero (or anti-hero), the humorous, sceptical but genial presence of the author himself as observer and commentator, the exposures of cant and hypocrisy – we are left with the ways in which *Don Juan* is different, a new invention in a new style, unlike anything else before or since. There are resemblances with some of the light verse of Byron's own time (e.g.

---

[1] John Galt was himself one of the most truly distinguished and original novelists of his period. *The Entail* takes its place with *Heart of Midlothian* as a Scottish novel of the period with qualities of greatness.

Hookham Frere), but these resemblances are superficial, as that light verse itself is. *Don Juan* is a great and original achievement, much greater than anything that could be described as light verse. Byron (now enjoying Italian scenes and poetry) certainly learned from Pulci, conceived himself as adapting the Pulcian mode, and (perhaps not so generally recognized) caught into his English poem something of the spirit of Mozartian and of Italian comic opera. There are resemblances also with Voltaire's *Candide* and more fundamentally with Goethe's *Faust*.[1] But in the end we have to recognize that *Beppo* (1818), *The Vision of Judgment* (1822) and *Don Juan* (1818–23) are a new thing in literature, unique as an expression of Byron's maturer personality. There are essential differences between *Don Juan* and either an 18th-century novel or an 18th-century poem. *Don Juan* is a highly personal and original production. It is different from anything by Byron's contemporaries and different from his own early work (not only from his early Romantic poetry but also from his juvenile Popeian imitation, *English Bards and Scotch Reviewers*). Among the verse of Byron's English contemporaries the nearest thing I can think of to *Don Juan* and *The Vision of Judgment* in some of their more essential qualities, is Shelley's *Peter Bell the Third* (Florence 1819), particularly the section on London life and the final section. It is worth noting the proximity of the dates of these poems of Shelley and Byron. Among the prose authors Peacock comes to mind (*Headlong Hall* 1816, *Nightmare Abbey* 1818) as offering some points of comparison, because of his lightness of touch, his sparkle and vivacity, as a humorous entertaining critic of the ideas and opinions, the intellectual fashions and interests of his time. But, above all, both as an expression of the developing individualism of the early 19th century and as something like a novel in verse, there is clearly a relation between the new thing that *Don Juan* is and the whole 19th-century development from poetry into the novel. Among the later 19th-century approximations to a novel in verse the most distinguished is Clough's *Amours de Voyage* (1849),[2] which has some qualities anticipatory

---

[1] Santayana's account of *Faust* in *Three Philosophical Poets* has some relevance to Byron's *Don Juan*.

[2] The relation between Browning's *The Ring and the Book* and Jacobean dramatic poetry seems to me too much that of Bowningesque mimicry, almost

of James (distorted by the mechanical effect of the unfortunately chosen metre). But by then, as the great novelists occupied the field, poetry as a whole had taken a turn away from the novel.[1]

If Byron is recognized – and justly – as a great poet, it is not because of the same poems which first made him famous in his own day throughout Europe, but because of the very different (and at the time unfashionable) poems of his final phase, *Beppo*, *The Vision of Judgment* and *Don Juan*. It is this (by contrast) 'anti-Romantic' poetry of Byron's conscious passage into middle age, not the Romantic poetry of his youth (culminating in the last two Cantos of *Childe Harold*), that has stood the test of time. In these final comic or satiric poems Byron is no longer the melancholy exile or histrionic Satanic rebel. Their spirit is more in accord with Goethe's dialogues between Mephisto and Faust than with Milton's Satan. He appears now rather to be enjoying his 'exile' in Italy, which has been discovered by him to be a new-found freedom rather than exile, freedom not only from English society but from his own earlier Romantic attitudes and rhetoric. Though his poetry is still largely an expression of himself, more sides of his complex personality are expressed and he can now regard not only the world but himself humorously ('a broken Dandy lately on my travels'), indeed look back on his Regency London days, the vanished social world of his Romantic youth, with more humour than regret. He has become able, in these final poems, to view and to present the world he has known as a comedy. It might be supposed, therefore, that these final poems of Byron would take their place with the two great anti-Romantics or (as they should more properly be called) non-Romantics of the early 19th century, Crabbe and Jane Austen (as well as with the lesser Peacock). The Romantic Byron appears suddenly to have changed into the anti-Romantic Byron.[2] But the differences

parody. Nevertheless Browning's shorter dramatic monologues are remarkable in the age of Tennyson.

[1] A poem – Pushkin's *Eugene Onegin* – might be said to have inaugurated the great Russian novel, and Pushkin's poem was partly inspired by Byron's *Don Juan*.

[2] If we say that Byron's *Don Juan* is an 'anti-Romantic' poem we imply the presence in it still of Romantic attitudes together with their opposites, whereas if we say of Crabbe's poetry that it is 'unromantic' we imply the absence from it of the qualities we are accustomed to associate with Romantic poetry.

between *Don Juan* and Crabbe's *Tales in Verse* or Jane Austen's novels are as radical as are the differences between *Don Juan* and the poetry of Pope. It is possible to see Crabbe and Jane Austen as still in the line from the Augustans, though developing in their art new psychological insights into the individual in relation to the family and to society. It is not possible to see the Byron of *Don Juan* (any more than it is possible to see the earlier Romantic Byron) in the Augustan line. The fact that *Don Juan* and *The Vision of Judgment* are comic and satiric poetry only emphasizes the completeness of their break with the Popeian. Byron in *Don Juan* continues to be a rebel and, in this and other respects, his attitudes, tone and manner are as foreign to Jane Austen and Crabbe as to Pope or Johnson or, indeed, Fielding. It is true that Byron has developed a sense of humour and a liveliness of wit in his middle age. He is also now, having broken loose, much more easy in tone and carefree in spirit. There are signs (from his letters etc.) that he always could be like this in his conversations with friends and that this side of him has come out at last in his poetry. This has evidently been made possible because he has found a conversational verse mode – a mode of talking easily in verse – in which more of his whole or real complex personality could be expressed.[1] It freed him from the compulsion to be continuously and monotonously solemn, rhetorical and declamatory in verse, stirring as is his recurrent note of lofty indignation at tyranny and oppression. But the defiance of social and moral conventions, cant, humbug and hypocrisy, is at least as vigorous (and far more effective) in the later gay and witty poetry as in the earlier gloomy Romantic poetry. This kind of radical assertion of the freedom of the individual associates Byron with (in their different ways) Dickens and Blake much more than with Crabbe or Jane Austen. The criticisms of their society and the concern for the individual life we meet with in Crabbe and Jane Austen are more equally balanced (and polite). They recognize that the forms and conventions of a society may become too rigid, may be felt to be constricting and cramping for the livelier or more intelligent individuals in it. But they retain a respect for the forms and conventions of civilized society, even while being critical of them.

---

[1] Thus we find in *Don Juan* an interplay between a wide range of sympathetic and antipathetic feelings and attitudes.

They can still see a necessity, an amenity, some value and good for the individual himself in their particular society, its manners, morals and tastes. It would have been difficult for them to conceive of a civilized human being without a society to live in.

Byron's admiration for Pope (sincere as no doubt it was and not simply an expression of his lordly disdain for much of the contemporary verse of his own time) is contradicted in almost every respect by the qualities of his own poetry, the qualities of *Beppo, The Vision of Judgment* and *Don Juan* no less than the qualities of his Romantic earlier poetry. It proves to have been an admiration for a poet in many respects his opposite, even considered as a satiric poet. This incompatibility can be detected already in Byron's juvenile imitation of Pope, his *English Bards and Scotch Reviewers*. But a comparison between Byron's mature comic or satiric poems and Pope turns out to be an almost complete contrast. It is no accident that in these poems Byron has developed a form of verse utterly different from the Popeian couplets. We need only call to mind the qualities of Pope and those of Byron (in his mature last poems) to realize the extent to which the two poets are opposites. There is the extreme formality of Pope, the informality of Byron, the compactness and balanced epigrammatic neatness of Pope, the diffusion, expansiveness and discursiveness of Byron, the strictness, the correctness, the regularity of Pope, the air of impromptu and casual improvisation of Byron, the concern for propriety, politeness and decorum of Pope, the improprieties, the irreverence, the indecorousness of Byron. The art of *Don Juan* or *The Vision of Judgment* is, of course, art, highly skilled art, though as different as could be imagined from the smoothly polished art of Pope. Byron's art is a highly personal expression of Byron's complex individuality, an art which cultivates a tone of careless improvisation and of free-and-easy, relaxed, unconstricted talking among men friends in which the poet can, as it were, say what he likes or whatever comes into his head. He has developed a kind of verse – apparently (though only apparently) slap dash, with its combinations of incongruous, unconventional, eccentric, ingenious rhymes – that makes it possible for him, as it were talking, casually to hit the tone he wants at the moment, to express his changing moods, his opinions and attitudes, to introduce his recollections, to exercise his wit as he looks round or back on the world, now sufficiently detached from it to be humorously or satirically critical of it. This verse mode of *Don Juan* (and the two other poems associated with it) is unmistakably itself an expression of Byron's personality, the individual kicking over the traces, his gay contempt and disdain for forms and conventions, such as would have been abhorrent to Pope and the Augustans. There is at least this element of consistency between the youthful melancholy poetry of Byron and the later humorous poetry of his middle age – the note of recklessness and defiance in both, the disregard of what had been the Augustan values of politeness, decorum and propriety. The Byron of *Don Juan* and *The Vision of Judgment* – as much and more effectively than the Romantic early Byron, with his indignant rhetorical declarations on behalf of freedom and against injustice – shares and carries to a radical extreme the early 19th century revolt of the individual against the conventions, the hypocrisies, the shams, the cant and humbug of society. Byron is the individual liberating himself from the mumbo-jumbo of society, in particular his own English society, its narrow morality, its illiberal politics, its insularity. He is part of the liberal revolt. This is the ultimate basis of the contrast between Byron and Pope. Pope was conscious of the responsibilities of the poet towards society as well as to the individual members of it, conscious that the poet had a place and a function in society, to refine and correct manners, morals and taste, conscious of poetry as a civilizing and humanizing influence. For Byron, on the other hand, poetry was the expression of the individual as such, a means of conscious liberation of the individual. In his own case the individual was in revolt against the constrictions and deadnesses of his own particular society (from which he personally had extricated himself). The disenchanted tone and satirical humour of the later poetry of Byron is tempered with the geniality and generosity of a free spirit, a warm sense of a common human fellowship that associates the aristocratic and cosmopolitan Byron with his Scottish predecessor, Burns, and the new democratic spirit of the age. This is in obvious respects a different bursting of the bonds from Blake's and different again, in obvious respects, from Dickens. But it can equally be regarded as again a bursting of the bonds, another of the versions of the 19th century breaking out, the effort to liberate as well as to understand more deeply the individual life as it develops from the child to the man or woman.

II

Beppo (published 1818) seems to have been the first poem in what was to become the *Don Juan* manner. It is astonishing the ease with which, it appears, Byron has fallen into this manner as if he had found his natural way of expressing himself, a way of talking easily in anything but simple verse. Jeffrey had to concede of *Beppo* 'the matchless facility with which he has cast into regular, and even difficult, versification the unmingled, unconstrained and unselected language of the most light, familiar and ordinary conversation. With great skill and felicity . . . running on in an inexhaustible series of good, easy, colloquial phrases, and finding them fall into verse by some unaccountable and happy fatality.' But *Beppo* is not simply the highly skilled, gay trifle it seemed to Jeffrey ('It is, in itself, absolutely a thing of nothing,' though, he added, 'very engaging' because of its 'gaiety' and 'good humour'). The tale may in itself be slight – an anecdote told, as it were, in the course of talk. But the anecdote is only the centre round which the conversation – on a range of subjects – revolves. The art here contrasts with the art of the short story in verse as practised by Crabbe, an art of compactness. While Byron carries his reader or auditor through a series of digressions ranging easily over a variety of interests and opinions, recollections and descriptions, the anecdote is held suspended until the moment of its surprising climax. This art of the digression – while keeping the reader in suspense as to the outcome of a tale begun – is an art in which Chaucer in several of his tales was a master, though Chaucer was also, in the *Canterbury Tales*, a master of compactness. Byron is freely and easily discursive, as if the tale itself were of secondary importance, maintaining the interest largely by the liveliness, wit and humour of his personal views and comments. *Beppo* carries the reader along by its gaiety, buoyancy of spirit and wit, a miraculous transformation in Byron's poetry after *Childe Harold* and his Romantic earlier poetry. The reader is interested by the companionable poet himself as much as by his anecdote. The light-heartedness is that of a Byron conscious of having burst out of what seems to him the gloom of England and his own Romantic gloom. Italy – the Carnival in Venice – provides not simply the picturesque setting for the anecdote; the contrast of England and Italy in the poem enables Byron to bring out vividly the merits and demerits of life as it is lived in both countries. As in Forster's *Where Angels Fear to Tread*, it makes possibly a critical comparison of two different styles of life, a comedy of contrasts of peoples and places.

The Venetian Carnival scene presented in the opening stanzas of *Beppo* lifts the reader out of England and out of Venice too into a cosmopolitan comedy world, a motley spectacle, a medley of masqueraders, Ancients and Moderns, Europeans and Orientals.

> 'Tis known, at least it should be, that throughout
>   All countries of the Catholic persuasion,
> Some weeks before Shrove Tuesday comes about,
>   The people take their fill of recreation,
> And buy repentance, ere they grow devout,
>   However high their rank, or low their station,
> With fiddling, feasting, dancing, drinking, masquing,
> And other things which may be had for asking.
>
> The moment night with dusky mantle covers
>   The skies (and the more duskily the better),
> The time less liked by husbands than by lovers
>   Begins, and prudery flings aside her fetter;
> And gaiety on restless tiptoe hovers,
>   Giggling with all the gallants who beset her;
> And there are songs and quavers, roaring, humming,
> Guitars, and every other sort of strumming.
>
> And there are dresses splendid, but fantastical,
>   Masks of all times and nations, Turks and Jews,
> And harlequins and clowns, with feats gymnastical,
>   Greeks, Romans, Yankee-doodles, and Hindoos;
> All kinds of dress, except the ecclesiastical.[1]

The contrast with the kind of society Byron has left behind is everywhere implicit where it is not explicit. There is the Italian Count whose accomplishments and tasks are lightly, easily and gaily sketched.

[1] Stanzas I–III.

And then he was a Count, and then he knew
　　Music, and dancing, fiddling, French and Tuscan;
The last not easy, be it known to you,
　　For few Italians speak the right Etruscan.
He was a critic upon operas, too,
　　And knew all niceties of the sock and buskin;
And no Venetian audience could endure a
Song, scene, or air, when he cried 'seccatura!'

His 'bravo' was decisive, for that sound
　　Hush'd 'Academie' sigh'd in silent awe;
The fiddlers trembled as he look'd around,
　　For fear of some false note's detected flaw;
The 'prima donna's' tuneful heart would bound,
　　Dreading the deep damnation of his 'bah!'
Soprano, basso, even the contra-alto,
Wish'd him five fathom under the Rialto.

He patronised the improvisatori,
　　Nay, could himself extemporise some stanzas,
Wrote rhymes, sang songs, could also tell a story,
　　Sold pictures, and was skilful in the dance as
Italians can be, though in this their glory
　　Must surely yield the palm to that which France has;
In short, he was a perfect cavaliero,
And to his very valet seem'd a hero.[1]

Byron's personal sense of enjoyment in finding himself in Italy
comes out.

With all its sinful doings, I must say,
　　That Italy's a pleasant place to me,
Who love to see the sun shine every day,
　　And vines (not nail'd to walls) from tree to tree
Festoon'd, much like the back scene of a play,
　　Or melodrame, which people flock to see,
When the first act is ended by a dance
In vineyards copied from the south of France.

I like on autumn evenings to ride out,
　　Without being forced to bid my groom be sure

[1] Stanzas XXXI–XXXIII.

My cloak is round his middle strapp'd about,
  Because the skies are not the most secure;
I know too that, if stopp'd upon my route,
  Where the green alleys windingly allure,
Reeling with *grapes* red waggons choke the way, –
In England 't would be dung, dust, or a dray.

I also like to dine on becaficas,
  To see the sun set, sure he'll rise to-morrow,
Not through a misty morning twinkling weak as
  A drunken man's eye in maudlin sorrow,
But with all heaven t' himself; that day will break as
  Beauteous as cloudless, nor be forced to borrow
That sort of farthing candlelight which glimmers
Where reeking London's smoky caldron simmers.[1]

The language too – 'I love the language, that soft bastard Latin'.
But though his 'love of England', as he recalls it in Italy, is
qualified, it is qualified humorously. There is no animosity.

'England! with all thy faults I love thee still,'
  I said at Calais, and have not forgot it;
I like to speak and lucubrate my fill;
  I like the government (but that is not it);
I like the freedom of the press and quill;
  I like the Habeas Corpus (when we've got it);
I like a parliamentary debate,
Particularly when 't is not too late;

I like the taxes, when they're not too many;
  I like a seacoal fire, when not too dear;
I like a beef-steak, too, as well as any;
  Have no objection to a pot of beer;
I like the weather, when it is not rainy;
  That is, I like two months of every year.
And so God save the Regent, Church, and King!
Which means that I like all and every thing.[2]

He can now regard himself (and his verse-making) humorously,
as would have seemed impossible for the Byron of *Childe Harold*.

[1] Stanzas XLI–XLIII.   [2] XLVII–XLVIII.

> But I am but a nameless sort of person
>   (A broken Dandy lately on my travels) . . .
> I've half a mind to tumble down to prose,
>   But verse is more in fashion – so here goes.[1]

The personal note, lightly and easily expressing his own opinions
as they occur, is present throughout. There is his personal prefer-
ence (now) for married ladies of all nations for the sake of their
good company and conversation –

> Because they know the world, and are at ease,
>   And, being natural, naturally please,[2]

in contrast to the awkwardness of 'your budding Miss ... So
much alarm'd, that she is quite alarming'.

> And glancing at *mamma*, for fear there's harm in
>   What you, she, it, or they, may be about.[3]

Byron can now (as later in *Don Juan*) play his own light-hearted
variations on the old theme of *contemptus mundi* – the world he
has known.

> The fashionable stare of twenty score
> Of well-bred persons, call'd '*the world*;' but I,
> Although I know them, really don't know why.

> This is the case in England; at least was.[4]

A Turk who stares at Laura (her returned husband in Carnival
disguise) not only gives a new turn to the anecdote but occasions
a digression (yet another) on the imagined advantages of being
a Turkish woman locked up and veiled. The cosmopolitan poet,
having been in Turkey once, can continue to introduce these
contrasts between the customs of nations. Provoked by the earn-
estness of English gentlewomen, Byron here plays the shocking
Philistine and satirizes their intellectual aspirations by comparison
with the total absence of such among the 'poor dear Mussul-
women'.

> No chemistry for them unfolds her gasses,
>   No metaphysics are let loose in lectures,

[1] LII.   [2] XXXVIII.   [3] XXXIX.   [4] LIX–LX.

No circulating library amasses
  Religious novels, moral tales, and strictures
Upon the living manners, as they pass us;
  No exhibition glares with annual pictures;
They stare not on the stars from out their attics,
Nor deal (thank God for that!) in mathematics.[1]

But in the next stanza the satiric mood is, it seems, already dissolving.

I fear I have a little turn for satire,
  And yet methinks the older that one grows
Inclines us more to laugh than scold, though laughter
Leaves us so doubly serious shortly after.[2]

He expresses disdain also for professional authors.

One hates an author that's *all author*, fellows
  In foolscap uniforms turn'd up with ink,
So very anxious, clever, fine, and jealous,
  One don't know what to say to them, or think,
Unless to puff them with a pair of bellows;
  Of coxcombry's worst coxcombs e'en the pink
Are preferable to these shreds of paper,
These unquench'd snuffings of the midnight taper.[3]

That stanza could not better illustrate the rapidity of movement and the flowing, bubbling loquacity of Byron that contrast with the measured dignity of Pope (a professional poet if ever there were one). The anecdote in *Beppo* is terminated with a comic theatrical effect that anticipates the one with which *Don Juan* breaks off (the discovery of 'her frolic grace Fitz-Fulke' in the friar's ghost): the confrontation of the Count and the seeming Turk followed by the latter's unmasking and disconcerting discovery of himself.

The Count and Laura found their boat at last,
  And homeward floated o'er the silent tide,
Discussing all the dances gone and past;
  The dancers and their dresses, too, besides;
Some little scandals eke: but all aghast

---

[1] LXXVIII.   [2] LXXIX.   [3] LXXV.

> (as to their palace stairs the rowers glide)
> Sate Laura by the side of her adorer,
> When lo! the Mussulman was there before her.
>
> 'Sir,' said the Count, with brow exceeding grave,
>   'Your unexpected presence here will make
> It necessary for myself to crave
>   Its import? But perhaps 't is a mistake;
> I hope it is so; and, at once to wave
>   All compliment, I hope so for *your* sake;
> You understand my meaning, or you *shall.*'
> 'Sir,' (quoth the Turk) ''t is no mistake at all:
> 'That lady is *my wife!*'[1]

III

There is little more that need be said about *The Vision of Judgment* after the critical analysis by Mr. Leavis in his note on Byron's satire in *Revaluation*. Clearly the poem was conceived and designed as a satiric poem (a parody of Southey's solemn poem), whereas satire comes into *Beppo* and into *Don Juan* casually at intervals in the flow, as it were, of the conversation.

There is the note of irreverence from the beginning, the sense of the dreariness, the boredom of the celestial establishment, though any attempt to break out from it, any nonconformities, any irregularities, any sportive liveliness on the part of any young rebel have to be checked and curbed.

> The angels all were singing out of tune,
>   And hoarse with having little else to do,
> Excepting to wind up the sun and moon,
>   Or curb a runaway young star or two,
> Or wild colt of a comet, which too soon
>   Broke out of bounds o'er the ethereal blue,
> Splitting some planet with its playful tail,
> As boats are sometimes by a wanton whale.[2]

It would be possible to extract lines or phrases from the poem which by themselves, out of their context, are indistinguishable from Byron's Romantic poetry. In his description of the funeral

---

[1] LXXXVII–LXXXIX.   [2] Stanza II.

of George III the satiric note momentarily almost disappears (certainly the humour does) in the lofty tone of indignant denunciation.

He died! – his death made no great stir on earth;
    His burial made some pomp; there was profusion
Of velvet, gilding, brass, and no great dearth
    Of aught but tears – save those shed by collusion.
For these things may be bought at their true worth;
    Of elegy there was the due infusion –
Bought also; and the torches, cloaks, and banners,
Heralds, and relics of old Gothic manners,

Form'd a sepulchral melo-drame. Of all
    The fools who flock'd to swell or see the show,
Who cared about the corpse? The funeral
    Made the attraction, and the black the woe.
There throbb'd not there a thought which pierced the pall;
    And when the gorgeous coffin was laid low,
It seem'd the mockery of hell to fold
The rottenness of eighty years in gold.[1]

On the other hand, if we singled out and considered by themselves the two lines

Who cared about the corpse? The funeral
    Made the attraction, and the black the woe

we might agree that, though the whole poem is so different, there is a hint here of Pope. The two lines are comparable with, for example, the couplet in Pope's *Elegy on an Unfortunate Lady*.

And bear about the mockery of wo
To midnight dances and the public show.

The different context makes most of the difference in each case. For Pope what matters is that the transient grief, if indeed it ever was real, has ceased to be felt long before the mourning costume is discarded ('Grieve for an hour, perhaps, then mourn a year') and therefore there is something especially indecorous, affronting good feeling and good taste, in continuing to wear the mourning black ('the mockery of wo') at dances and on other public

[1] IX–X.

occasions. For Byron what more simply matters is that there is no natural grief, no real grief at all for George III at his gorgeous funeral. Even if there had been, the funeral pageantry would be merely a Gothic spectacle. The personal Byronic defiance that rings throughout the poem (so utterly unlike Pope) is expressed frankly a stanza or two later.

> I know this is unpopular; I know
>   'Tis blasphemous; I know one may be damn'd
> For hoping no one else may e'er be so;
>   I know my catechism; I know we are cramm'd
> With the best doctrines.[1]

It would seem, indeed, that Byron has not lost anything in his later poetry but has involved his earlier qualities in a more complex poetry, more various as well as more wide-ranging. The combination of fantasy with farcical humour, for example, associates *The Vision of Judgment* not simply with the English caricaturists but with Dickens, as in the episode of the arrival of George III at the gate where St. Peter is the porter (stanzas XVI–XVIII).

> '*What George? what Third?*' 'The king of England,' said
>   The angel. 'Well! he won't find kings to jostle
> Him on his way; but does he wear his head?
>   Because the last we saw here had a tussle,
> And ne'er would have got into heaven's good graces,
> Had he not flung his head in all our faces.'[2]

It need hardly be added that the burlesque or mock heroic aspect of the poem implies more interesting poems than Southey's, in particular, Dante's vision and Milton's epic – as Pope's mock epics imply the Homeric epics. We might guess from Byron's poetry the appeal for him of Milton's Satan, the rebel angel.

Before turning to *Don Juan* we may note again in passing the affinities between this later poetry of Byron (1818–23) and Shelley's *Peter Bell the Third* (1819). Byron and Shelley are here in their satiric poetry (as well as of course in their other poetry) much nearer to one another than either is to Pope and the English Augustans. If there is such a thing as a Romantic satiric

---

[1] XIV.   [2] XVIII.

poetry, even if we call it an anti-Romantic satiric poetry, both descriptions – Romantic or anti-Romantic – would imply the presence in this satiric poetry of Romantic elements with other elements in mutual opposition. It is apparent also from *The Vision of Judgment* and from *Peter Bell the Third* that Byron and Shelley were both acquainted with Goethe's *Faust*, as well as with Dante and Milton. Part III of Shelley's poem:

> Hell is a city much like London –
> A populous and a smoky city,

offers not only a useful comparison with Byron's cantos in *Don Juan* about London life (as well as with Dickens's London) but with *The Vision of Judgment*.

> Lawyers – judges – old hobnobbers
>   Are there – bailiffs – chancellors –
> Bishops – great and little robbers –
>   Rhymesters – pamphleteers – stockjobbers –
>   Men of glory in the wars, –
>
> Things whose trade is, over ladies
>   To lean, and flirt, and stare, and simper,
> Till all that is divine in woman
> Grows cruel, courteous, smooth, inhuman,
>   Crucified 'twixt a smile and whimper.
>
> Thrusting, toiling, wailing, moiling,
>   Frowning, preaching – such a riot!
> Each with never-ceasing labour,
> Whilst he thinks he cheats his neighbour,
>   Cheating his own heart of quiet.
>
> And all these meet at levees; –
>   Dinners convivial and political: –
> Suppers of epic poets; – teas,
> Where small talk dies in agonies; –
>   Breakfasts professional and critical;
>
> Lunches and snacks so aldermanic
>   That one would furnish forth ten dinners,
> Where reigns a Cretan-tonguèd panic,

> Lest news Russ, Dutch, or Alemannic
> Should make some losers, and some winners; –
>
> At conversazioni – balls –
> Conventicles – and drawing-rooms –
> Courts of law – committees – calls
> Of a morning – clubs – book-stalls –
> Churches – masquerades – and tombs.
>
> And this is Hell – and in this smother
> All are damnable and damned;
> Each one damning, damns the other;
> They are damned by one another,
> By none other are they damned.

The Shelleyan note is more high-pitched, sharper, intenser than Byron's. The satire here comes near to merging – as it intensifies – into the kind of near-Blakeian vision that Shelley's *Mask of Anarchy* is. Byron's London life is recalled in *Don Juan* with easy, genial humour. The movement, the animation of its transient life, are recalled by Byron with zest and even enjoyment as a kaleidoscopic comedy world, without any suggestion of the nightmarishness of Shelley's (or of Dickens's) London.

But again, in these stanzas, Shelley is much more like Byron (for all the differences between their personalities) than he is like Pope. There is in Shelley as in Byron the irreverent and disrespectful note towards established authority and institutions ('the tyranny of church and state'), the note of personal rebellion and defiance. This shows in the verse itself and the rhymes, the effect of knockabout and consciously shocking irregularity.

IV

The gay, high-spirited comedy of the opening canto of *Don Juan* is a wonderful thing, and unexpected, if we come to it after *Childe Harold* and the earlier Romantic Byron. Canto I captures the attention and the imagination partly by the element in it of pantomimic farce (the bedroom scene, in particular) as the early Falstaff scenes do in *Henry IV, Part I*, and the early episodes (the tilting at windmills, for example) do in *Don Quixote*. Thereafter, in the latter parts of these three works there is a settling down (as in the Justice Shallow scenes in *Henry IV, Part II*) to the level of the unexaggerated comic observation of life as it more ordinarily is. One can see, particularly in the London cantos, how *Don Juan* anticipates in some respects Henry James's comedies of London life in his time.

The traditional Don Juan –

> We all have seen him, in the pantomime,
> Sent to the devil somewhat ere his time –[1]

and the traditional Faust have, of course, a good deal in common. These legends seem, indeed, often to have partially merged in popular tradition and entertainment. But there is nothing diabolic, nothing that could be associated with the Devil and Hell about Byron's hero or anti-hero, nor any dabbling with magic or the supernatural. There is indeed rather a 19th-century innocence about him through all his youthful adventures or misadventures. In Canto I we view his development from boyhood through adolescence. In the later cantos we view the youth growing into manhood which, in Byron's poem, necessitates an involvement with and knowledge of 'the world'. The treatment in *Don Juan* of the development of the individual human being from childhood to manhood – one of the main themes of 19th century poetry and novels – is of course very different, as Byron's own experience had been different, from that of *The Prelude*. Byron's (as his Juan's) 'world' is mainly his contemporary Regency social world, Wordsworth's is that of the mountains of his native region, the people who lived there, and the universe. Clearly this Juan, Byron's Juan, is very largely the youthful Byron humorously viewed in retrospect by his middle-aged self. Byron's poem is almost as autobiographical as is *The Prelude*, though Byron's 'recollected experiences' could not be more different from Wordsworth's.

The character of Donna Inez, a comic paragon, learned, moral and mathematical, is the first to stand out from Canto I. As young Juan's mother she is largely responsible for his education, which proves to be not an education for life and the world. But first the account of the domestic squabbles between her and her husband, Don José, with its references to the activities of meddling and

---

[1] Canto I, Stanza I.

uncharitable friends and relations and, of course, predatory
lawyers is a scarcely disguised translation into a comic opera
world of Byron's personal domestic and public disaster. Byron is
able now in retrospect and in Italy to treat even that lightly and
detachedly as a comedy rather than a tragedy.

> Don José and his lady quarrell'd – *why*,
>   Not any of the many could divine,
> Though several thousand people chose to try,
>   'T was surely no concern of theirs nor mine;[1]

and so on, through many stanzas, in the same light tone, till

>   The lawyers did their utmost for divorce,
>   But scarce a fee was paid on either side
>   Before, unluckily, Don José died.[2]

Juan's education (presided over now by his mother) is the
conventional upper-class education of the period, as recollected
by Byron, a humorous criticism of what that education had
amounted to. A grounding in the Classics, of course, formed (as
in the 18th century) a large part of it. The problem of how to fit
the Classics (even as expurgated) into a moral education is gaily
commented on. 'Moral' means in effect that the boy should learn
as little as possible about actual human nature, remain as ignorant
as possible about his own nature.

> For Donna Inez dreaded the Mythology.

Naturally the boy Juan's inner nature asserts itself and he passes
through a Wordsworthian (and Coleridgean) adolescence – as
Byron suggests, though it may strike the reader as more Shelleyan
than Wordsworthian.

> Young Juan wander'd by the glassy brooks,
>   Thinking unutterable things; he threw
> Himself at length within the leafy nooks
>   Where the wild branch of the cork-forest grew;
> There poets find materials for their books,
>   And every now and then we read them through,
> So that their plan and prosody are eligible,
> Unless, like Wordsworth, they prove unintelligible.

[1] Canto I, Stanza XXIII.   [2] Canto I, Stanza XXXII.

He, Juan (and not Wordsworth), so pursued
   His self-communion with his own high soul,
Until his mighty heart, in its great mood,
   Had mitigated part, though not the whole,
Of its disease; he did the best he could
   With things not very subject to control,
And turn'd, without perceiving his condition,
Like Coleridge, into a metaphysician.

He thought about himself, and the whole earth,
   Of man the wonderful, and of the stars,
And how the deuce they ever could have birth;
   And then he thought of earthquakes and of wars,
How many miles the moon might have in girth,
   Of air-balloons, and of the many bars
To perfect knowledge of the boundless skies; –
And then he thought of Donna Julia's eyes.[1]

Juan's adolescent passion for Julia – who is almost as ignorant of
herself as Juan is of himself, though she happens to be married –
is treated with the knowledge and hindsight of maturity. (Cf.
Stendhal's treatment of Julien's affair with Madame de Renal in
Le Rouge et le Noir.)

   Some of the best things in the first canto, as throughout *Don
Juan*, are, of course, the digressions and comments by the way.
The whole poem is largely Byron talking, the Juan story he tells
being a part only of the talk. The episodes and characters of the
Juan narrative are interspersed freely and copiously with Byron's
lively personal opinions and observations, largely about con-
temporary life. It is here that his gift for handling ideas lightly
finds expression. His now humorous view of the world discovers
abundant matter for comedy in the age, including its inventions
and novelties.

Man's a strange animal, and makes strange use
   Of his own nature, and the various arts,
And likes particularly to produce
   Some new experiment to show his parts;
This is the age of oddities let loose.[2]

[1] Canto I, Stanzas XC–XCII.   [2] Canto I, Stanza CXXVIII.

> This is the patent-age of new inventions
>   For killing bodies, and for saving souls,
> All propagated with the best intentions;
>   Sir Humphry Davy's lantern, by which coals
> Are safely mined for in the mode he mentions,
>   Tombuctoo travels, voyages to the Poles,
> Are ways to benefit mankind, as true,
> Perhaps, as shooting them at Waterloo.[1]

This particular digression on the oddities and incongruities of the age intervenes, as an easy pause, before the comic (or farcical) climax of Canto I. It prepares us for any absurdity to happen in a topsy-turvy world and, promptly, such does happen. This is the scene, very much in the gay spirit of comic opera, of the invasion of Donna Julia's bedroom at midnight by her jealous husband (Don Alfonso) with 'half the city', a rabble of friends, servants and neighbours.

> It surely was exceedingly ill-bred,
>   Without a word of previous admonition,
> To hold a levee round his lady's bed,
>   And summon lackeys, arm'd with fire and sword,
> To prove himself the thing he most abhorr'd.[2]

There follows one of those comic chaoses into which (as in several of Chaucer's tales) comedy sometimes explodes and in which the ordinary conventional world, that is too much with us, is turned upside down. Noisy and confused action breaks out (as in the great world of public affairs) to no rational purpose or practical effect. There is a quick succession of skilfully stage-managed comic climaxes and anticlimaxes.

> *He* search'd, *they* search'd, and rummaged every where,
>   Closet and clothes' press, chest and window-seat,
> And found much linen, lace, and several pair
>   Of stockings, slippers, brushes, combs, complete,
> With other articles of ladies fair,
>   To keep them beautiful, or leave them neat:
> Arras they prick'd and curtains with their swords,
> And wounded several shutters, and some boards.

[1] Canto I, Stanza CXXXII.   [2] Canto I, Stanza CXXXIX.

Under the bed they search'd, and there they found –
No matter what – it was not that they sought.[1]

The comic verve of the scene is exhilarating. It mounts and soars
in the outraged Donna Julia's indignant, heroic, scornful, ora-
torical tirade in the (burlesque) grand manner which puts her
husband quite out of countenance – though she is, of course, not
in fact an injured innocent (the boy Juan being hidden by the
quick-witted serving-maid under the heaped bedclothes).

'Was it for this that no Cortejo e'er
   I yet have chosen from out the youth of Seville?
Is it for this I scarce went any where,
   Except to bull-fights, mass, play, rout, and revel?
Is it for this, whate'er my suitors were,
   I favour'd none – nay, was almost uncivil?
Is it for this that General Count O'Reilly,
Who took Algiers, declares I used him vilely?

'Did not the Italian musico Cazzani
   Sing at my heart six months at least in vain?
Did not his countryman, Count Corniani,
   Call me the only virtuous wife in Spain?
Were there not also Russians, English, many?
   The Count Strongstroganoff I put in pain,
And Lord Mount Coffeehouse, the Irish peer,
Who kill'd himself for love (with wine) last year.

'Have I not had two bishops at my feet?
   The Duke of Ichar, and Don Fernan Nunez,
And is it thus a faithful wife you treat?
   I wonder in what quarter now the moon is:
I praise your vast forbearance not to beat
   Me also, since the time so opportune is –
Oh, valiant man! with sword drawn and cock'd trigger,
Now, tell me, don't you cut a pretty figure?

'Was it for this you took your sudden journey,
   Under pretence of business indispensable,
With that sublime of rascals your attorney,
   Whom I see standing there, and looking sensible

[1] Canto I, Stanzas CXLIII–CXLIV.

Of having play'd the fool? though both I spurn, he
 Deserves the worst, his conduct's less defensible,
Because, no doubt, 't was for his dirty fee,
And not from any love to you nor me.

'If he comes here to take a deposition,
 By all means let the gentleman proceed;
You've made the apartment in a fit condition: –
 There's pen and ink for you, sir, when you need –
Let everything be noted with precision,
 I would not you for nothing should be fee'd –
But, as my maid's undrest, pray turn your spies out.'
'Oh!' sobb'd Antonia, 'I could tear their eyes out.'[1]

The attorney alone remains complacent, knowing he thrives on domestic discord.

So there were quarrels, cared not for the cause,
Knowing they must be settled by the laws.[2]

There are Chaucerian mock indignant asides.

No sooner was it bolted, then – Oh! shame!
 O son! O sorrow! and O womankind!
How can you do such things and keep your fame,
 Unless this world, and t' other too, be blind?[3]

When all seems safely over there is, of course, yet another surprise, the unexpected discovery and exposure

When, lo! he stumbled o'er a pair of shoes.

A pair of shoes! – what then? not much, if they
 Are such as fit with ladies' feet, but these
(No one can tell how much I grieve to say)
 Were masculine.[4]

Thus the canto comes round again at the end to the theme of yet another divorce that provides yet another pleasant public scandal.

The pleasant scandal which arose next day,
 The nine days' wonder which was brought to light,

---

[1] Canto I, Stanzas CXLVIII–CLII.   [2] Canto I, Stanza CLIX.
[3] Canto I, Stanza CLXV.   [4] Canto I, Stanzas CLXXX–CLXXXI.

And how Alfonso sued for a divorce,
Were in the English newspapers, of course.[1]

So Juan (as Byron was) is sent on his travels and Byron, looking back now on his own case, gives himself some advice.

You've pass'd your youth not so unpleasantly,
    And if you had it o'er again – 't would pass –
So thank your stars that matters are no worse,
And read your Bible, sir, and mind your purse.[2]

The appropriate comment on Juan comes at the beginning of the next Canto (Canto II).

A lad of sixteen causing a divorce
Puzzled his tutors very much, of course.

I can't say that it puzzles me at all,
    If all things be consider'd: first, there was
His lady-mother, mathematical,
    A —— never mind; – his tutor, an old ass;
A pretty woman – (that's quite natural,
    Or else the thing had hardly come to pass);
A husband rather old, not much in unity
With his young wife – a time, and opportunity.[3]

As for Donna Inez she 'now sets up a Sunday school' – a neat concluding irony.

The great success of Juan's education
Spurr'd her to teach another generation.[4]

v

It is not possible here to comment at equal length on all the cantos of the immense entertaining diffusion which is *Don Juan* (contrast, again, Pope's compactness). The most important cantos (to my mind) are the later ones about Don Juan in England (Cantos XI to the end) because of their criticism of life in the Regency society which Byron had known. I shall, therefore, only briefly touch on a few things in the intervening cantos (up to Canto X).

[1] Canto I, Stanza CLXXXVIII.
[2] Canto I, Stanza CCXX.
[3] Canto II, Stanzas II–III.
[4] Canto II, Stanza X.

Canto II is chiefly notable for the unromantic grim realism of the tempest, the shipwreck and the exposure of the survivors on the raft. The Romantic youth is exposed to the anti-Romantic effects of these not merely unpleasant but terrible experiences at sea, none the less 'realistic' because of the element of grim humour in the descriptions. There is first described the efficacy of seasickness as a cure for Romantic feelings (stanzas XIII–XXIII). As the tempest develops there are exhibited the behaviour and demeanour of the individual members of the motley crew and passengers, each responding in character. Even in the teeth of death – the devouring jaws of the sea – the comedy of life grimly persists.

> There's nought, no doubt, so much the spirit calms
>   As rum and true religion: thus it was,
> Some plunder'd, some drank spirits, some sung psalms,
>   The high wind made the treble, and as bass
> The hoarse harsh waves kept time; fright cured the qualms
>   Of all the luckless landsmen's sea-sick maws:
> Strange sounds of wailing, blasphemy, devotion,
> Clamour'd in chorus to the roaring ocean.[1]
>
> The ship was evidently settling now
>   Fast by the head; and, all distinction gone,
> Some went to prayers again, and made a vow
>   Of candles to their saints – but there were none
> To pay them with; and some look'd o'er the bow;
>   Some hoisted out the boats; and there was one
> That begg'd Pedrillo for an absolution,
> Who told him to be damn'd – in his confusion.
>
> Some lash'd them in their hammocks; some put on
>   Their best clothes, as if going to a fair.[2]

There is the macabre farce of the end of Juan's tutor (Pedrillo) eaten by his famished fellows on the raft.

The conclusion of Canto II and the Cantos that follow (Cantos III–V) recall, within the flow and diversity of Byron talking, as Juan's adventures, Byron's own youthful voyages to

---

[1] Canto II, Stanza XXXIV.   [2] Canto II, Stanzas XLIV–XLV.

the Aegean, his fresh discovery there of the lands and islands of
the Classical reading of his schooldays and the picturesqueness of
the Islamic East. As now looked back upon in middle age these
places and peoples seem both to have recovered for Byron their
early freshness and to have mellowed in memory. In the modern
epic Juan is washed ashore on an island as Odysseus was; Haidee
is his Nausicaa. The episode of the boy and girl love of Juan and
Haidee in the primitive paradisiacal setting of an Aegean island is,
as a pastoral idyll, an unexpected interlude in *Don Juan* (would be
more so if the poem were not full of the unexpected and changes
of tone and mood). It is Byron's version of the Age of Innocence,
the State of Nature, a boy and girl love that is simply natural and,
as such, not invalidated by its context in *Don Juan* (for all the
nonsense that has been talked about Byron's cynicism). On the con-
trary it seems easily to find its place there in the course of the
humorous, genial, man-of-the-world talk. It is presented by the
middle-aged poet with the gentleness and tenderness with which
the very young man may often be regarded by one who is no
longer young, who is himself sadly experienced in the world,
disenchanted, humorous, sceptical in his view of the world but
not sceptical about simple human naturalness. If a recovered Eden
can be imagined, for Byron evidently it could most easily be
imagined in one of those remembered Greek islands of his youth.

The humour of the episode – again at times a grim humour – is
in fact centred on the not-so-innocent character and actions of
old Lambro, Haidee's piratical papa, not on the young lovers.
Byron's partiality for an outlaw is still strong. Haidee is the 'only
daughter'

> Of an old man, who lived upon the water.

> A fisherman he had been in his youth,
>   And still a sort of fisherman was he;
> But other speculations were, in sooth,
>   Added to his connection with the sea,
> Perhaps not so respectable, in truth:
>   A little smuggling, and some piracy,
> Left him, at last, the sole of many masters
> Of an ill-gotten million of piastres.[1]

[1] Canto II, Stanzas CXXIV–CXXV.

We hear more of him in the following Canto (Canto III).

> Let not his mode of raising cash seem strange,
>   Although he fleeced the flags of every nation,
> For into a prime minister but change
>   His title, and 't is nothing but taxation;
> But he, more modest, took a humbler range
>   Of life, and in an honester vocation
> Pursued o'er the high seas his watery journey,
> And merely practised as a sea-attorney.[1]

> French stuffs, lace, tweezers, toothpicks, teapot, tray,
>   Guitars and castanets from Alicant;
> All which selected from the spoil he gathers,
> Robb'd for his daughter by the best of fathers.[2]

His unexpected return to his island home after being supposed to be dead is, of course, partly reminiscent of the return of Odysseus combined with Byron's remembered impressions of the colourful Eastern Mediterranean.

> He saw his white walls shining in the sun,
>   His garden trees all shadowy and green;
> He heard his rivulet's light bubbling run,
>   The distant dog-bark; and perceived between
> The umbrage of the wood so cool and dun
>   The moving figures, and the sparkling sheen
> Of arms (in the East all arm) – and various dyes
> Of colour'd garbs, as bright as butterflies.

> And further on a group of Grecian girls,
>   The first and tallest her white kerchief waving,
> Were strung together like a row of pearls,
>   Link'd hand in hand, and dancing.[3]

The comedy is in old Lambro's being utterly disconcerted by what he finds at home, a scene of merry-making, an island festival, that is (to his sense) outrageous. The old pirate has also his conventions. The effect of his discovering himself to the revellers is equally disconcerting. (Cf. Polixenes in Act 3 of *A Winter's*

---

[1] Canto III, Stanza XIV.   [2] Canto III, Stanza XVII.
[3] Canto III, Stanzas XXVII, XXX.

Tale.) He returns in fact to spoil joy. Should we, then, the English reader (asks Byron) condemn his savagery and treachery? The irony of the answer is directed at society.

> You're wrong. – He was the mildest-manner'd man
>   That ever scuttled ship or cut a throat;
> With such true breeding of a gentleman,
>   You never could divine his real thought;
> No courtier could, and scarcely woman can
>   Gird more deceit within a petticoat;
> Pity he loved adventurous life's variety,
> He was so great a loss to good society.[1]

A shift in the kaleidoscope to Turkish scenes, again with comic opera episodes, follows next in Juan's swift-moving peregrinations (Cantos IV–VI). The presence of an Italian opera company among Juan's fellow-captives on the ship taking them up the Hellespont as cargo to be sold in the slave-market of Constantinople re-introduces the comic opera note. They are each described by the buffo of the company, with rather malicious humour, exposing their seamy, seedy side. But the comic operatic spirit fills the verse with light-hearted gaiety, carrying it buoyantly along (aided by the rhyming and chiming together of sonorous Italian names).

> The little fellow really look'd quite hearty,
>   And bore him with some gaiety and grace,
> Showing a much more reconciled demeanour
> Than did the prima donna and the tenor.
>
> In a few words he told their hapless story,
>   Saying, 'Our Machiavellian impresario,
> Making a signal off some promontory,
>   Hail'd a strange brig; Corpo di Caio Mario!
> We were transferr'd on board it in a hurry,
>   Without a single scudo of salario;
> But if the Sultan has a taste for song,
> We will revive our fortunes before long.
>
> 'The prima donna, though a little old,
>   And haggard with a dissipated life,

[1] Canto III, Stanza XLI.

And subject, when the house is thin, to cold,
   Has some good notes; and then the tenor's wife,
With no great voice, is pleasing to behold;
   Last carnival she made a deal of strife
By carrying off Count Cesare Cicogna
From an old Roman princess at Bologna.

'And then there are the dancers; there's the Nini,
   With more than one profession gains by all;
Then there's that laughing slut the Pelegrini,
   She, too, was fortunate last carnival,
And made at least five hundred good zecchini,
   But spends so fast, she has not now a paul;
And then there's the Grotesca – such a dancer!
Where men have souls or bodies she must answer.'[1]

and so on through half-a dozen stanzas more. Juan's misadventures as a slave with the Sultana (the favourite Sultana) culminate in the comic operatic unexpected entrance of the Sultan in procession – a recurrence amidst more exotic and extravagant scenes of the invasion of Julia's bedroom in the first canto, for history repeats itself in various shapes and disguises, human nature remaining basically the same.

His peace was making, but before he ventured
Further, old Baba rather briskly enter'd:

'Bride of the Sun! and sister of the Moon!'
   ('T was thus he spake,) 'and Empress of the Earth!
Whose frown would put the spheres all out of tune,
   Whose smile makes all the planets dance with mirth,
Your slave brings tidings – he hopes not too soon –
   Which your sublime attention may be worth:
The Sun himself has sent me, like a ray,
To hint that he is coming up this way.'

'Is it,' exclaim'd Gulbeyaz, 'as you say?
   I wish to Heaven he would not shine till morning!
But bid my women form the milky way.
   Hence, my old comet! give the stars due warning –
And Christian! mingle with them as you may,

[1] Canto IV, Stanzas LXXXI–LXXXIV.

> And as you'd have me pardon your past scorning –'
> Here they were interrupted by a humming
> Sound, and then by a cry, 'The Sultan's coming!'[1]

The Turkish episodes are, of course, like all the Juan episodes throughout the whole poem, again freely interspersed with Byron's personal comments, opinions and reminiscences. This easy, familiar flow of English talk contrasts with and (being English) relieves the exotic and bizarre Oriental scenes. Byron pleasantly recalls his own early travels in Asia Minor, his own visit to the site of Troy, his youthful feelings there about Mutability and the Ruins of Time, the incongruity of his finding the place and people there now not Greek but Islamic.

> ... but where I sought for Ilion's walls,
> The quiet sheep feeds, and the tortoise crawls;
>
> Troops of untended horses; here and there
>   Some little hamlets, with new names uncouth;
> Some shepherds (unlike Paris), led to stare
>   A moment at the European youth
> Whom to the spot their school-boy feelings bear;
>   A Turk, with beads in hand, and pipe in mouth,
> Extremely taken with his own religion,
> Are what I found there – but the devil a Phrygian.[2]

There are inevitably wry reflections also on how he himself and his world have changed.

> What! can I prove 'a lion' then no more?
> A ball-room bard, a foolscap, hot-press darling?[3]
>
> A neat snug study on a winter's night,
>   A book, friend, single lady, or a glass
> Of claret, sandwich, and an appetite,
>   Are things which make an English evening pass;
> Though *certes* by no means so grand a sight
>   As is a theatre lit up by gas.
> I pass my evenings in long galleries solely,
> And that's the reason I'm so melancholy.[4]

[1] Canto V, Stanzas CXLIII–CXLV.
[2] Canto IV, Stanzas LXXXVII–LXXXVIII.
[3] Canto IV, Stanza CIX.   [4] Canto V, Stanza LVIII.

The exotic Turkish scenes are further relieved by the presence of a real, live, typical Englishman – a version of the Englishman abroad that has been made more familiar later in novels. He shares the same predicament with Juan – for sale in the slave-market.

> Which for himself he seem'd to deem no worse
>   Than any other scrape, a thing of course.
>   'My boy!' – said he, 'amidst this motley crew
>   Of Georgians, Russians, Nubians, and what not,
>   All ragamuffins differing but in hue,
>   With whom it is our luck to cast our lot,
>   The only gentlemen seem I and you;[1]

His name is Johnson, a namesake of the great Englishman whom Byron admired.

VI

The Turkish scenes are wound up in Canto VI – Juan in yet another comic opera situation, in female disguise, with Lolah, Katinka and Dudu. But the Cantos that follow (Cantos VII and VIII) are quite a different matter. There we are presented with a realistic – and anti-Romantic and anti-Epic – view of war, the actuality of war, which anticipates not only Stendhal (Fabrice at Waterloo) but Tolstoy. Byron involves Juan (together with the Englishman) in one of the wars between the Russians and the Turks. The details of the Siege of Ismail are taken (according to Byron's preface) from a French historical work. But, though Byron had had himself no direct experience of war, his imagination makes it immediately present as what it is really like to an individual mixed up in it, stripped of Romantic or Heroic Epic idealizing notions of it, a butcher's business.

> History can only take things in the gross;
>   But could we know them in detail, perchance
> In balancing the profit and the loss,
>   War's merit it by no means might enhance.[2]

> The groan, the roll in dust, the all-white eye
>   Turn'd back within its socket, – these reward

---

[1] Canto V, Stanzas XII–XIII.   [2] Canto VIII, Stanza III.

> Your rank and file by thousands, while the rest
> May win, perhaps, a riband at the breast![1]

Byron's frequent references throughout his work to Waterloo make it plain that he had begun to take an anti-Romantic view of war as senseless carnage, a butchery, a shambles. So it is represented here in these cantos of *Don Juan*. He draws attention to the horror and pity of it for the real men of flesh and blood who get slain or maimed. The glory reduces itself to the names in the Gazette.

> He fell, immortal in a bulletin.

War is already matter for newspapers. An anti-Romantic view of war, as well as an anti-Romantic view of love, finds a place, therefore, in the whole anti-Romantic view of the world presented in *Don Juan*. The light, witty, sardonic, irreverent tone of the talk in which these events are recounted is exactly calculated to produce the deflating effect. What makes the realism of the narrative and descriptions possible is in fact partly this colloquial, familiar tone, anti-Grand Manner and, therefore, the more closely matter-of-fact.

> But then the fact's a fact – and 't is the part
> Of a true poet to escape from fiction.[2]

This is what Crabbe might have said. Here is the inexperienced, innocent youth, Juan, in his first military engagement.

> When after a good deal of heavy firing,
> He found himself alone, and friends retiring.

> Juan, who had no shield to snatch, and was
>   No Caesar, but a fine young lad, who fought
> He knew not why, arriving at this pass,
>   Stopp'd for a minute, as perhaps he ought
> For a much longer time; then, like an ass –
>   (Start not, kind reader, since great Homer thought
> This simile enough for Ajax, Juan
> Perhaps may find it better than a new one); –

[1] Canto VIII, Stanza XIII.   [2] Canto VIII, Stanza LXXXV.

Then, like an ass, he went upon his way,
    And, what was stranger, never look'd behind;
But seeing, flashing forward, like the day
    Over the hills, a fire enough to blind
Those who dislike to look upon a fray,
    He stumbled on, to try if he could find
A path, to add his own slight arm and forces
To corps, the greater part of which were corses.

Perceiving then no more the commandant
    Of his own corps, nor even the corps, which had
Quite disappear'd – the gods know how! (I can't
    Account for every thing which may look bad
In history; but we at least may grant
    It was not marvellous that a mere lad,
In search of glory, should look on before,
Nor care a pinch of snuff about his corps;) –

Perceiving nor commander nor commanded,
    And left at large, like a young heir, to make
His way to – where he knew not – single-handed;
    As travellers follow over bog and brake
An 'ignis fatuus;' or as sailors stranded
    Unto the nearest hut themselves betake;
So Juan, following honour and his nose,
Rush'd where the thickest fire announced most foes.

He knew not where he was, nor greatly cared,
    For he was dizzy, busy, and his veins
Fill'd as with lightning – for his spirit shared
    The hour, as is the case with lively brains;
And where the hottest fire was seen and heard,
    And the loud cannon peal'd his hoarsest strains,
He rush'd, while earth and air were sadly shaken
By thy humane discovery, Friar Bacon![1]

It may be remarked again that throughout all his misadventures
in love and war Juan in Byron's poem remains essentially an
innocent. The old Don Juan story is reversed, it is the world that
is worldly not Juan. That Byron's Juan is not the cynical Don

---

[1] Canto VIII, Stanzas XXVII–XXXIII.

Juan of tradition could not be more strikingly illustrated than by
the episode of the child he preserves from the slaughter, respond-
ing naturally to the deep human appeal of the unprotected child.
In dry, matter-of-fact, rapid narrative and dialogue this is (iron-
ically) how Byron's Don Juan comes to have his 'first child':

> Up Johnson came, with hundreds at his back
>   Exclaiming: – 'Juan! Juan! On, boy! brace
> Your arm, and I'll bet Moscow to a dollar
> That you and I will win St. George's collar.
>
> 'The Seraskier is knock'd upon the head,
>   But the stone bastion still remains, wherein
> The old Pacha sits among some hundreds dead,
>   Smoking his pipe quite calmly 'midst the din
> Of our artillery and his own: 't is said
>   Our kill'd, already piled up to the chin,
> Lie round the battery; but still it batters,
> And grape in volleys, like a vineyard, scatters.
>
> 'Then up with me!' – But Juan answer'd, 'Look
>   Upon this child – I saved her – must not leave
> Her life to chance; but point me out some nook
>   Of safety, where she less may shrink and grieve,
> And I am with you.' – Whereon Johnson took
>   A glance around – and shrugg'd – and twitch'd his sleeve
> And black silk neckcloth – and replied, 'You're right;
> Poor thing! what's to be done? I'm puzzled quite.'
>
> Said Juan – 'Whatsoever is to be
>   Done, I'll not quit her till she seems secure
> Of present life a good deal more than we.' –
>   Quoth Johnson – '*Neither* will I quite ensure;
> But at the least *you* may die gloriously.' –
>   Juan replied – 'At least I will endure
> Whate'er is to be borne – but not resign
> This child, who is parentless, and therefore mine.'[1]

Cantos VII and VIII, then, present Byron's mature view of war.
It causes the comic poem to sharpen occasionally into satire and
invective.

[1] Canto VIII, Stanzas XCVII–C.

Cockneys of London! Muscadins of Paris!
Just ponder what a pious pastime war is.

Think how the joys of reading a gazette
    Are purchased by all agonies and crimes.[1]

Still there is one object of sublime national satisfaction:

Gaunt famine never shall approach the throne –
Though Ireland starve, great George weighs twenty stone.[2]

The image recalls the political caricatures and lampoons of the
period, particularly those of Gillray.

Cantos VII and VIII on war have their final comment in the
opening stanzas of Canto IX, the satiric invective against
Wellington.

You are 'the best of cut-throats:' – do not start;
    The phrase is Shakspeare's, and not misapplied: –
War's a brain-spattering, windpipe-slitting art,
    Unless her cause by right be sanctified.
If you have acted *once* a generous part,
    The world, not the world's masters, will decide,
And I shall be delighted to learn who,
Save you and yours, have gain'd by Waterloo?

I am no flatterer – you've supp'd full of flattery:
    They say you like it too – 't is no great wonder.
He whose whole life has been assault and battery,
    At last may get a little tired of thunder;
And swallowing eulogy much more than satire, he
    May like being praised for every lucky blunder,
Call'd 'Saviour of the Nations' – not yet saved,
And 'Europe's Liberator' – still enslaved.

I've done. Now go and dine from off the plate
    Presented by the Prince of the Brazils,
And send the sentinel before your gate
    A slice or two from your luxurious meals:
He fought, but has not fed so well of late.
    Some hunger, too, they say the people feels: –

---

[1] Canto VIII, Stanzas CXXIV–CXXV.   [2] Canto VIII, Stanza CXXVI.

There is no doubt that you deserve your ration,
But pray give back a little to the nation.[1]

It is as effectively direct in its conversational way as Shelley's
more earnest and intense, more high-pitched, *Mask of Anarchy*,
with its nightmare vision, or some of the things in Blake –

And the hapless soldier's sigh
Runs in blood down palace walls.

If Byron thrusts home the blade unfairly here, too personally, it
can be accounted for as the indignant recoil of a warmly generous
nature at the thought of humanity subjected to injustice, tyranny
and wrong.

Cantos IX and X go on thereafter to present, always in the
midst of the flow of Byron's personal talk, Juan in Petersburg at
the Court of Catherine the Great, another shift of the kaleido-
scope and another succession of comic opera scenes. Dressed up
in extravagant Russian uniform by an army tailor – like a tailor's
model – Juan reappears in yet another costume in the comic
carnival of the cosmopolitan great world.

Behold him placed as if upon a pillar! He
Seems Love turn'd a lieutenant of artillery![2]

and so on through several stanzas of brilliant, gay description. As
such a dazzling youthful figure, Juan, of course, takes the eye of
the great Catherine.

But in such matters Russia's mighty empress
Behaved no better than a common sempstress.

The whole court melted into one wide whisper,
    And all lips were applied unto all ears!
The elder ladies' wrinkles curl'd much crisper
    As they beheld; the younger cast some leers
On one another, and each lovely lisper
    Smiled as she talk'd the matter o'er; but tears
Of rivalship rose in each clouded eye
Of all the standing army who stood by.

All the ambassadors of all the powers
    Inquired, who was this very new young man,

Who promised to be great in some few hours?
  Which is full soon (though life is but a span):
Already they beheld the silver showers
  Of rubles rain, as fast as specie can,
Upon his cabinet, besides the presents
Of several ribands, and some thousand peasants.[1]

But when the levee rose, and all was bustle
  In the dissolving circle, all the nations'
Ambassadors began as 't were to hustle
  Round the young man with their congratulations.
Also the softer silks were heard to rustle
  Of gentle dames, among whose recreations
It is to speculate on handsome faces,
Especially when such lead to high places.[2]

Though the widely travelled Byron had never himself been to
Petersburg, the extravaganza of these scenes makes pantomime or
comic opera again of the 'great world' of the society he *had*
known. These scenes of the world, for all their dazzle and glitter
and the gaiety with which they are rapidly sketched, are recog-
nized in the commentary that accompanies them to be, of course,
vanity. There is indeed something of the Hamlet mood (one of
the prevailing moods in the 19th century) underlying the wit of
the Byronic commentary here. The seeds of death are in 'the
world'.

Sovereigns may sway materials, but not matter,
And wrinkles, the d——d democrats, won't flatter. . .[3]

He lived (not Death, but Juan) in a hurry
  Of waste, and haste, and glare, and gloss, and glitter. . .[4]

Oh for a *forty-parson power* to chant
  Thy praise, Hypocrisy! Oh for a hymn
Loud as the virtues thou dost loudly vaunt,
  Not practise! Oh for trumps of cherubim!
Or the ear-trumpet of my good old aunt,
  Who, though her spectacles at last grew dim,

[1] Canto IX, Stanzas LXXVII–LXXIX.   [2] Canto IX, Stanza LXXXII.
[3] Canto X, Stanza XXIV.   [4] Canto X, Stanza XXVI.

Drew quiet consolation through its hint,
When she no more could read the pious print.

She was no hypocrite at least, poor soul![1]

It is not wholly accidental, perhaps, that there are allusions to
Hamlet in Canto IX – and to Montaigne (who had, some readers
feel, something to do with *Hamlet*) –

So little do we know what we're about in
This world, I doubt if doubt itself be doubting.[2]

Scepticism and a knowledge of human weakness can, however,
and do in Byron (as in the great Montaigne) go together with a
tolerant and humane spirit, even with geniality and generosity.
The Petersburg scenes are relieved (as were the Turkish scenes)
by the homely note of Byron's personal talk and reminiscences,
as in the stanzas (in Canto X) which bring back Byron's early
memories of Scotland and turn the poem in a homeward direction.

And all our little feuds, at least all *mine*,
    Dear Jeffrey, once my most redoubted foe
(As far as rhyme and criticism combine
    To make such puppets of us things below),
Are over: Here's a health to 'Auld Lang Syne!'
    I do not know you, and may never know
Your face – but you have acted on the whole
Most nobly, and I own it from my soul.

And when I use the phrase of 'Auld Lang Syne!'
    'T is not address'd to you – the more's the pity
For me, for I would rather take my wine
    With you, than aught (save Scott) in your proud city.
But somehow, – it may seem a schoolboy's whine,
    And yet I seek not to be grand nor witty,
But I am half a Scot by birth, and bred
    A whole one, and my heart flies to my head, –

As 'Auld Lang Syne' brings Scotland, one and all,
    Scotch plaids, Scotch snoods, the blue hills, and clear
                                                    streams

[1] Canto X, Stanzas XXXIV–XXXV.   [2] Canto IX, Stanza XVII.

The Dee, the Don, Balgounie's brig's *black wall*,
    All my boy feelings, all my gentler dreams
Of what I *then dreamt*, clothed in their own pall,
    Like Banquo's offspring; – floating past me seems
My childhood in this childishness of mine:
    I care not – 't is a glimpse of 'Auld Lang Syne.'

And though, as you remember, in a fit
    Of wrath and rhyme, when juvenile and curly,
I rail'd at Scots to show my wrath and wit,
    Which must be own'd was sensitive and surly,
Yet 't is in vain such sallies to permit,
    They cannot quench young feelings fresh and early:
I '*scotch'd* not kill'd' the Scotchman in my blood,
And love the land of 'mountain and of flood.'

Don Juan, who was real, or ideal, –
    For both are much the same, since what men think
Exists when the once thinkers are less real
    Than what they thought, for mind can never sink,
And 'gainst the body makes a strong appeal;
    And yet 't is very puzzling on the brink
Of what is call'd eternity, to stare,
And know no more of what is here, than there.[1]

VII

Canto X culminates with Juan's eager arrival in England full of youthful hopes and idealistic illusions as to what he will find there. The cantos that follow are (to my mind) for all their surface lightness of tone and touch Byron's most solid achievement, a large-scale comic criticism of English life as Byron had intimately known it. As a comedy of Regency high life, it may be said to supplement Jane Austen's and Crabbe's portrayals of the very different English provincial life and society they were familiar with. The device of seeing English life through the eyes and in relation to the presence of a foreign visitor can be, and is in *Don Juan*, a means of getting the sense of a fresh and unbiased look at it, free from the prejudices and insularity of the natives. We find it also, of course, in Goldsmith's *Citizen of the World*, in

[1] Canto X, Stanzas XVI–XX.

Arnold's *Friendship's Garland*, in the presence of Herr Klesmer in *Daniel Deronda* and, above all, in James's Americans in England and in Europe (as well as, of course, his Europeans in America). But essentially Byron in these cantos is himself looking back, with the detachment provided him by his residence in Italy, by an interval of years and by his ripening middle-aged maturity, on the Regency aristocratic society – 'the great world' – in which in his youth he himself had made a figure and cut a dash. Cantos XI and XII present vivid and witty recollections and evocations of London life. Cantos XIII–XVI (the last to be completed before Byron's death) do the same for the country house-party that up to James's day continued to be a feature of English high life and continued to offer a subject – a motley collection of people – for the comic observer. All these English cantos, indeed, in some ways anticipate not only the subject matter but the spirit of witty comedy of such of James's novels as are specifically criticisms of English life as he observed it in his time, *What Maisie Knew*, *The Awkward Age* and many of his most brilliant short stories. One of the great differences is that James's sense of the complexity of life is such that in his work comedy is never simply comedy but simultaneously tragedy, often deeply poignant.

The stanzas (towards the conclusion of Canto X) that rapidly convey Juan across Europe (through Courland, Poland, Germany and the Low Countries) on his Russian diplomatic mission to England not only recapture a sense of swift movement and youthful exhilaration but suggest a kaleidoscope of landscapes, the diverse countries of the world that shift, change and pass by. The climax of the journey is Juan's first sight of England, the familiar one at Dover, and his impressions as the coach rolls him through Kent to his first sight of London. Here is London as sketched from Shooter's Hill:

> A mighty mass of brick, and smoke, and shipping,
>   Dirty and dusky, but as wide as eye
> Could reach, with here and there a sail just skipping
>   In sight, then lost amidst the forestry
> Of masts; a wilderness of steeples, peeping
>   On tiptoe through their sea-coal canopy;

A huge dun cupola, like a foolscap crown
On a fool's head – and there is London Town![1]

But this is not exactly London as young Juan sees it.

> But Juan saw not this: each wreath or smoke
>   Appear'd to him but as the magic vapour
> Of some alchymic furnace, from whence broke
>   The wealth of worlds (a wealth of tax and paper):
> The gloomy clouds, which o'er it as a yoke
>   Are bow'd, and put the sun out like a taper,
> Were nothing but the natural atmosphere,
> Extremely wholesome, though but rarely clear.[2]

He sees it through a haze not simply of smoke but of enchantment, for he arrives full of glorious illusions about England. The concluding stanzas of Canto X announce the poet's intention of stripping away such illusions – not only Juan's but those of the English people about themselves, as being, for example, 'a moral people'. Byron is now proposing a more serious criticism of life than in the earlier cantos – English life directly observed, though still detachedly and as comedy.

>   at least I'll try
> To tell you truths *you* will not take as true,
>   Because they are so; – a male Mrs. Fry,
> With a soft besom will I sweep your halls,
> And brush a web or two from off the walls.
>
> Oh, Mrs. Fry! Why go to Newgate? Why
>   Preach to poor rogues? And wherefore not begin
> With Carlton, or with other houses? Try
>   Your hand at harden'd and imperial sin.
> To mend the people's an absurdity,
>   A jargon, a mere philanthropic din,
> Unless you make their betters better: – Fy!
> I thought you had more religion, Mrs. Fry.[3]

[1] Canto X, Stanza LXXXII. Contrast this comedy image with the tragic solemnity of Wordsworth's image:

> Our haughty life is crowned with darkness
> Like London with its own black wreath.

[2] Canto X, Stanza LXXXIII.   [3] Canto X, Stanzas LXXXIV–LXXXV.

Canto X had opened with a gay dismissal of Newton's Physics and the scientific development and inventions that have followed[1] (cf. Blake's rejection of Newtonian Science). Canto XI (the first of the two cantos on London life) opens with an equally light treatment of Berkeley's Metaphysics.

> When Bishop Berkeley said 'there was no matter,'
>   And proved it – 't was no matter what he said:
> They say his system 't is in vain to batter,
>   Too subtle for the airiest human head;
> And yet who can believe it? I would shatter
>   Gladly all matters down to stone or lead,
> Or adamant, to find the world a spirit,
> And wear my head, denying that I wear it.[2]

Evidently Byron is firmly in a mood to take a matter-of-fact, down-to-earth, unenchanted look at English life. Yet a comparison with, for example, Crabbe will remind us that there are more ways than one of being matter-of-fact, as there is more than one idiom of wit. The light-hearted irreverent gaiety of Byron's informal conversational comedy is a very different note from Crabbe's.

Juan's heartfelt but high-flown oration on England, home of freedom and the domestic virtues, as he looks down on London from Shooter's Hill is anticlimaxed, rudely cut short by footpads.

> Here – ' he was interrupted by a knife,
> With, 'Damn your eyes! your money or your life!'[3]

The episode might be from a Fielding or Smollett novel but was evidently the kind of thing that happened. It ends not Juan but Tom, a very English footpad. ('O Jack! I'm floor'd by that 'ere bloody Frenchman!') Byron's warm uncynical human sympathies, his frank, open, generous kindred feeling for common humankind – thieves and other lawless characters of course included – associates him with Burns and with Dickens (and also, of course, with Shakespeare, if we recall, for example, the Falstaff scenes).

---

[1] Quoted in Chapter Three (Wordsworth: *The Prelude*), p. 98.
[2] Canto XI, Stanza I.   [3] Canto XI, Stanza X.

> Poor Tom was once a kiddy upon town,
>   A thorough varmint, and a *real* swell.[1]

Thus, as Dickens might have done, Byron creates an elegy for
Tom out of Tom's own thieves' slang, a wonderful flow of such
language that reproduces with its comic verve the swagger and
dash of such a life.

> He from the world had cut off a great man,
>   Who in his time had made heroic bustle,
> Who in a row like Tom could lead the van,
>   Booze in the ken, or at the spellken hustle?
> Who queer a flat? Who (spite of Bow-street's ban)
>   On the high toby-spice so flash the muzzle?
> Who on a lark, with black-eyed Sal (his blowing),
> So prime, so swell, so nutty, and so knowing?[2]

As Juan rolls into London his first visual impressions of the
great city are those of Byron's own recollections of it. The
animation, the bustle, the confusion of the streets are enjoyably
present again in recollection, but without excluding the seamy,
seedy side of it. These vivid impressions are, therefore, not simply
what young Juan would see but also what, if he does see, he is not
yet experienced or informed enough to interpret. Juan would see
London rather as the young Romantic Byron might first have
seen it. The irony depends on the discrepancy between the vision
of the enchanted youth and that of disenchanted middle age,
though the scene itself is the same. Yet what gives added zest and
amusement to Byron's recollections of London is evidently a re-
captured sense of once youthful raptures and carefree high
spirits.

The pace seems to gather speed as Juan is caught up (as Byron
himself had been) a figure in the whirl of the fashionable 'great
world', the dizzying round.

> In the great world, – which, being interpreted,
>   Meaneth the west or worst end of a city,
> And about twice two thousand people bred
>   By no means to be very wise or witty,
> But to sit up while others lie in bed,

----

[1] Canto XI, Stanza XVII.   [2] Canto XI, Stanza XIV.

And look down on the universe with pity, –
Juan, as an inveterate patrician,
Was well received by persons of condition.[1]

But Juan was a bachelor – of arts,
    And parts, and hearts: he danced and sung, and had
An air as sentimental as Mozart's
    Softest of melodies; and could be sad
Or cheerful, without any 'flaws or starts,'
    Just at the proper time; and, though a lad,
Had seen the world – which is a curious sight,
And very much unlike what people write.[2]

Then dress, then dinner, then awakes the world!
    Then glare the lamps, then whirl the wheels, then roar
Through street and square fast-flashing chariots, hurl'd
    Like harness'd meteors; then along the floor
Chalk mimics painting; then festoons are twirl'd;
    Then roll the brazen thunders of the door,
Which opens to the thousand happy few
An earthly paradise of 'or-molu'.

There stands the noble hostess, nor shall sink
    With the three-thousandth curtsey; there the waltz,
The only dance which teaches girls to think,
    Makes one in love even with its very faults.
Saloon, room, hall, o'erflow beyond their brink,
    And long the latest of arrivals halts,
'Midst royal dukes and dames condemn'd to climb,
And gain an inch of staircase at a time.[3]

But this won't do, save by and by; and he
    Who, like Don Juan, takes an active share,
Must steer with care through all that glittering sea
    Of gems and plumes and pearls and silks, to where
He deems it is his proper place to be;
    Dissolving in the waltz to some soft air,
Or proudlier prancing with mercurial skill
Where Science marshals forth her own quadrille.

[1] Canto XI, Stanza XLV.   [2] Canto XI, Stanza XLVII.
[3] Canto XI, Stanzas LXVI–LXVII.

Or, if he dance not, but hath higher views
 Upon an heiress or his neighbour's bride,
Let him take care that that which he pursues
 Is not at once too palpably descried.
Full many an eager gentleman oft rues
 His haste: impatience is a blundering guide
Amongst a people famous for reflection,
Who like to play the fool with circumspection.

But, if you can contrive, get next at supper;
 Or, if forestall'd, get opposite and ogle: –
Oh, ye ambrosial moments! always upper
 In mind, a sort of sentimental bogle,
Which sits for ever upon memory's crupper,
 The ghost of vanish'd pleasures once in vogue! Ill
Can tender souls relate the rise and fall
Of hopes and fears which shake a single ball.[1]

The gay humour and amusement – not merely nostalgia or con-
tempt – with which these past scenes are evoked seem again to
arise from the poet's new-found detachment from them. Such a
tone and attitude towards that world have clearly been made
possible for him by a sense of liberation from it – from the
oppressive conventionalities and falsities underlying its dazzling,
glittering surface, its sparkling effervescence. He can recall it now
with a certain enjoyment and zest as a remembered brilliant
spectacle, with a delight in its absurdities, because he is at last
himself freed from it. He no longer regards it as anything of real
worth and therefore no longer takes it (or himself) seriously, as it
takes itself. He is no longer deceived by the bright illusion of it.
He can be humorously or satirically critical of it in retrospect as a
comedy world. He can now all the more freely relish his memories
of it, even in some degree regret, naturally enough, the vanishing
of what had once been a portion of his own youth. These vividly
recalled past scenes are rapidly sketched in what appears to be
improvised, finely careless verse, happy-go-lucky rhyming and
easy, familiar colloquial language which all together combine to
produce an effect of humorous irreverence towards their subject-
matter. But it is after all merely 'the great world' that is being

[1] Canto XI, Stanzas LXIX–LXXI.

gaily and wittily insulted or shocked. In the midst of the comic
flow there is, indeed, here and there an occasional momentary
assumption or resumption of the earlier Romantic Byron's
lordly grandeur of attitude, disdainful or indignant tone. But
these elements are now absorbed into the complex whole which is
Byron's middle-aged humorous version of *contemptus mundi*.
There are, he observes, perpetually shifting, changing fashions in
poetry itself as in everything else. The personal familiar reminis-
cent note comes out again particularly pleasantly in the stanzas in
Canto XI about the poets, his contemporaries. He can regard
humorously his own displacement from among the poets of the
age – 'the eighty greatest living poets' who are never the same
ones for long, in fashionable favour.

> Even I – albeit I'm sure I did not know it,
>   Nor sought of foolscap subjects to be king, –
> Was reckon'd, a considerable time,
>   The grand Napoleon of the realms of rhyme.[1]

> Sir Walter reign'd before me; Moore and Campbell
>   Before and after; but now, grown more holy,
> The Muses upon Sion's hill must ramble
>   With poets almost clergymen, or wholly;
> And Pegasus hath a psalmodic amble
>   Beneath the very Reverend Rowley Powley.[2]

But the essence of Byron's complex feeling about the world he
had known, and that had already vanished with his youth, is
expressed most memorably in the *tempus fugit* stanzas with which
Canto XI culminates.

> 'Where is the world?' cries Young, at *eighty* – 'Where
>   The world in which a man was born?' Alas!
> Where is the world of *eight* years past? *'T was there* –
>   I look for it – 't is gone, a globe of glass!
> Crack'd, shiver'd, vanish'd, scarcely gazed on, ere
>   A silent change dissolves the glittering mass.
> Statesmen, chiefs, orators, queens, patriots, kings,
> And dandies, all are gone on the wind's wings.

[1] Canto XI, Stanza LV.   [2] Canto XI, Stanza LVII.

Where is Napoleon the Grand? God Knows:
   Where little Castlereagh? The devil can tell:
Where Grattan, Curran, Sheridan, all those
   Who bound the bar or senate in their spell?
Where is the unhappy Queen, with all her woes?
   And where the Daughter, whom the Isles loved well?
Where are those martyr'd saints the Five per Cents.?
And where – oh, where the devil are the rents?

Where's Brummel? Dish'd. Where's Long Pole Wellesley?
                                                  Diddled.
   Where's Whitbread? Romilly? Where's George the
                                                  Third?
Where is his will? (That's not so soon unriddled.)
   And where is 'Fum' the Fourth, our 'royal bird?'
Gone down, it seems, to Scotland, to be fiddled
   Unto by Sawney's violin, we have heard:
'Caw me, caw thee' – for six months hath been hatching
This scene of royal itch and loyal scratching.

Where is Lord This? And where my Lady That?
   The Honourable Mistresses and Misses?
Some laid aside like an old opera-hat,
   Married, unmarried, and remarried: (this is
An evolution oft perform'd of late.)
   Where are the Dublin shouts – and London hisses?
Where are the Grenvilles? Turn'd, as usual. Where
My friends the Whigs? Exactly where they were.[1]

and so on, through half-a-dozen brilliant stanzas more, con-
cluding:

But 'carpe diem,' Juan, 'carpe, carpe!'
   To-morrow sees another race as gay
And transient, and devour'd by the same harpy.
   'Life's a poor player,' – then 'play out the play,
Ye villains!' and above all keep a sharp eye
   Much less on what you do than what you say:
Be hypocritical, be cautious, be
Not what you *seem*, but always what you *see*.[2]

---

[1] Canto XI, Stanzas LXXV–LXXVIII.   [2] Canto XI, Stanza LXXXV.

The Mutability theme, of course, had run through Byron's youthful Romantic rhetoric. But here, in the *Don Juan* humorous conversational mode, the theme is as deeply and sincerely felt by a more experienced and mature mind. In fact it may be said that here again the *Don Juan* mode incorporates the earlier Byronic Romantic attitudes together with his now dominent anti-Romantic attitudes in a much more complex and varied poetry. The line, for example,

> Where is the unhappy Queen with all her woes

with its heroic ring might, taken by itself, have come from one of the Romantic poems. There are also occasional lines or phrases that are in resonance with Shelley (at least the Shelley of *The Mask of Anarchy*) not only in subject-matter but in their lofty tone of indignation at hypocrisy, injustice, tyranny and oppression.

> I have seen the people ridden o'er like sand
> By slaves on horseback.[1]

But these lines have now their context in the complex whole, with its many varying notes, a full mature expression of Byron's mature personality.

VIII

The mercenary side of the 'great world' shows through the comedy and is exposed in Canto XII. We are taken into some of the intricacies of aristocratic 'London life', the match-making and the gossip and scandal that accompany it, particularly as these involve the young heiress or eligible bachelor. But first, expressed in the opening stanzas of the canto, we have the recognition that money (not love) rules the world, the political world as well as the social. ('Who hold the balance of the world?' The answer is the financiers.) But money, we discover, also rules love. Though Jane Austen, too, shows something of this in her society (as do her 18th century predecessors), Byron here anticipates Dickens's grimmer exhibition of the money-power in his contemporary England, its deadly blight on individual human lives. Byron can still afford, however, to treat the subject with a lighter irony,

[1] Canto XI, Stanza LXXXIV.

though with clear unenchanted knowledge. (Avarice, he says with irony, is one of the few substantial pleasures left to middle age. 'Why call the miser miserable?' 'The frugal life is his.' He is as ascetic as the saint or cynic. But he has power over the world and all that is in it.

> While he, despising every sensual call,
> Commands – the intellectual lord of all.[1]

'He is your only poet.' He lives by the imagination. 'What visions spring from each cheese-paring.')

This introduces the main subject of this canto – the matrimonial market, the love-making and match-making of 'the great world' of aristocratic society as Byron had known it, its worldliness, hardness, heartlessness and cynicism. The subject-matter and its treatment as high-spirited comedy anticipate the James of *The Awkward Age* and his other comedies critical of English high life in his time. The tone of *entre nous* chatter, for example, is perfectly caught, caught up (in Byron) in the verse and rhyming which has a further enlivening and animating effect.

> Quicksilver small talk, ending (if you note it)
> With the kind world's amen – 'Who would have thought it?'[2]

> How all the needy honourable misters,
>   Each out-at-elbow peer, or desperate dandy,
> The watchful mothers, and the careful sisters
>   (Who, by the by, when clever, are more handy
> At making matches, where ''t is gold that glisters,'
>   Than their *he* relatives), like flies o'er candy
> Buzz round '*the* fortune' with their busy battery,
> To turn her head with waltzing and with flattery![3]

> Some are soon bagg'd, and some reject three dozen.
>   'T is fine to see them scattering refusals
> And wild dismay o'er every angry cousin
>   (Friends of the party), who begin accusals
> Such as – 'Unless Miss (Blank) meant to have chosen
>   Poor Frederick, why did she accord perusals

---

[1] Canto XII, Stanza IX.   [2] Canto XII, Stanza XXVI.
[3] Canto XII, Stanza XXXII.

To his billets? *Why* waltz with him? Why, I pray,
Look *yes* last night, and yet say *no* to-day?

'Why? – Why? – Besides, Fred really was *attach'd*;
　'T was not her fortune – he has enough without:
The time will come she'll wish that she had snatch'd
　So good an opportunity, no doubt: –
But the old marchioness some plan had hatch'd,
　As I'll tell Aurea at to-morrow's rout:
And, after all, poor Frederick may do better –
Pray did you see her answer to his letter?'

Smart uniforms and sparkling coronets
　Are spurn'd in turn, until her turn arrives,
After much loss of time, and hearts, and bets
　Upon the sweepstakes for substantial wives;
And when at last the pretty creature gets
　Some gentleman, who fights, or writes, or drives,
It soothes the awkward squad of the rejected
To find how very badly she selected.[1]

This is the world which Leila (the child whom Juan rescued, adopted as his daughter and brought to England) is now growing up into, a young Oriental-type beauty and also 'a good match'. Consequently

　　So first there was a generous emulation,
　　　And then there was a general competition
　　To undertake the orphan's education.[2]

– rivalry also as to who shall 'bring her out' when the time comes. Her education has, therefore, to be 'an education for the world' (unlike, if we remember, Juan's own education which proved to have deficiencies in this respect). For such an education Juan sensibly chooses, as the child's mentor, one who has herself in her time had experience of the world (Lady Pinchbeck) and may therefore be supposed to know how to put her innocent charge on guard against its perils and deceptions. This was again to be one of James's subjects. The character of the Lady Pinchbeck (brilliantly and wittily sketched in stanzas XLII et seq.)

[1] Canto XII, Stanzas XXXIV–XXXVI.　　[2] Canto XII, Stanza XXX.

anticipates, in its broader outlines, James's veterans of the world (in the long line from Pope and earlier).

But we are now to be shown Juan himself (not only his adopted daughter) as having become (as Byron had been) 'a match', largely unconscious of being so, of course, and of the risks he is running.

> Perhaps you'll have a letter from the mother,
> To say her daughter's feelings are trepann'd;
> Perhaps you'll have a visit from the brother,
> All strut, and stays, and whiskers, to demand
> What 'your intentions are?' – One way or other
> It seems the virgin's heart expects your hand:
> And between pity for her case and yours,
> You'll add to Matrimony's list of cures.[1]

The traps and pitfalls in such a deceiving world may be disastrous for the young and innocent – especially the girl – in 'this moral nation'.

> But in old England, when a young bride errs,
> Poor thing! Eve's was a trifling case to hers.[2]

Only the expert in this kind of complicated game, with its complicated rules and conventions, can expect to cheat disaster.

> But they who blunder thus are raw beginners;
> A little genial sprinkling of hypocrisy
> Has saved the fame of thousand splendid sinners,
> The loveliest oligarchs of our gynocracy;
> You may see such at all the balls and dinners,
> Among the proudest of our aristocracy,
> So gentle, charming, charitable, chaste –
> And all by having *tact* as well as taste.[3]

But Byron notes that human nature itself, at all ages, even the well-brought-up English girl, is explosive and unpredictable.

> And if in fact she takes to a 'grande passion,'
> It is a very serious thing indeed:
> Nine times in ten 't is but caprice or fashion,

---

[1] Canto XII, Stanza LX.   [2] Canto XII, Stanza LXIV.
[3] Canto XII, Stanza LXVI.

> Coquetry, or a wish to take the lead,
>   The pride of a mere child with a new sash on,
>   Or wish to make a rival's bosom bleed:
>   But the tenth instance will be a tornado,
>   For there's no saying what they will or may do.[1]

In this way Byron holds up the unflattering mirror of truth not only to 'that microcosm on stilts . . . the Great World' but to 'this moral nation' as a whole.

> But now I'm going to be immoral; now
>   I mean to show things really as they are.[2]

To 'this moral nation' it is 'immoral', it seems, to 'show things as they really are'. But how 'moral' is 'this moral nation' is the question which, we may say, Byron's poem now asks that nation to ask itself.

IX

In Canto XIII the scene of the comedy shifts, with the end of the London season, to the country. The house party that assembles in the great country house is again 'the great world' that re-assembles there, outside the season, as in other of the great houses throughout the land. There, in this typically English setting of the great house and its landscape garden in the heart of the English country, the comedy of English aristocratic life goes on through the remaining completed cantos of *Don Juan* (Cantos XIII–XVI).

The canto opens on the familiar personal note once again.

> I now mean to be serious; – it is time,
>   Since laughter now-a-days is deem'd too serious.
> A jest at Vice by Virtue 's call'd a crime.[3]

The announcement is, of course, not entirely not serious. The tone continues to be light, but in these English cantos (beginning already with the London cantos) there builds up a substantial comedy that amounts to a formidable criticism of aspects of English life. The apparently casual references to 'Rough Johnson,

---

[1] Canto XII, Stanza LXXVII.   [2] Canto XII, Stanza XL.
[3] Canto XIII, Stanza I.

the great moralist', although 'Perhaps the fine old fellow spoke in jest' and to Cervantes, who in *Don Quixote* 'smiled Spain's chivalry away', are among the hints which suggest that Byron would have his comedy of English life understood to have, perhaps, a weighty import for all its lightness of tone. A further reason for its being a time to be serious – though not too serious – is his recognition again here in these opening stanzas, as recurrently through the whole poem, that he is now middle-aged.

> While those who are not beginners should have sense
>   Enough to make for port, ere time shall summon
> With his grey signal-flag; and the past tense,
>   The dreary *'fuimus'* of all things human,
> Must be declined, while life's thin thread's spun out
> Between the gaping heir and gnawing gout.[1]

After youth and love (romantic love) are past there remains, then, middle age. Though middle age is a condition to which we should not (he suggests) attach too much importance or in which we should not attach too much importance to ourselves (as the pompous middle-aged are prone to do) it does provide a new viewpoint on human life. Byron has, of course, no illusions about the middle-aged state himself. (There is irony, in the context, in the phrase 'walk in wisdom's ways'.)

> And after that serene and somewhat dull
>   Epoch, that awkward corner turn'd for days
> More quiet, when our moon's no more at full,
>   We may presume to criticise or praise;
> Because indifference begins to lull
>   Our passions, and we walk in wisdom's ways;
> Also because the figure and the face
> Hint, that 't is time to give the younger place.[2]

There are those, however, – including the great public figures on the world's stage – who would postpone the inevitable decline or at least compensate by private indulgences or by occupying themselves with various public affairs.

> But then they have their claret and madeira
>   To irrigate the dryness of decline;

[1] Canto XIII, Stanza XL.   [2] Canto XIII, Stanza IV.

And county meetings, and the parliament,
And debt, and what not, for their solace sent.
And is there not religion, and reform,
    Peace, war, the taxes, and what's call'd the 'Nation!'
The struggle to be pilots in a storm!
    The landed and the money'd speculation?[1]

The references in these last lines to the affairs of 'the Nation'
begin to invoke the great public figure, the English great lord as
county magnate and political personage. Such a one presently
makes his appearance in the poem, Lord Henry Amundeville,
together with his wife, the Lady Adeline (who is evidently
destined to play a complicating part in Juan's English misadven-
tures). The poet sees himself as, on the contrary, reduced in his
middle age to being 'a mere spectator':

For my part, I am but a mere spectator.

In these words Byron (with a modesty of tone that contrasts with
his youthful Romantic arrogance) indicates his relation to the
comedy he can now detachedly observe and represent, as no
longer a participant. In that comedy of English aristocratic life the
presiding presences (as host and hostess to their country house
party) are, throughout the remaining cantos, Lord Henry and his
wife, Lady Adeline. The latter begins, in these remaining cantos,
to unfold as the more interesting of the two, more interesting as a
psychological study. The initial sketches of Adeline and of her
husband, Lord Henry (in that order), are introduced as if casually
in Canto XIII in the flow of the poet's talk. The sketches are then
filled in and developed in the succeeding cantos into a larger and
fuller portrait of (as they at first seem) a typical English patrician
couple.

Chaste was she, to detraction's desperation,
    And wedded unto one she had loved well –
A man known in the councils of the nation,
    Cool, and quite English, imperturbable,
Though apt to act with fire upon occasion,
    Proud of himself and her: the world could tell

<hr>

[1] Canto XIII, Stanzas V–VI.

Nought against either, and both seem'd secure –
She in her virtue, he in his hauteur.[1]

Lord Henry has, of course, his house in town.

Lord Henry's mansion was in Blank-Blank Square.[2]

It is better to keep the name anonymous (Byron 'explains') to avoid any risk of its being touched by any of the scandals that so frequently rock the 'best society'.

Such I might stumble over unawares,
Unless I knew the very chastest squares.[3]

But the effect of the repeated 'Blank-Blank Square' inevitably further suggests a blankness about the appearance, perhaps not only the outward appearance, of the house and of its London square (cf. Dickens's mansions of the moneyed genteel middle class in his London).

There are hints already in these first sketches that Adeline might (as she begins to do in the succeeding cantos) break out of her portrait as simply a type, hints that there is an individual woman behind the façade of her rank and position, her social and public role as the correct, the perfect wife of Lord Henry.

There also was of course in Adeline
That calm patrician polish in the address,
Which ne'er can pass the equinoctial line
Of any thing which nature would express;
Just as a mandarin finds nothing fine, –
At least his manner suffers not to guess
That any thing he views can greatly please.
Perhaps we have borrow'd this from the Chinese.[4]

But Adeline was not indifferent: for
(*Now* for a common-place!) beneath the snow,
As a volcano holds the lava more
Within – *et caetera*. Shall I go on? – No!
I hate to hunt down a tired metaphor,
So let the often-used volcano go.

[1] Canto XIII, Stanza XIV. [2] Canto XIII, Stanza XXV.
[3] Canto XIII, Stanza XXVI. [4] Canto XIII, Stanza XXXIV.

Poor thing! How frequently, by me and others,
It hath been stirr'd up till its smoke quite smothers!

I'll have another figure in a trice: –
    What say you to a bottle of champagne?
Frozen into a very vinous ice,
    Which leaves few drops of that immortal rain,
Yet in the very centre, past all price,
    About a liquid glassful will remain;
And this is stronger than the strongest grape
Could e'er express in its expanded shape.[1]

The tone here is, of course, light and flippant. But there is what
promises to be (in the succeeding cantos begins to be) a subtle
psychological study, as in a novel. In these final cantos it becomes
transparent that Adeline, the correct lady and correct wife, is
another who but imperfectly knows herself, imperfectly under-
stands what is happening to her or the exact nature of her
developing feelings for Juan. But this is of course to anticipate –
although it is to anticipate what might be guessed from the
initial sketches.

To return to the 'action' of the Juan story there is first in
Canto XIII the sudden exhilarating sense of the break-up at the
end of the London season, the excitement and movement of the
departure of 'the great world' for its country seats, the prelude to
the change of scene for the comedy. As the carriage of Lord
Henry and Lady Adeline sweeps proudly away with the stream of
other carriages it seems to brush aside debts to tradesmen, the
tradesmen themselves and other disagreeables with what seems
insolent and cynical disregard for 'the lower orders' – for, in fact,
the human cares and needs of indigent people dependent for their
livelihoods on the favours of the great.

And tradesmen, with long bills and longer faces
Sigh – as the postboys fasten on the traces.

But these are trifles. Downward flies my lord,
    Nodding beside my lady in his carriage.
Away! away! 'Fresh horses!' are the word,
    And changed as quickly as hearts after marriage.[2]

                    [1] Canto XIII, Stanzas XXXVI–XXXVII.
                    [2] Canto XIII, Stanzas XLIV, XLVI.

Once again Byron expresses the cynicism of the aristocratic order
to which he belongs – or had belonged – a cynicism which as an
individual of generous human sympathies he does not share. That
he does not share the cynicism comes out in the irony with which
he notes that the announcements of social events of 'the great
world' take precedence in the newspapers over the lists of killed
and wounded.

> 'We understand the splendid host intends
>   To entertain, this autumn, a select
> And numerous party of his noble friends;
>   'Midst whom, we have heard from sources quite correct,
> The Duke of D—— the shooting season spends,
>   With many more by rank and fashion deck'd;
> Also a foreigner of high condition,
> The envoy of the secret Russian mission.'. . .[1]
>
> 'T is odd, but true, – last war the news abounded
> More with these dinners than the kill'd or wounded; –
>
> As thus: 'On Thursday there was a grand dinner;
>   Present, Lords A. B. C.' – Earls, dukes, by name
> Announced with no less pomp than victory's winner:
>   Then underneath, and in the very same
> Column: date, 'Falmouth. There has lately been here
>   The slap-dash regiment, so well known to fame;
> Whose loss in the late action we regret:
> The vacancies are fill'd up – see *Gazette*.'[2]

Norman Abbey is, of course, Newstead recollected in Italy.
The beautiful Gothic place with its landscape garden setting
(Romantic rather than 18th century) is the remembered place of
Byron's youth in the mellowing light of affectionate memory.
The description through many delightful stanzas (stanzas LV et
seq.) is essentially serious in mood, responding to the Romantic
picturesque Gothic appeal of the place, though done with a light
touch as in some of the sketches and the water-colours of the
period. There is an absence here of the heavy Romantic rhetorical
melancholy. Equally (though conversational in tone) there is an
absence here of the comic or satiric – unless in an occasional
touch –

[1] Canto XIII, Stanza LII.   [2] Canto XIII, Stanzas LIII–LIV.

> it lies perhaps a little low,
> Because the monks preferr'd a hill behind,
> To shelter their devotion from the wind.[1]

which may, perhaps, be an echo of Pope's

> a lake behind
> Improves the keenness of the northern wind.

It is the diverse mixed company assembled there who provide the comedy. There is, of course, throughout these final cantos an element of burlesque of Gothicism and there are resemblances in this and in other respects (as well as differences) to Peacock's *Nightmare Abbey* and to Jane Austen's *Northanger Abbey*.

The important part 'the great house' and its civilization have played in English civilization as a whole has inevitably been reflected throughout English literature. We need only recall Ben Jonson's *To Penshurst* and Marvell's *Appleton House*. Pope's Timon's Villa is, of course, the great house and its formal gardens (in this case the much too great house and the much too formal gardens) as the kind of thing they should not be, outsize, disproportionate, ostentatious, inhuman (e.g. nature violated in the too formal garden

> 'The suffering eye inverted nature sees.').

But Pope's viewpoint in this satiric poetry is that of a poet who had positive ideals of what the great house and garden should and could be in the English country, an ideal of humane and civilized living (as well as a feeling for landscape gardening and domestic architecture). Jane Austen's perceptively critical appreciation of the late 18th-century civilization of Mansfield Park – a civilization tending to become rigidified – belongs in this line. We can, indeed, trace the line right through George Eliot to James's equally perceptive critical appreciation of the civilization of the English great house in its latter days when a degenerating philistine or barbarian society is now often to be discovered occupying these beautiful English places. It is in this line that Byron's cantos on the Regency house party at Norman Abbey belong. It is not the beautiful place but the company assembled there that is the subject of Byron's satiric comedy, the people of the Regency 'great

[1] Canto XIII, Stanza LV.

world' in their annual temporary sojourn in the country, their annual displacement from London. It does seem a displacement for the Regency aristocracy (as well as for their associated circle and hangers-on) as it would not have seemed, perhaps, for their 18th century and earlier predecessors, whose lives, purposes, interests and responsibilities were firmly based and centred in their country estates. The final cantos certainly suggest this change from the old patriarchal order.

> Society is now one polish'd horde,
> Form'd of two mighty tribes, the *Bores* and *Bored*.[1]

There is also in Byron's description of Norman Abbey a sense of the past, a feeling of the relation of the place to English history from the Middle Ages through the centuries to the Restoration and the 18th century (reminding one that Byron was a contemporary of Scott). The note receives a further emphasis from the portraits in the galleries. With the portraits the note of comedy also returns. The subjects of the portraits are characters in the human comedy through the centuries: their costumes change fantastically but (as Dryden comments on the Canterbury Pilgrims) are recognizably those of English people at all times, and at any time, beneath their various disguises in the human procession.

> Steel barons, molten the next generation
>   To silken rows of gay and garter'd earls,
> Glanced from the walls in goodly preservation:
>   And Lady Marys blooming into girls,
> With fair long locks, had also kept their station:
>   And countesses mature, in robes and pearls:
> Also some beauties of Sir Peter Lely,
> Whose drapery hints we may admire them freely.[2]

They are all, of course, portraits of the great and their ladies, Judges, Bishops, Generals, massive public characters who pass in the slow procession through time and look down now on their living Regency counterparts and successors in the continuing human comedy.

The guests now assembling in the great house, the guests of

---

[1] Canto XIII, Stanza XLV.   [2] Canto XIII, Stanza LXVIII.

the present, are themselves ripe fruits of time in the English autumn country scene, amidst its abundance and plenty, stored for their exclusive enjoyment.

> The mellow autumn came, and with it came
>   The promised party, to enjoy its sweets.
> The corn is cut, the manor full of game;
>   The pointer ranges, and the sportsman beats
> In russet jacket: – lynx-like in his aim;
>   Full grows his bag, and wonder*ful* his feats.
> Ah, nut-brown partridges! Ah, brilliant pheasants!
> And ah, ye poachers! – 'T is no sport for peasants.
>
> An English autumn, though it hath no vines,
>   Blushing with Bacchant coronals along
> The paths, o'er which the fair festoon entwines
>   The red grape in the sunny lands of song,
> Hath yet a purchased choice of choicest wines;
>   The claret light, and the madeira strong.
> If Britain mourn her bleakness, we can tell her,
> The very best of vineyards is the cellar.[1]

Thus the comedy of Regency English high life is viewed in the perspective of historical time and also in relation to the cosmopolitan world. The comparison of the English autumn with the Italian is not here fortuitous and is here equally appreciative of both lands.

The guests are then listed and presented.

> The noble guests, assembled at the Abbey,
>   Consisted of – we give the sex the *pas* –
> The Duchess of Fitz-Fulke; the Countess Crabby;
>   The Ladies Scilly, Busey; – Miss Eclat,
> Miss Bombazeen, Miss Mackstay, Miss O'Tabby.[2]

Byron's Regency mixed assemblage is noticeably similar to those of Peacock's novels and (as in Peacock) includes a Scottish and Irish admixture (e.g. the two 'wits', 'Longbow from Ireland, Strongbow from the Tweed').

---

[1] Canto XIII, Stanzas LXXV–LXXVI.   [2] Canto XIII, Stanza LXXIX.

There was the young bard Rackrhyme, who had newly
    Come out and glimmer'd as a six weeks' star.
There was Lord Pyrrho, too, the great freethinker;
And Sir John Pottledeep, the mighty drinker.[1]

There was Dick Dubious, the metaphysician,
    Who loved philosophy and a good dinner;
Angle, the soi-disant mathematician;
    Sir Henry Silvercup, the great race-winner.
There was the Reverend Rodomont Precisian,
    Who did not hate so much the sin as sinner;
And Lord Augustus Fitz-Plantagenet,
Good at all things, but better at a bet.

There was Jack Jargon, the gigantic guardsman;
    And General Fireface, famous in the field,
A great tactician, and no less a swordsman,
    Who ate, last war, more Yankees than he kill'd.
There was the waggish Welsh Judge, Jefferies Hardsman,
    In his grave office so completely skill'd,
That when a culprit came for condemnation,
He had his judge's joke for consolation.[2]

Such heterogeneity, bizarre mixture of all sorts of people ('Good
company's a chess-board'), is of the essence of comedy. So, too,
perhaps, is the sense of having nothing much to do, the sense of
time passing slowly, drifting by, the sense of having to devise
ways of passing the time, the sense of infinite leisure and idleness.
Time often hangs heavy on the hands in the worlds of comedy,
as it seems to do ('under the shade of melancholy boughs') in the
forest in *As You Like It*[3] (and as distinct from farces where the
quick succession of knockabout actions gives us no time to think
of time, producing at least the illusion of a world of desperately
earnest, purposeful action, making 'time run'). The daily round
at Norman Abbey (as it is described) certainly comprehends a
variety of ways of filling in time. But boredom, *ennui*, descends,

---

[1] Canto XIII, Stanza LXXXIV.

[2] Canto XIII, Stanzas LXXXVII–LXXXVIII.

[3] Compare the leisurely opening movement of Marvell's *Coy Mistress* where the
fancy plays with what it would be like supposing we had an amplitude of space and
time as in Eden or the Golden Age, supposing time did not, as in fact it does, press.

at least among the many guests whose youthful zest has gone, the middle-aged and the elderly. It is a sad picture.

> The gentlemen got up betimes to shoot,
>   Or hunt: the young, because they liked the sport —
> The first thing boys like, after play and fruit;
>   The middle-aged, to make the day more short;
> For *ennui* is a growth of English root,
>   Though nameless in our language: — we retort
> The fact for words, and let the French translate
> That awful yawn which sleep can not abate.

> The elderly walk'd through the library,
>   And tumbled books, or criticised the pictures,
> Or saunter'd through the gardens piteously,
>   And made upon the hot-house several strictures,
> Or rode a nag which trotted not too high,
>   Or on the morning papers read their lectures,
> Or on the watch their longing eyes would fix,
> Longing at sixty for the hour of six.[1]

The ladies are in not much better case, at least in the daytime, jaded in the mornings. They are very apparently town ladies of the leisured class.

> The ladies — some rouged, some a little pale —
>   Met the morn as they might. If fine, they rode,
> Or walk'd; if foul, they read, or told a tale,
>   Sung, or rehearsed the last dance from abroad;
> Discuss'd the fashion which might next prevail,
>   And settled bonnets by the newest code,
> Or cramm'd twelve sheets into one little letter,
> To make each correspondent a new debtor.[2]

The evenings — the long evenings — are described:

> With evening came the banquet and the wine;
>   The conversazione; the duet,
> Attuned by voices more or less divine
>   (My heart or head aches with the memory yet).
> The four Miss Rawbolds in a glee would shine;
>   But the two youngest loved more to be set

---

[1] Canto XIII, Stanzas CI–CII.   [2] Canto XIII, Stanza CIV.

Down to the harp – because to music's charms
They added graceful necks, white hands and arms.

Sometimes a dance (though rarely on field-days,
    For then the gentlemen were rather tired)
Display'd some sylph-like figures in its maze;
    Then there was small-talk ready when required;
Flirtation – but decorous; the mere praise
    Of charms that should or should not be admired.
The hunters fought their fox-hunt o'er again,
And then retreated soberly – at ten.

The politicians, in a nook apart,
    Discuss'd the world, and settled all the spheres;
The wits watch'd every loop-hole for their art,
    To introduce a bon-mot head and ears:
Small is the rest of those who would be smart,
    A moment's good thing may have cost them years
Before they find an hour to introduce it,
And then, even *then*, some bore may make them lose it.

But all was gentle and aristocratic
    In this our party; polish'd, smooth, and cold,
As Phidian forms cut out of marble Attic.
    There now are no Squire Westerns, as of old;
And our Sophias are not so emphatic,
    But fair as then, or fairer to behold:
We have no accomplish'd blackguards, like Tom Jones,
But gentlemen in stays, as stiff as stones.[1]

The impression is of 'a society' for the most part not at home in
the country, out of place there, a social life without purpose and
(except for the very young who can enjoy themselves anywhere)
without zest. To some extent this is no doubt simply Byron's
expression of one of his own middle-aged moods. The world is
never what it was when we were young. He brings in the contrast
with the robust, warm-blooded vitality of Fielding's 18th-century
English squires and their sons and daughters. English high
society (as he portrays it in these lines) has become dully decorous

[1] Canto XIII, Stanzas CVII–CX.

and coldly formal – a neo-Classic contrast to the Gothic place. Byron's personal revolt against English conventionality may have affected the picture here. But perhaps he (being wonderfully skilful) designs the scene to be really not altogether believable, to prepare for the effect, in the cantos to follow, of the social surface about to be cracked by some scandal. Something (we are certainly made to feel) must happen, human nature being what underneath it is, something (comically) outrageous, scandalous. Some lively spirit, some natural creature, must break bounds to break the deadening monotony and contribute to the gaiety of nations with some comic catastrophe.

X

In this social state of things it would be surprising if there did not develop 'a situation' and if it did not involve, once again, Juan. It does so, in Cantos XIV and XV, through the presence among the heterogeneous guests of the scandalous Duchess of Fitz-Fulke ('her frolic Grace') and her noticeable attentions to Juan. 'The situation' also involves, in no simple way, their hostess, Adeline. Further, there is drawn into 'the situation' Miss Aurora Raby, a pleasant unattached girl with whom Juan begins to form a genuine attachment. This attachment (we have reason to apprehend) will be threatened by 'the situation' as it develops or as disaster is precipitated by some 'folly' of the Duchess of Fitz-Fulke. The irony is that none of these characters really knows what is happening to them or what they are about, except the Duchess of Fitz-Fulke.

But it is Adeline's complicated state of mind, rather than 'the situation', which in these cantos is the subject of what begins to be a psychological study of some interest and insight (indicating explosive materials beneath Adeline's wonderful social surface). This is a subject – inner states of mind – that is more fully explored in the greater 19th-century novels (as in Shakespeare). But Byron recognizes this psychological subject, though it is not his intention in his comedy to explore it deeply but rather – by means of irony – to hint at its depths.

> 'T is sad to hack into the roots of things,
> They are so much intertwisted with the earth . . .

> To trace all actions to their secret springs
>   Would make indeed some melancholy mirth.[1]

He makes this plain enough again in the concluding stanzas of
Canto XIV.

> 'T is strange, – but true; for truth is always strange;
>   Stranger than fiction: if it could be told,
> How much would novels gain by the exchange!
>   How differently the world would men behold!
> How oft would vice and virtue places change!
>   The new world would be nothing to the old,
> If some Columbus of the moral seas
> Would show mankind their souls' antipodes.

> What 'antres vast and deserts idle' then
>   Would be discover'd in the human soul!
> What icebergs in the hearts of mighty men,
>   With self-love in the centre as their pole!
> What Anthropophagi are nine of ten
>   Of those who hold the kingdoms in control!
> Were things but only call'd by their right name,
> Caesar himself would be ashamed of fame.[2]

Canto XIV resumes (in its opening stanzas) the flow of Byron's
personal talk, personal commentary on life and light play of
philosophical ideas.

> Nothing more true than *not* to trust your senses;
> And yet what are your other evidences?[3]

The reader is drawn again into an intimate familiar relationship
with the poet talking. In the course of the talk the Juan tale is, as
if casually, resumed and borne along on the stream.

In the daily (and nightly) round of the great country house
party Juan continues at the height of his brilliant social success in
England, the gay attractive young foreigner and accomplished
gentleman, who has the art of living in all climes with ease. He
is still, however, not like the Don Juan of tradition:

[1] Canto XIV, Stanza LIX.   [2] Canto XIV, Stanzas CI–CII.
                [3] Canto XIV, Stanza II.

His manner was perhaps the more seductive,
  Because he ne'er seem'd anxious to seduce;
Nothing affected, studied, or constructive
  Of coxcombery or conquest.[1]

At dancing, of course, he excels Englishmen.

And then he danced; – all foreigners excel.[2]

It is not surprising, therefore, that he is especially attractive to Englishwomen. Nor is it surprising that he becomes involved unawares in a complicated 'situation'. This is brought about by the introduction upon the scene of the amorous, licentious Duchess of Fitz-Fulke, a sensual woman on the largest, fullest, richest scale (in these respects another Empress Catherine the Great).

She was a fine and somewhat full-blown blonde,
  Desirable, distinguish'd, celebrated
For several winters in the grand *grand monde*.
  I'd rather not say what might be related
Of her exploits, for this were ticklish ground:
  Besides there might be falsehood in what's stated:
Her late performance had been a dead set
At Lord Augustus Fitz-Plantagenet.[3]

The names themselves are enough to suggest a couple almost grotesquely large-scale within the relatively small 'great world'. That the Duchess has, of course, also a husband seems a matter of lesser importance. The Duke has the habit of staying conveniently or obligingly out of the way.

Theirs was the best of unions, past all doubt,
  Which never meets, and therefore can't fall out.[4]

The Duchess of Fitz-Fulke's new-found interest in Juan is too public not to be noticed and commented on.

The circle smiled, then whisper'd, and then sneer'd;
  The misses bridled, and the matrons frown'd;

Some hoped things might not turn out as they fear'd;
    Some would not deem such women could be found;
Some ne'er believed one half of what they heard;
    Some look'd perplex'd, and others look'd profound;
And several pitied, with sincere regret,
Poor Lord Augustus Fitz-Plantagenet.[1]

Among those who notice is Adeline, with somewhat undue personal concern. It is thus discovered in the poem that Adeline's feelings towards Juan are more complicated and stronger than she herself knows or understands.

But, oh! that I should ever pen so sad a line!
    Fired with an abstract love of virtue, she,
My Dian of the Ephesians, Lady Adeline,
    Began to think the duchess' conduct free;
Regretting much that she had chosen so bad a line,
    And, waxing chiller in her courtesy,
Look'd grave and pale to see her friend's fragility,
For which most friends reserve their sensibility.

There's nought in this bad world like sympathy:
    'T is so becoming to the soul and face,
Sets to soft music the harmonious sigh,
    And robes sweet friendship in a Brussels lace.
Without a friend, what were humanity,
    To hunt our errors up with a good grace!
Consoling us with – 'Would you had thought twice!
Ah! if you had but follow'd my advice!' . . .[2]

But Juan also shared in her austerity,
    But mix'd with pity, pure as e'er was penn'd:
His inexperience moved her gentle ruth,
And (as her junior by six weeks) his youth.[3]

But Adeline was far from that ripe age,
    Whose ripeness is but bitter at the best:
'T was rather her experience made her sage,
    For she had seen the world and stood its test,
As I have said in – I forget what page.[4]

[1] Canto XIV, Stanza XLIV.   [2] Canto XIV, Stanzas XLVI–XLVII.
[3] Canto XIV, Stanza LI.   [4] Canto XIV, Stanza LIV.

The irony is continued in the stanzas that convey her brief biography – her coming out, marriage and brilliant social and public career and status, virtuous and correct.

> At sixteen she came out; presented, vaunted,
>   She puts all coronets into commotion:
> At seventeen, too, the world was still enchanted
>   With the new Venus of their brilliant ocean:
> At eighteen, though below her feet still panted
>   A hecatomb of suitors with devotion,
> She had consented to create again
> That Adam, call'd 'The happiest of men.'
>
> Since then she had sparkled through three glowing winters,
>   Admired, adored; but also so correct,
> That she had puzzled all the acutest hinters,
>   Without the apparel of being circumspect;
> They could not even glean the slightest splinters
>   From off the marble, which had no defect.[1]

The irony extends to her husband, Lord Henry, when she consults him for advice and counsel on the matter of Juan and the Duchess. That great English public character, statesman, man of affairs, proves comically inadequate on affairs of the human heart. On that complex subject his indifference is matched by his ignorance. He addresses his wife as if he were addressing the House of Lords on state affairs in a succession of clichés and commonplaces.

> And first, in the o'erflowing of the heart,
>   Which really knew or thought it knew no guile,
> She call'd her husband now and then apart,
>   And bade him counsel Juan. With a smile
> Lord Henry heard her plans of artless art
>   To wean Don Juan from the siren's wile;
> And answer'd, like a statesman or a prophet,
> In such guise that she could make nothing of it.
>
> Firstly, he said, 'he never interfered
>   In any body's business but the king's:'
> Next, that 'he never judged from what appear'd,

[1] Canto XIV, Stanzas LV–LVI.

Without strong reason, of those sorts of things:'
Thirdly, that 'Juan had more brain than beard,
    And was not to be held in leading-strings;'
And fourthly, what need hardly be said twice,
'That good but rarely came from good advice.'

And, therefore, doubtless to approve the truth
    Of the last axiom, he advised his spouse
To leave the parties to themselves, forsooth –
    At least as far as *bienséance* allows:
That time would temper Juan's faults of youth;
    That young men rarely made monastic vows;
That opposition only more attaches –
But here a messenger brought in despatches:

And, being of the council called 'the Privy,'
    Lord Henry walk'd into his cabinet,
To furnish matter for some future Livy
    To tell how he reduced the nation's debt;
And if their full contents I do not give ye,
    It is because I do not know them yet;
But I shall add them in a brief appendix,
To come between mine epic and its index.

But ere he went, he added a slight hint,
    Another gentle common-place or two,
Such as are coin'd in conversation's mint,
    And pass, for want of better, though not new:
Then broke his packet, to see what was in 't,
    And having casually glanced it through,
Retired; and, as he went out, calmly kiss'd her,
Less like a young wife than an aged sister.

He was a cold, good, honourable man,
    Proud of his birth, and proud of every thing...

But there was something wanting on the whole –
    I don't know what, and therefore cannot tell –
Which pretty women – the sweet souls! – call *soul*.
    Certes it was not body; he was well
Proportion'd, as a poplar or a pole,
    A handsome man, that human miracle;

And in each circumstance of love or war
Had still preserved his perpendicular.[1]

So Adeline is left much where she is and where exactly that is it is
clear she does not know.

She knew not her own heart; then how should I?
    I think not she was *then* in love with Juan:
If so, she would have had the strength to fly
    The wild sensation, unto her a new one:
She merely felt a common sympathy
    (I will not say it was a false or true one)
In him, because she thought he was in danger, –
Her husband's friend, her own, young, and a stranger,

She was, or thought she was, his friend.[2]

These ironies continue throughout the next canto (Canto XV).
The virtuous Adeline's motives as she actively plans and schemes
to save Juan from the Duchess continue to be obscure to herself.

She 'gan to ponder how to save his soul.

And morally decided, the best state is
For morals, marriage; and, this question carried,
She seriously advised him to get married.[3]

Once Adeline has 'determined Juan's wedding', the whole
problem seems to be reduced to a practical matter (including, of
course, considerations of 'means', according to the advice of
Malthus, 'Thou shalt not marry unless *well*'). The gay comic
opera note returns (as it recurrently does throughout *Don Juan*)
with the list of eligible Misses.

But then, with whom? There was the sage Miss Reading,
    Miss Raw, Miss Flaw, Miss Showman, and Miss Knowman
And the two fair co-heiresses Giltbedding.
    She deem'd his merits something more than common:
All these were unobjectionable matches,
And might go on, if well wound up, like watches.[4]

---

[1] Canto XIV, Stanzas LXV–LXXI.   [2] Canto XIV, Stanzas XCI–XCII.
[3] Canto XV, Stanzas XXVIII–XXIX.   [4] Canto XV, Stanza XL.

There are also Miss Millpond, Miss Audacia Shoestring – and
Aurora Raby?

> Now it so happen'd, in the catalogue
>   Of Adeline, Aurora was omitted.[1]

Aurora, the one whom Juan himself will find truly appealing (and
justly so because of the girl's genuinely good qualities) is dis-
approved of by Adeline, again for obscure reasons, obscure at
least to herself. The real reasons are plain enough. Adeline
instinctively preceives that Aurora will appeal to Juan.

> Why Adeline had this slight prejudice –
>   For prejudice it was – against a creature
> As pure as sanctity itself from vice,
>   With all the added charm of form and feature,
> For me appears a question far too nice,
>   Since Adeline was liberal by nature;
> But nature's nature, and has more caprices
> Than I have time, or will, to take to pieces.
>
> Perhaps she did not like the quiet way
>   With which Aurora on those baubles look'd,
> Which charm most people in their earlier day...
>
> It was not envy – Adeline had none;
>   Her place was far beyond it, and her mind.
> It was not scorn – which could not light on one
>   Whose greatest *fault* was leaving few to find.
> It was not jealousy, I think but shun
>   Following the 'ignes fatui' of mankind.
> It was not – but 't is easier far, alas!
> To say what it was not than what it was.[2]

All considerations, except material ones, seem suddenly dis-
placed by the description in the middle of Canto XV of the great
dinner party, a massive Homeric feast that maintains the comic
epic aspect and scale of the poem. There are the inevitable mock
heroic suggestions –

[1] Canto XV, Stanza XLVIII.   [2] Canto XV, Stanzas LII–LIV.

Great things were now to be achieved at table,
    With massy plate for armour, knives and forks
For weapons[1]

– though the rhyming French names for dishes (as in the earlier cantos Italian names) lighten the description with again a comic operatic note. Byron himself makes it plain he prefers (like Horace) simpler fare, olives and bread, as once

    The grass my table-cloth, in open air,
On Sunium or Hymettus.[2]

These massed material enjoyments, the heavily laden table –

Amidst this tumult of fish, flesh, and fowl[3]

– are rendered the more incongruous by Juan's finding himself in the difficult position of being seated between the watchful Adeline and Aurora. We are thus returned to the human comedy as Juan attempts to win the attention of the latter who remains provokingly cool and 'correct'.

To his gay nothings, nothing was replied,
    Or something which was nothing, as urbanity
Required. Aurora scarcely look'd aside,
    Nor even smiled enough for any vanity.
The devil was in the girl![4]

Aurora (who is 'very young, although so very sage') is however less indifferent to Juan than she seems. There are other things developing beneath the social surface for which as yet Juan is without the clue. It only requires the ingredient of the Gothic supernatural to complicate and further enrich the comedy, intensify the suspense and provide the surprising. The concluding stanzas of Canto XV – a return of the personal note – prepare us for Canto XVI (the last canto to be completed).

The night – I sing by night – sometimes an owl,
    And now and then a nightingale – is dim,
And the loud shriek of sage Minerva's fowl
    Rattles around me her discordant hymn:

[1] Canto XV, Stanza LXII.
[2] Canto XV, Stanza LXXIII.
[3] Canto XV, Stanza LXXIV.
[4] Canto XV, Stanza LXXVIII.

Old portraits from old walls upon me scowl –
   I wish to Heaven they would not look so grim;
The dying embers dwindle in the grate –
I think too that I have sate up too late:

And therefore, though 't is by no means my way
   To rhyme at noon – when I have other things
To think of, if I ever think – I say
   I feel some chilly midnight shudderings,
And prudently postpone, until mid-day,
   Treating a topic which, alas! but brings
Shadows; – but you must be in my condition
Before you learn to call this superstition.

Between two worlds life hovers like a star,
   'Twixt night and morn, upon the horizon's verge.
How little do we know that which we are!
   How less what we may be! The eternal surge
Of time and tide rolls on, and bears afar
   Our bubbles.[1]

The humorous mood suddenly changes into the serious. That final stanza is like a voice from the past, the momentary presence again of the seriously Romantic Byron.

XI

The last completed Canto of *Don Juan* (Canto XVI) is to my mind one of the best. It has in itself a range, variety and liveliness that seem to show that Byron's powers and skill were not declining. A large part of his living whole as a man has gone into this final canto. If the poem had to be broken off, it could not have done so with more dramatic effect than with the climax (or anticlimax that has the effect of a climax) with which the canto (and the whole poem) concludes.

Byron the middle-aged 'philosopher' and comic poet beautifully combine throughout this last canto in the light-hearted interplay on the 'natural' and 'supernatural', the material and the immaterial, the substantial and the insubstantial aspects of the life that is presented, the Gothic monk's ghost discovered, in the final surprise, to be lusty flesh and blood. The allusion in the

[1] Canto XV, Stanzas XCVII–XCIX.

opening stanzas to St. Augustine's belief in the impossible because it is so helps to prepare our minds.

> Who nibble, scribble, quibble, he
> Quiets at once with *'quia impossibile.'*[1]

After the too, too solid Homeric feast described in the preceding canto the company has vanished like ghosts, as if already into the past, melted into air, into thin air.

> The song was silent, and the dance expired:
> The last thin petticoats were vanish'd – gone
>   Like fleecy clouds into the sky retired,
> And nothing brighter gleam'd through the saloon
> Than dying tapers – and the peeping moon.[2]

The poetry here would have appealed to Hardy – though less, perhaps, the Byronic intermixture of humorous irreverence with the sadness.

> The evaporation of a joyous day
> Is like the last glass of champagne.[3]

Certainly the portraits of the dead – among them the living beauties of other days – assume in the moonlight a Hardyesque quality (transmuted from Scott).

> But by dim lights the portraits of the dead
> Have something ghastly, desolate, and dread.

> The forms of the grim knight and pictured saint
>   Look living in the moon; and as you turn
> Backward and forward to the echoes faint
>   Of your own footsteps – voices from the urn
> Appear to wake, and shadows wild and quaint
>   Start from the frames which fence their aspects stern,
> As if to ask how you can dare to keep
> A vigil there, where all but death should sleep.

> And the pale smile of beauties in the grave,
>   The charms of other days, in starlight gleams,
> Glimmer on high; their buried locks still wave
>   Along the canvass; their eyes glance like dreams.[4]

[1] Canto XVI, Stanza V.   [2] Canto XVI, Stanza VIII.
[3] Canto XVI, Stanza IX.   [4] Canto XVI, Stanzas XVII–XIX.

This is, of course, as Juan sees them. He has retired for the night — the Romantic sleepless melancholy lover in the Gothic mansion in the anti-Romantic comedy — ('Below his window waved (of course) a willow.')

> Juan felt somewhat pensive, and disposed
>> For contemplation rather than his pillow:
> The Gothic chamber, where he was enclosed,
>> Let in the rippling sound of the lake's billow,
> With all the mystery by midnight caused:
>> Below his window waved (of course) a willow;
> And he stood gazing out on the cascade
> That flash'd and after darken'd in the shade.[1]

He walks the gallery in the moonlight among the portraits — as in a Gothic romance.

> As Juan mused on mutability,
>> Or on his mistress — terms synonymous —
> No sound except the echo of his sigh
>> Or step ran sadly through that antique house;
> When suddenly he heard, or thought so, nigh,
>> A supernatural agent — or a mouse,
> Whose little nibbling rustle will embarrass
> Most people as it plays along the arras.

> It was no mouse, but lo! a monk, array'd
>> In cowl and beads, and dusky garb, appear'd,
> Now in the moonlight, and now lapsed in shade.[2]

The physical (or metaphysical) problems that this appearance (which glances on him 'a bright eye') presents Juan with are formidable.

> And did he see this? or was it a vapour?

> Once, twice, thrice pass'd, repass'd — the thing of air,
>> Or earth beneath, or heaven, or t' other place,
> And Juan gazed upon it with a stare,
>> Yet could not speak or move; but, on its base
> As stands a statue, stood: he felt his hair
>> Twine like a knot of snakes around his face;

[1] Canto XVI, Stanza XV.   [2] Canto XVI, Stanzas XX–XXI.

He tax'd his tongue for words, which were not granted,
To ask the reverend person what he wanted.

The third time, after a still longer pause,
   The shadow pass'd away – but where? the hall
Was long, and thus far there was no great cause
To think his vanishing unnatural:
Doors there were many, through which, by the laws
   Of physics, bodies whether short or tall
Might come or go; but Juan could not state
Through which the spectre seem'd to evaporate.[1]

He finds it hard to recover his equanimity, to assure himself of
the everyday world:

                he took up an old newspaper;
The paper was right easy to peruse;
He read an article the king attacking,
And a long eulogy of 'patent blacking'.[2]

This savour'd of this world; but his hand shook.

We are returned to the reassuring social world of next day and
next evening – the world also of flirtations – in which Gothicism
is no more than a fashion, a fashion for thrills and shivers, though
it is not surprising that Juan looks all day and evening as if he had
seen a ghost.

   The Duchess of Fitz-Fulke play'd with her veil,
     And look'd at Juan hard.[3]

Adeline renders for her guests the ballad 'Beware! Beware of the
Black Friar' – a ballad sufficiently consciously calculated to be (in
its *Don Juan* context) near burlesque. The songs rendered by the
ladies in the evening are, of course, typically those of the age of
Romantic sentiment.

   Oh! the long evenings of duets and trios!
     The admirations and the speculations;
The 'Mamma Mia's!' and the 'Amor Mio's!'
   The 'Tanti Palpiti's' on such occasions:

[1] Canto XVI, Stanzas XXII–XXIV.   [2] Canto XVI, Stanza XXVI.
         [3] Canto XVI, Stanza XXXI.

The 'Lasciami's,' and quavering 'Addio's!'
    Amongst our own most musical of nations;
With 'Tu mi chamas's' from Portingale,
To soothe our ears, lest Italy should fail.

In Babylon's bravuras – as the home
    Heart-ballads of Green Erin or Grey Highlands,
That bring Lochaber back to eyes that roam
    O'er far Atlantic continents or islands.[1]

A day in the public life of Lord Henry and his Lady follows.
They have their public life also in the country. We could not be
more back in the unghostly mundane sphere. This would be more
reassuring if Lord Henry's public life even in the country were
not so exposible to satiric comedy that leaves us with few illusions
as to its real human worth. Lord Henry is still, of course, main-
taining with grand gestures (in these latter days) his inherited
18th century role and responsibilities as great patriarchal land-
owner, great country gentleman as well as metropolitan states-
man. As a patron and connoisseur of the arts he has, in the course
of the day, to see a picture-dealer about buying a picture and to
see an architect about

New buildings of correctest conformation,
    And throw down old, which he call'd *restoration*.[2]

Then there are his lawyers to see on several vexed matters. Then

There was a prize ox, a prize pig, and ploughman,
    For Henry was a sort of Sabine showman.[3]

Then two poachers are brought before him, as justice of the peace,
and a country girl for the crime of having been made pregnant (a
'poacher upon Nature's manor'). The warm human, democratic
sympathies that occasionally associate Byron with Burns break
through the light comedy tone and idiom here.

Poor soul! for she was country born and bred,
    And knew no better in her immorality
Than to wax white – for blushes are for quality.[4]

[1] Canto XVI, Stanzas XLV–XLVI.   [2] Canto XVI, Stanza LVIII.
[3] Canto XVI, Stanza LX.   [4] Canto XVI, Stanza LXIV.

There is always, of course, for the Lord Henrys within the British Constitution the necessary public duty of electioneering for his Party. There is some acute Byronic political satire here.

> Lord Henry was a great electioneerer,
>> Burrowing for boroughs like a rat or rabbit.
> But county contests cost him rather dearer,
>> Because the neighbouring Scotch Earl of Giftgabbit
> Had English influence, in the self-same sphere here;
>> His son, the Honourable Dick Dicerabbit,
> Was member for the 'other interest' (meaning
> The same self-interest, with a different leaning).

> Courteous and cautious therefore in his country,
>> He was all things to all men, and dispensed
> To some civility, to others bounty,
>> And promises to all – which last commenced
> To gather to a somewhat large amount, he
>> Not calculating how much they condensed;
> But what with keeping some, and breaking others,
> His word had the same value as another's.

> A friend to freedom and freeholders – yet
>> No less a friend to government – he held,
> That he exactly the just medium hit
>> 'Twixt place and patriotism – albeit compell'd,
> Such was his sovereign's pleasure (though unfit,
>> He added modestly, when rebels rail'd),
> To hold some sinecures he wish'd abolish'd,
> But that with them all law would be demolish'd.

> He was 'free to confess' – (whence comes this phrase?
>> Is't English? No – 't is only parliamentary) –
> That innovation's spirit now-a-days
>> Had made more progress than for the last century.
> He would not tread a factious path to praise,
>> Though for the public weal disposed to venture high;
> As for his place, he could but say this of it,
> That the fatigue was greater than the profit.

Heaven, and his friends, knew that a private life
    Had ever been his sole and whole ambition.[1]

The satire has moved easily into parody of parliamentary oratory,
the kind of thing Lord Henry would say and the way he would
say it in his political speeches – self-interest and self-preservation
eloquently disguised (no doubt also from himself) in lofty senti-
ments and phrases about patriotism, love of freedom, reform. In
his 'false position' as reforming Lord –

    To hold some sinecures he wish'd abolish'd –

Byron's Lord Henry in some ways anticipates James's Lord
Warburton. Warburton is, of course, a pleasant, decent and like-
able English gentleman. He is much more sympathetically created
than Lord Henry, with a gentle, subtle, understanding irony, as a
human character. But Warburton is also the English Radical Lord
of a later period who seems politically to be working for his own
abolition (typically English in this as in other respects) and whom
Isabel Archer, as an American girl, feels that to marry would be
too like marrying an institution or marrying into a system.

    The old tradition of free hospitality and entertaining the
tenants is kept up by Lord Henry and Lady Adeline on the weekly
or fortnightly 'public feast' and 'public day'. But the old rustic
custom has become in many ways a strain for all concerned,
everybody out of his sphere and ill-at-ease.

    But 't was a public feast and public day, –
        Quite full, right dull, guests hot, and dishes cold,
    Great plenty, much formality, small cheer,
    And every body out of their own sphere.

    The squires familiarly formal, and
        My lords and ladies proudly condescending;
    The very servants puzzling how to hand
        Their plates – without it might be too much bending
    From their high places by the sideboard's stand –
        Yet, like their masters, fearful of offending.
    For any deviation from the graces
    Might cost both men and masters too – their *places*.

[1] Canto XVI, Stanzas LXX–LXXIV.

There were some hunters bold, and coursers keen,
　　Whose hounds ne'er err'd, nor greyhounds deign'd to
　　　　　　　　　　　　　　　　　　　　　　lurch;
Some deadly shots too, Septembrizers, seen
　　Earliest to rise, and last to quit the search
Of the poor partridge through his stubble screen.
　　There were some massy members of the church,
Takers of tithes, and makers of good matches,
And several who sung fewer psalms than catches.

There were some country wags too – and, alas!
　　Some exiles from the town, who had been driven
To gaze, instead of pavement, upon grass,
　　And rise at nine in lieu of long eleven,
And lo! upon that day it came to pass,
　　I sate next that o'erwhelming son of heaven,
The very powerful parson, Peter Pith,
The loudest wit I e'er was deafen'd with.

I knew him in his livelier London days,
　　A brilliant diner-out, though but a curate;
And not a joke he cut but earn'd its praise,
　　Until preferment, coming at a sure rate,
(O Providence! how wondrous are thy ways!
　　Who would suppose thy gifts sometimes obdurate?)
Gave him, to lay the devil who looks o'er Lincoln,
A fat fen vicarage, and nought to think on.

His jokes were sermons, and his sermons jokes;
　　But both were thrown away amongst the fens;
For wit hath no great friend in aguish folks.
　　No longer ready ears and short-hand pens
Imbibed the gay *bon mot*, or happy hoax:
　　The poor priest was reduced to common sense,
Or to coarse efforts, very loud and long,
To hammer a hoarse laugh from the thick throng.[1]

In this comic sketch of the metamorphosis of the town wit into the country parson, Byron is much more reminiscent of Dryden than of Pope – perhaps consciously so.

[1] Canto XVI, Stanzas LXXVIII–LXXXIII.

To hammer a hoarse laugh from the thick throng.

The line (though not an Alexandrine) sounds like one of Dryden's Alexandrines, heavily stressed, and the broad coarse caricature effects throughout these stanzas are generally more reminiscent of Dryden with his feeling for matter and mass. The 'thickness' of the 'thick throng' is both physical and mental. But Dryden (like Pope) would always have been too conscious of his public and social responsibilities as a satirist, a corrector of manners and morals, or a reconciler of political and religious divisions, to have dared the reckless Byronic tone and air of humorous shocking irreverence.

Byron's satire here on 'the great' extends, of course, to Adeline's manner and demeanour as she goes through her exhausting duties, her performance of her part as the great public hostess, in the interests of her husband.

> Juan, when he cast a glance
> On Adeline while playing her grand *rôle*,
>   Which she went through as though it were a dance,
> Betraying only now and then her soul
>   By a look scarce perceptibly askance
> (Of weariness or scorn), began to feel
> Some doubt how much of Adeline was *real*;
>
> So well she acted all and every part
>   By turns – with that vivacious versatility,
> Which many people take for want of heart:
>   They err – 't is merely what is call'd mobility,
> A thing of temperament and not of art,
>   Though seeming so, from its supposed facility;
> And false – though true; for surely they 're sincerest
> Who are strongly acted on by what is nearest.[1]

The departing crowd have, however, been duly impressed.

> Delighted with their dinner and their host,
> But with the Lady Adeline the most.[2]

What she thinks of them, tired as she is after her day's exertions in being so successfully agreeable, is of course very different.

[1] Canto XVI, Stanzas XCVI–XCVII.   [2] Canto XVI, Stanza XCI.

Meanwhile sweet Adeline deserved their praises,
    By an impartial indemnification
For all her past exertion and soft phrases,
    In a most edifying conversation,
Which turn'd upon their late guests' miens and faces,
    And families, even to the last relation;
Their hideous wives, their horrid selves and dresses,
And truculent distortion of their tresses.[1]

Here then, very much with us, is the solid, substantial world of 'bodies', if not of 'souls'.

They little knew, or might have sympathised,
    That he the night before had seen a ghost,
A prologue which but slightly harmonised
    With the substantial company engross'd
By matter, and so much materialised,
    That one scarce knew at what to marvel most
Of two things – how (the question rather odd is)
Such bodies could have souls, or souls such bodies.[2]

This prepares, by way of contrast, for the final scene of the comedy, the Gothic ghostliness that is unexpectedly discovered to be not so.

But apprehensive of his spectral guest,
    He sate with feelings awkward to express
(By those who have not had such visitations),
    Expectant of the ghost's fresh operations.

And now in vain he listen'd; – Hush! what's that?
    I see – I see – Ah, no! – 't is not – yet 't is –
Ye powers it is the – the – the – Pooh! the cat!
    The devil may take that stealthy pace of his!
So like a spiritual pit-a-pat,
    Or tiptoe of an amatory miss,
Gliding the first time to a rendezvous,
And dreading the chaste echoes of her shoe.[3]

A noise like to wet fingers drawn on glass,
    Which sets the teeth on edge; and a slight clatter

---

[1] Canto XVI, Stanza CIII.   [2] Canto XVI, Stanza XC.
[3] Canto XVI, Stanzas CXI–CXII.

> Like showers which on the midnight gusts will pass,
>   Sourding like very supernatural water,
> Came over Juan's ear, which throbb'd, alas!
>   For immaterialism's a serious matter;
> So that even those whose faith is the most great
> In souls immortal, shun them tête-à-tête.
>
> Were his eyes open? – Yes, and his mouth too.
>   Surprise has this effect – to make one dumb,
> Yet leave the gate which eloquence slips through
>   As wide as if a long speech were to come.
> Nigh and more nigh the awful echoes drew,
>   Tremendous to a mortal tympanum:
> His eyes were open, and (as was before
> Stated) his mouth. What open'd next? – the door.[1]

So, through the suspense of several more stanzas, we are carried
to the supreme surprise of that final stanza:

> A dimpled chin, a neck of ivory, stole
>   Forth into something much like flesh and blood;
> Back fell the sable frock and dreary cowl,
>   And they reveal'd – alas! that e'er they should!
> In full, voluptuous, but *not o'er*grown bulk,
> The phantom of her frolic Grace – Fitz-Fulke![2]

The climax (or anticlimax) involves the contrast between ghostli-
ness and flesh and blood, ascetic monk and ripe female beauty,
romanticism suddenly brushed aside by common sense. If the
curtain had to come down on *Don Juan* it could not have done so
with greater theatrical effect than on that anti-Romantic climax of
the comedy.

[1] Canto XVI, Stanzas CXIV–CXV.   [2] Canto XVI, Stanza CXXIII.

CHAPTER SEVEN
POETRY INTO NOVEL

I

The three poets of the beginning of the 19th century who have seemed to me to have most affinities with the novelists are Wordsworth, Crabbe (the Crabbe of his *Verse Tales*) and Byron (the Byron of *Don Juan*). These three poets have, therefore, engaged the greater part of the attention in this book. But, at the same time, the pervasive and profound creative effect of Shakespeare on both the poets and the novelists of the 19th century, working on the novelists through the poets as well as directly, could not be ignored. The chapters on Wordsworth, Crabbe and Byron have, therefore, been preceded by a chapter on Blake and Shakespeare, Coleridge and Shakespeare, Keats and Shakespeare. The chapters on Wordsworth will suggest the extent of the effect of Shakespeare in Wordsworth's poetry also. The best passages of *The Borderers* show that already, at the beginning of his development, Wordsworth had learned more from Shakespeare than he learned from Spenser and Milton, particularly about how to make his own poetry out of the idioms and rhythms of the spoken language.

Of all these poets it is certainly Blake who is the most original genius, the more remarkably so because he was the earliest of them, the most isolated, and because in his *Songs of Experience* and his other great short poems and fragments we witness a renewal in the language of what may properly be called a Shakespearian poetic or imaginative creativeness (as well as Blake's revolt against Newtonian Physics and Lockeian Philosophy) in what was still the 18th century.

Nevertheless it is Wordsworth who occupies the most extensive place in this book. This is not only because he seems to me (when all qualifications have been made) the greatest English poet of the 19th century (after Blake) but because his effect on the novelists, especially on George Eliot, seems to me to have been the most pervasive and profound. Wordsworth himself could never have been a novelist. His interest did not take him in that direction and he lacked some of the gifts that we generally think of as essential for a novelist (or dramatist). But he did have insights as a poet which revealed new possibilities for the novelists. There are his insights into the nature of the human mind, into the development of the individual human being from infancy to maturity, into the relationship between states of mind and the external world. There are also his sense of a living connection between the individual being and the universe and, generally, his sense of the mystery of things. These psychological, moral and religious insights had undoubtedly a deepening effect on the novel in the 19th century and must have had to do with the greatness of the greater novels. Wordsworth's poetry extended the conception of the nature of man as not simply the 18th-century 'rational' or 'social man' but as an imaginative, creative being and as having unexplored depths ('the mystery, the depth of human souls'). In these respects we may justly recognize the poet Wordsworth as a predecessor of George Eliot and Lawrence. This is again another way of saying that in these respects what had been recovered, rediscovered by Blake and Wordsworth and the poets of their generation, was a Shakespearian sense of the complexity and depth of human nature and of life and a corresponding Shakespearian development of language. This is what is developed also in the great novels, developed in their language. (The indivisibility of literature comes home to me more and more and, consequently, the risks there may be in the present academic insistence on 'specialization' in a single period.)

It is no accident, for example, that the child ('the new individual') and the adolescent, the pains of growing up and of arriving at mature manhood or womanhood, are one of the main recurrent themes in the novels of the 19th century, including the greater novels of the Brontës, Dickens, George Eliot and finally Lawrence. It is a theme that the poets – Wordsworth again and, before him, Blake – had already begun to explore. It has to do with the 19th-century interest in the developing individual, the individual's struggle for liberation not only from external oppressions but from his own imprisoning states of mind. Wordsworth's recollections of childhood experiences have (as I have indicated in the chapter on *The Prelude*) nothing to do with a nostalgic wish to be a child again. This is in general true of the treatment of the theme by the greater 19th-century authors (though not by the inferior authors and this is a sign of their inferiority). Some of the childhood and boyhood experiences recollected in *The Prelude* are in fact painful and disturbing – shocks, frights, the sense of being lost – and such as no one would wish to live through again, except imaginatively. Their importance for Wordsworth – and for his readers – is the clearer understanding they provide into the nature of man, in particular into the nature of the man who has developed into manhood from and through such experiences.

In addition to Wordsworth, the two other poets discussed in this book extensively and in some detail are Crabbe and Byron. If I had wished simply to illustrate the diversity of the poetry (indeed of the whole literature) of the period that still goes under the simplifying name 'the Romantic Period', I could not have done better than set these three poets side by side. But my main reason here for choosing the Crabbe of his *Verse Tales* and the Byron of *Don Juan* is that they are – at first sight more obviously than Wordsworth – the poets of the period who are nearest to being, in their verse, themselves novelists. In the *Verse Tales* of Crabbe the poet exhibits the gifts of a novelist (as well as of a master of the short story in verse). The novelist whom Crabbe may most readily be associated with is Jane Austen. He is much more like Jane Austen than he is like Byron, even the Byron of *Don Juan*. In Crabbe as in Jane Austen there is still a good deal of the 18th century. But in Crabbe's *Verse Tales*, as in Jane Austen's novels, there is also the developing 19th century moral and psychological analytical interest in the individual, together with the individual's relation to other individuals, to his or her family and whole society. This is the interest that is greatly developed in *Middlemarch* and the few other great novels of the 19th century.

Byron is the third of my poets because *Don Juan* is the one long poem of the period that is, at least in some ways, most like 'a novel in verse'.[1] Here again the contrast with Crabbe (and with Jane Austen) could hardly be more complete, notwithstanding that all three could be regarded (rather simply) as viewing human

[1] Santayana, *Three Philosophical Poets*, in the section on Goethe, also calls it so.

life unromantically as comedy. *Don Juan* has of course, some resemblances to the 18th-century kind of novel. But, for all Byron's admiration for Pope and Fielding, he is radically a 19th-century personality and *Don Juan* (unlike a poem of Pope) is a very personal expression of the poet's personality. In this way it is essentially a 19th-century poem. It is indeed much more completely and authentically an expression of Byron's personality, his whole complex personality, with its fluctuating moods and attitudes, the 'flow and recoil' of his sympathies, than his earlier 'Romantic' verse tales and poems. Further, Byron is 'a rebel' as neither Crabbe nor Jane Austen could possibly have been, have thought of themselves as being or ever wanted to be. But *Don Juan* is not merely an expression of personal rebellion and defiance it is genuinely and gaily liberating in effect, a liberation of the human spirit from the mumbo-jumbo of rigidifying social and moral conventions and institutions (as they existed in the England and Europe of his time). Strangely in this respect – the individual shaking himself free, bursting his bonds – we can more readily associate Byron, even the anti-Romantic Byron of *Don Juan*, with Blake and Dickens than with Crabbe and Jane Austen.

In so far as the 'comic spirit' is based on a 'commonsense' view of human life we may agree that there is here, in *Don Juan*, still a connection with the great 18th-century authors. But if so, it is a connection that goes back through the 18th century to an older world, in the line of the great comic authors through all the centuries. The radical difference from the 18th century[1] is that in Byron as in Burns 'good sense' is no longer equated with 'decorum'. On the contrary, conventions together with 'decorum' are observed to be often in practice absurdly at variance with human nature. In this respect again *Don Juan* proves to be more in accord with the new (or renewed) interest in the individual human being.

The effect of the poetry of the early 19th century can be seen already in the non-novelistic prose of the period – at least the poetry and the prose can be seen to be closely associated – in the development of imaginativeness and introspectiveness and the expression of an individual's states of mind, notably in De Quincey. Some of Lamb's personal impressions of the London

[1] As suggested in my book *The Scots Literary Tradition*.

scene and its characters also come near to resembling paragraphs from a 19th-century novel, for all his humorous 'literary' affectations, personal idiosyncrasies and whimsical 17th-century stylistic reminiscences. There are passages in the non-novelistic prose which are much more like passages from the 19th-century novels than from the 18th-century novels. There is as interesting a relation between the prose of De Quincey, Hazlitt and Lamb and that of the 19th-century novelists as there is between the *Tatler* and *Spectator* and the 18th-century novelists. This evidently begins from the relation between the prose of De Quincey, Hazlitt and Lamb and the poetry of their contemporaries.

II

The aspect of Dickens which particularly relates him to the poets is, of course, his imaginativeness, an imaginativeness inseparable from his comic creativeness. If we look for a characteristic essence of Dickens it is here, in his combination of his often grim, even macabre humour, with his imaginative fertility and exuberance. The characteristic scenes and dialogues of the Dickensian comedy are part of the Dickensian poetry, generated out of it, out of his poetic creative use of the English language. His comic imaginative genius is wholly identified (like Shakespeare's poetic dramatic genius) with the genius of the living English language. But for all his original and originating genius it is also certain that Dickens's novels would not be as they are but for the enlarged scope for the creative imagination which the poets, beginning with Blake, Wordsworth and Coleridge, had recently recovered after the 18th century's insistence on the rational and prosaic as its norm. We have only to compare the Dickensian novels with those of Smollett or Fielding to see the difference. The 'Romantic' imagination as it works in the early 19th-century poets had (I suggest) as much as the line of English caricaturists (up to and including his own illustrators) to do with the way Dickens's imagination sees.

Dickens has, of course, his individual vision, his vision of human life in London, his vision of London itself. The Gothicism which was an element in the early 19th-century poetry, as well as in the Gothic romances, may be recognized to have been one of the elements incorporated and transmuted in Dickens's vision of his contemporary London. The ghost-haunted churchyard or half-ruined castle of Gothicism or of the humorous burlesques of Gothicism (at their most distinguished in Peacock's *Nightmare Abbey* or Jane Austen's *Northanger Abbey*) is transmuted in the Dickensian novels into the nightmarish city, labyrinthine London as it seems (or seemed in Dickens's time) when immersed in smoky fog. The difference is, of course, the Dickensian comic creativeness, exuberance and zest. Though at times Dickens's vivid sense of London becomes magnified in the Dickensian imagination to the semblance of an enormous labyrinth or prison (the most inclusive of the many prisons in his novels), it is also animated and swarming, bursting with life and characters; it encloses and involves an abundance and diversity of intensely living individual 'characters'. Dickens's London is as much his vision of London as is Blake's in his poem, *London*.

It might indeed as truly be said of Dickens as Eliot says of Blake that he had a gift of 'hallucinated vision'. The prose of his novels is at its creative best whenever the novelist is most fully possessed by his imaginative comic vision. Dickens was a fully conscious artist in the important sense that he evidently lived imaginatively in each novel as he created it, seeing and hearing it all happen, dramatizing as he composed. It is the poetry (not the 'plot') which is the reality of a Dickens novel, the poetry of which the characters are themselves a part, out of which they are created.

The affinities between Dickensian art and Shakespearian, arising from their creative mastery of the living English language in their time, are now frequently remarked on. There is a sense in which Dickens's art is of the 'people', has its source in the imagination, the humour, the speech of the people, and has a long ancestry. Dickens, for example, shares with the people, as Shakespeare can – in so far as there still was a 'people', a 'folk' in the old sense, in so far as there still was a 'popular culture' persisting into the 19th century – that macabre humour which seems to arise from some profound as well as ancient association of birth and death. In Dickens's novels, funerals, marriages and baptisms are often associated festivals. We need only recall the funereal baptism of Little Paul in *Dombey and Son* (immediately preceded both by a funeral and a marriage). There are many such Dickensian scenes of radically the same kind of macabre humour as those

of the grave-diggers in *Hamlet*, the porter in *Macbeth*, the rural
fellow with the basket of figs in *Antony and Cleopatra*. Mistress
Quickly and Justice Shallow in the Falstaff comedy might almost
come straight out of Dickensian comedy.

We cannot, of course, read Dickens without being conscious
also of a relationship between his novels and the theatre. The
important thing is that Dickens's art greatly transcends the art of
the theatre of his time, as Shakespeare's art greatly transcends the
art of the theatre of *his* time. There are the obvious elementary
theatrical parallels in Dickens, the clowning and melodramatic
episodes, the rhetorical speeches, the histrionic gestures and
poses, the occasional entrances and exits of stagy characters.
Shakespearian productions were popular entertainment still in
Victorian England (as opera was in Italy). Victorian productions
of *Richard III* (even of the great tragedies) seem often to have
been very near Victorian melodrama, *A Midsummer Night's
Dream* very near Victorian pantomime, and as such no doubt not
only crude but robust. Certainly Dickens's novels, whole epi-
sodes of them, seem as if composed for performance, as evidently
he himself performed them in imagination as he composed,
acting out for himself the imagined characters, scenes and dia-
logues. The theatrical bent of his genius is obvious enough. But,
at a deeper level, his creativeness is fully and substantially dramatic
and poetic, the novelist as dramatic poet. At its creative best,
Dickensian English is no superficial rhetorical imitation or echo
from the 19th-century theatrical productions; it has its own
characteristic dramatic poetic vitality and fertility, comic zest and
imaginative flow. The whole spoken language of the English
people, not simply the jargon of the theatre, is being drawn upon
as its source, as it had been the source of the language of Shake-
speare and of Chaucer before Shakespeare.

In his novels Dickens views the Victorian world – in the sense
of the now dominant moneyed middle-class Victorian world –
its false money values and genteel pretensions, its rigid conven-
tions and hypocrisies. Of course, the Dickensian hypocrites,
frauds and humbugs can be traced right back through the English
comic tradition to Ben Jonson (through the European to Molière)
and much earlier. But hypocrisy, cant and humbug (including
deluges of sanctimonious 'uplift' e.g. Chadband) had assumed a

specific contemporary force and meaning for Dickens in his Victorian world.

There was so much in his contemporary world of the post-Industrial Revolution that Dickens (as did other great Victorians and, nearer our own time, Lawrence) recognized as 'the negation of life', the poverty, the ugliness, the brutality, the moral and physical squalor, worst of all the hypocrisy, the cant, the shams and pretences, especially among those who by their own self-defensive accumulations of wealth caused or aggravated the poverty and hideousness. The Dickens novels, in their own way as novels, are expressions of humanity against the deadening, dehumanizing force of the entrenched and established false values that produced these things, not least the valuation of money as a supreme good, its consequent unnatural hardening effect on human nature. But the novels have also, as in Bunyan, a more permanent universal import as a vision of the individual human being in 'this world' – 'world' in almost the old traditional religious sense, as in the phrase 'the World, the Flesh and the Devil'. It is through the poetry of his novels that Dickens also embodies (as Blake, Burns and Byron do) the sense of a shared, common humanity, the values of human naturalness, spontaneity and impulsive generosity and love.

It has often been noticed that Dickens reacts most strongly, in his novels, against any form of oppression or tyranny over the individual life, more especially the vulnerable, growing individual, the child. Partly from his own personal early experience Dickens was painfully conscious of the oppression of children, as was Blake before him (e.g. Blake's *Chimney Sweep* and his *Holy Thursday* of the *Songs of Experience*). The oppressed child becomes in his novels almost a symbol of imprisoned human nature, as in Blake. The prison image recurs throughout the novels[1] in various forms, including the institutions and conventions of society, the Law, schools ('Shades of the prison house begin to close upon the growing boy'), money and class – even

---

[1] I was thinking here in particular of the later, greater novels, *Dombey and Son, Bleak House, Hard Times, Little Dorrit, Great Expectations, Our Mutual Friend*. The prison in various forms and shapes, external and in the mind, is pervasive in these novels. But his early novels too have these different kinds of oppressive prisons.

the sense of the whole enclosing labyrinth of London itself when for groping foot-passengers or pale gazers from murky windows of gloomy, funereal houses it is submerged in smoky fog. But the most deadly prisons of all, in the novels, are those of the mind itself. It is especially from these imprisoning, inhibiting states of mind that Dickens, like Blake, feels that the individual man is most in need of liberation, the bursting of the bonds, the rising from the tomb. The mind constructs its own prisons and these include (for Dickens) also those external constructions of the collective mind, the institutions and conventions of what he vividly felt to be a false, hard-hearted society.

These imprisoning states of mind in individuals and these imprisoning constructions of society are (in the Dickensian imaginative vision) 'the negation of life', manifold forms and shapes of death. As such they are as much present, part of the poetry of the novels, as are the images of life in its variety and plenitude, which they menace and oppose. These negative or destructive forces or powers, falsities or inertias – in the mind itself as well as in the external or social world – thwart and impede, deform and petrify the spontaneous impulsive life, the generous sympathies, the creativeness which are, for Dickens, the essence of the nature of 'man alive'. In the imaginative vision of the novels they assume many various shapes and they can seem to become nightmarish, oppressive presences. To say that Dickens has as 'vivid' a sense of death as of life – and of life as of death – is, then a paradox which states a significant fact about Dickensian art. His most funereal or macabre scenes are often those in which his imaginative exuberance and comic zest are most apparent, inherent in the imagery and rhythm, the very texture and structure, of his prose. The characteristic Dickensian macabre humour may itself (as I have suggested) be understood as the expression of an ebullience of life, never more so than in the immediate presence of death, physical or moral, in a multitude of ghastly or ghostly shapes and disguises.

The final emphasis should, therefore, still be on Dickens's triumphant evocation of the diversity and plenitude of human life, perpetually generated and regenerated, an unending multitude and procession of comically incongruous and idiosyncratic characters who in their uniqueness magnificently do not 'fit in', do not 'adjust', struggling both with tyrannical external oppressions and inertias and with self-destructive urges and blindnesses, delusions and inhibitions in themselves.

If I were to begin to illustrate, in its variety and abundance, the poetry of Dickens I should never stop. I shall choose one or two passages only – from the chapter in *Little Dorrit* which conveys Clennam's impressions and feelings on his return to his mother's gloomy house and the gloomy London Sunday of his childhood. The conventional Gothic ingredients, the ghostly face at the window and so on, are present, as in other passages, but as always in Dickens with the immense difference produced by his individual exuberant imagination. There is in this passage in particular the magical effect of the lamplighter.

'He sat in the same place as the day he died, looking at the dull houses opposite, and thinking, if the disembodied spirits of former inhabitants were ever conscious of them, how they must pity themselves for their old places of imprisonment. Sometimes a face would appear behind the dingy glass of a window, and would fade away into the gloom as if it had seen enough of life and had vanished out of it. Presently the rain began to fall in slanting lines between him and those houses, and people began to collect under cover of the public passage opposite, and to look out hopelessly at the sky as the rain dropped thicker and faster. Then wet umbrellas began to appear, draggled skirts, and mud. What the mud had been doing with itself, or where it came from, who could say? But it seemed to collect in a moment, as a crowd will, and in five minutes to have splashed all the sons and daughters of Adam. The lamplighter was going his rounds now; and as the fiery jets sprang up under his touch, one might have fancied them astonished at being suffered to introduce any show of brightness into such a dismal scene.'

The interior of the Clennam house is, if anything, more dismal than the external scene. But here a sudden contrast is introduced by the recollection of the things and qualities that are absent from its funereal rooms. The effect is of a surprise irruption of the missing colours, the missing brightness, the diversity of shapes and forms from the excluded world of life, a vivid momentary recall of the expelled magic of life.

'The gaunt rooms, deserted for years upon years, seemed to have settled down into a gloomy lethargy from which nothing could rouse them again. The furniture, at once spare and lumbering, hid in the rooms rather than furnished them, and there was no colour in all the house; such colour as had ever been there, had long ago started away on lost sunbeams – got itself absorbed, perhaps, into flowers, butterflies, plumage of birds, precious stones.'

The imaginative and fanciful exuberance has here, once again, paradoxically a liberating effect from the oppressiveness of the presented dark horrors. The Dickensian imaginative sense of life lifts the grim macabre scene into fantastic poetry. The funereal pageantry, as if assuming a witchlike life of its own, becomes animated (as in Romantic or indeed Shakespearian poetry).

'There was not one straight floor, from the foundation to the roof; the ceilings were so fantastically clouded by smoke and dust, that old women might have told fortunes in them better than in grouts of tea; the dead-cold hearths showed no traces of having ever been warmed, but in heaps of soot that had tumbled down the chimneys, and eddied about in little dusky whirlwinds when the doors were opened. In what had once been a drawing-room, there were a pair of meagre mirrors, with dismal processions of black figures carrying black garlands, walking round the frames; but even these were short of heads and legs, and one undertaker-like Cupid had swung round on his own axis and got upside down, and another had fallen off altogether.'

The Dickensian combination of exuberant fancy and humour arrives here at an unexpected bizarre and grotesque climax. The funereal pageantry breaks out into pantomimic or circus clowning, images of death changing into images of life.

III

If we now glance at Emily and Charlotte Brontë, in their chronological place in between Jane Austen and George Eliot, we see that in their novels also there is already a profound connection with the poetry of the beginning of the 19th century. Narrowly constricted as they themselves were in their personal lives the poetic imagination deepens and extends the scope of their novels (above all in Emily's achievement of genius, *Wuthering Heights*). The 19th-century theme of the growing pains of the individual from childhood through adolescence to manhood or womanhood, the passionate individual woman breaking out from her prison and having to achieve mature relationships with other individuals and with the external world, is one of their main concerns. This theme (or variations of it – the girl who, more lively or intelligent than her family or neighbours though she may be, has herself painfully to mature and to find a *modus vivendi* in her society) was already, of course, one of Jane Austen's concerns. The differences are in the treatment, the different ways in which the general theme is developed in the novels. There is certainly in the Brontës still the interplay between what might be called 18th-century 'sense' and 19th-century Romantic 'sensibility'. But a Brontë novel is much nearer a kind of poetry, the poetry of the early 19th-century poets, than is Jane Austen. The psychological insights of the later novelists are defined and communicated through a use of language that is more imaginatively poetic (though we miss the controlling, detaching Jane Austen irony and wit in the line from the Augustan 'idiom of wit'). The way, for example, the heroine's inner states of mind are rendered more distinct to her own consciousness (and the reader's) through her sense of her involvement with her external surroundings, with houses and rooms, with the country ('nature' in that sense) in its changing seasons and hours and weathers, could be illustrated from many passages in *Jane Eyre* and *Villette*. Here is, for example, Jane's desolation after the shock of the prevention of her marriage (Chapter 26):

'A Christmas frost had come at midsummer; a white December storm had whirled over June; ice glazed the ripe apples, drifts crushed the blowing roses; on hay-field and corn-field lay a frozen shroud: lanes which last night blushed full of flowers, today were pathless with untrodden snow; and the woods, which twelve hours since waved leafy and fragrant as groves between the tropics, now spread, waste, wild and white as pine-forests in wintry Norway. My hopes were all dead – struck with a subtle doom, such as, in one night, fell on all the first-born in the land of Egypt. I looked on my cherished wishes, yesterday so blooming and glowing: they lay stark,

chill, livid corpses . . . I looked at my love . . . it shivered in
my heart, like a suffering child in a cold cradle.'
The note of confinement and constriction is struck in the opening
paragraphs of the novel:
'There was no possibility of taking a walk that day . . .
Folds of scarlet drapery shut in my view to the right.'
The whole novel, of course, traces, from within Jane's conscious-
ness, her development from the oppressed rebellious orphan child
of the opening chapters to mature womanhood. In this respect
there is an obvious relationship between the Brontë novels (as
between novels so different as *Great Expectations*, *The Mill on the
Floss*, *The Rainbow*) and *The Prelude*.

IV

But the great English novelist of the century – other than
Dickens and before James – is, of course, George Eliot. There is
again an unmistakable relationship between her work as a novelist
and the poets and Shakespeare. Her profound moral and psycho-
logical insight into the complexities of the human mind and human
life is essentially an imaginative insight, as in Shakespearian
dramatic poetry.

The way the creative and exploring imagination works could
be illustrated from many passages throughout her novels. There
is, for example, in *Middlemarch* the rendering of Dorothea's
dawning consciousness of what she has done in marrying Casau-
bon. There is the great passage in Chapter 20 about Dorothea's
honeymoon in Rome, in which the English provincial girl's
consciousness of Rome, the accumulations and wreckage of the
civilizations of the centuries there (the 'stupendous fragmentari-
ness', 'the oppressive masquerade of the ages', 'the weight of
unintelligible Rome') is involved with her bewildered, painfully
emerging recognition of what is happening in herself, the tragic
mistake her marriage is already beginning to reveal itself as being.
This is not so much psychological analysis as a dramatic poetic
rendering of a complex state of mind, from the inside, the girl's
groping, struggling consciousness of her strange unfamiliar situ-
ation. There is nothing comparable in the 18th-century novels,
even in Richardson. The development can only be related (within
literature at least) to the intervening poetry and the new ways of

reading and realizing Shakespeare. But the passage has now become well known and is unforgettable. Instead, therefore, I shall quote (for comparison also with the much simpler Charlotte Brontë) parts of the opening of the chapter (Chapter 28) about Dorothea's return to the Rectory after her honeymoon in Rome. The poetry here – for it is again essentially poetry – expresses Dorothea's sense of the frozen world of a married lady's gentility (a 19th century married lady) in which she feels her warm young life has been strangely imprisoned (cf. 'The pale virgin shrouded in snow').

'A light snow was falling as they descended at the door, and in the morning, when Dorothea passed from her dressing-room into the blue-green boudoir that we know of, she saw the long avenue of limes lifting their trunks from a white earth, and spreading white branches against the dun and motionless sky. The distant flat shrank in uniform whiteness and low-hanging uniformity of cloud. The very furniture in the room seemed to have shrunk since she saw it before: the stag in the tapestry looked more like a ghost in his ghostly blue-green world; the volumes of polite literature in the book-case looked more like immovable imitations of books. The bright fire of dry oak-boughs burning on the dogs seemed an incongruous renewal of life and glow – . . . As she laid the cameo-cases on the table in the bow-window, she unconsciously kept her hands on them, immediately absorbed in looking out on the still, white enclosure which made her visible world . . . Meanwhile there was the snow and the low arch of dun vapour – there was the stifling oppression of that gentlewoman's world, where everything was done for her and none asked for her aid – where the sense of connection with a manifold pregnant existence had to be kept up painfully as an inward vision, instead of coming from without in claims that would have shaped her energies. – "What shall I do?" "Whatever you please, my dear:" . . . Her blooming full-pulsed youth stood there in a moral imprisonment which made itself one with the chill, colourless, narrowed landscape, with the shrunken furniture, the never-read books, and the ghostly stag in a pale fantastic world that seemed to be vanishing from the daylight.'

The second of the quotations I shall allow myself from George

Eliot shall be from one of the chapters in *Daniel Deronda* (Chapter 54) in which another newly married couple float about in a boat on the Mediterranean. To outward appearance they are an idyllic couple enjoying an amplitude of leisure and pleasure: in reality each is the other's hell from which neither can escape. The following brief quotation may be sufficient to recall something of the complex whole of their situation, their mutual self-imprisonment.

' "A – just ring, please, and tell Gibbs to order some dinner for us at three," said Grandcourt, as he too rose, took out a cigar, and then stretched his hand towards the hat that lay near. "I'm going to send Angus to find me a little sailing-boat for us to go out in; one that I can manage, with you at the tiller. It's uncommonly pleasant these fine evenings – the least boring of anything we can do."

'Gwendolen turned cold: there was not only the cruel disappointment – there was the immediate conviction that her husband had determined to take her because he would not leave her out of his sight; and probably this dual solitude in a boat was the more attractive to him because it would be wearisome to her. They were not on the plank-island; she felt it the more possible to begin a contest. But the gleaming content had died out of her. There was a change in her like that of a glacier after sunset.

' "I would rather not go in the boat," she said. "Take some one else with you."

' "Very well; if you don't go, I shall not go," said Grandcourt. "We shall stay suffocating here, that's all."

' "I can't bear going in a boat," said Gwendolen, angrily.

' "That is a sudden change," said Grandcourt, with a slight sneer. "But since you decline, we shall stay indoors."

'He laid down his hat again, lit his cigar, and walked up and down the room, pausing now and then to look out of the windows.'

Grandcourt's grand manner, his tone of languid superiority, his boredom – you can hear it in his voice – are associated with a deadening triviality of soul, a destructive obstinacy of will, in which Gwendolen finds herself involved and imprisoned. Whatever Gwendolen, the spoilt child, deserved, she did not deserve

this. But she also, fortunately now for her self-preservation, likes
to have her own way. Hence the terrible conflict of wills as she
and Grandcourt float about on the summer Mediterranean, the
boat their prison. Though his drowning, which releases her, is an
accident, it is an accident which Gwendolen knows, with a sense
of guilt, she wished. She is in fact capable of tragic stature be-
cause she is capable of such feelings, capable of remorse, has 'a
root of conscience in her'.

These or similar passages from George Eliot might well be
compared with the chapter in *Portrait of a Lady* (Chapter 42)
which renders Isabel Archer's state of mind as she begins to
recognize and to explore, in her own mind, her situation – a
situation still obscure to herself – what her marriage with Osmond
really is, who and what Osmond and Madame Merle really are
('She had suddenly found the infinite vision of a multiplied life to
be a dark, narrow alley with a dead wall at the end'). She is
another of the heroines who had expected that her marriage
would open out a larger life and who finds herself trapped.

This is not, of course, the place to develop the whole compari-
son between George Eliot and Henry James even in their differ-
ing treatments of similar themes. But one significant difference is
that George Eliot's Gwendolen is embedded in English provincial
society unlike Isabel. The density of English life in *Daniel
Deronda*, as in all the novels of George Eliot (above all in
Middlemarch), is much greater than in James, fuller and more
solid, presented with greater specificity ('the deep rich English
tone, in which so many notes seemed blended together' is James's
own characteristic description of it as he admired it in *Daniel
Deronda*). James had his own particular advantages as an Ameri-
can observer looking at and into England and Europe, able to
note the significant differences between people of different
cultural and social backgrounds and to make discriminating
critical comparisons. What he lost in solidity (it might be said) he
gained through his gift – again essentially poetic imaginative –
for seizing impressions and essences, perceiving shades and
distinctions, detecting moral significances in appearances. On the
other hand one of George Eliot's advantages over James as a
portrayer of English life is that she herself, like Jane Austen, had
grown up in it, in provincial England, though sufficiently de-

tached from it by an interval of years and her London life to observe it, vividly recollected, as a novelist.

In her 19th-century English circumstances Gwendolen, George Eliot's English girl, unlike James's American girl, is under powerful, almost irresistible pressures from without, as well as from within herself, to accept the brilliant match, family and economic pressures. In these respects at least Isabel *is*, or is able to suppose herself to be, a 'free agent'. Gwendolen has also, of course, her personal ambition, as an individual with a strong will of her own, for a larger life for herself, more scope in which she (as Grandcourt's wife) would be a great lady, in which *she* would command and do good to large numbers of less fortunate people. It weighs with her in making her choice (as it would not with Isabel) that Grandcourt is a great landowner, a county magnate, occupying as such a great place in the English system. As a personality Grandcourt is clearly the counterpart of Osmond in James's novel. But Osmond, of course, has 'nothing' – nothing but his pose and pretensions as an 'aesthete'. Isabel brings him *his* fortune. The irony is that the fortune which was intended to ensure her independence, her 'freedom of choice', is exactly what attracts the predatory woman of the world, Madame Merle. For Isabel, too, as for Gwendolen (and Dorothea) life had seemed to be opening out ever more widely. She too had her idealism, her generosity of spirit, to rescue with her fortune, rescue from sordid worldly considerations, the impoverished artistic gentleman of fine sensibility and taste and to share with him an enlarged, disinterested, unworldly, cultured life. In reality no one is, of course, more worldly than Osmond. His pose of being an artist, or at least artistic, a connoisseur of the arts, and therefore superior, more refined than other people, is a sham. He creates nothing. Beneath his smooth, polished surface he is ruthlessly possessive. He puts (or hopes to do so) the bright, spontaneous girl into his collection of *objets d'art* ('a portrait of a lady' in that sense also), his most ornamental piece. There is nothing spontaneous about Osmond. Both Osmond and Grandcourt, in their respective novels, and in their different settings are thus studies in egoism, uncreative and sterile in themselves, beneath their deceiving surfaces of sophisticated manners and tastes, negating and nullifying life in others. But Gwendolen is capable of recognizing that her tragedy is partly her own fault, the consequence of her own morally wrong choice. She knew much more fully what she was doing than Isabel does and therefore her fault is tragically the greater. Isabel's tragedy – in so far as she is not (as she so largely is) deceived – is the consequence of an error of judgement rather than a moral fault. Eager, full of curiosity and interest, generous, sanguine and trusting, a spontaneous and fresh young life, her innocence is as yet largely ignorance, ignorance of 'the world'. She does not know enough. She only thinks she chooses. We have here, therefore, another Jamesian variation on the meanings of 'innocence' and 'sophistication' (cf. Blake's Innocence and Experience). Madame Merle, the sophisticated social animal, is 'deep' (she is unhappy too) and it is she who really arranges the marriage making 'a convenience' of the girl. There is, therefore, less reason for James's heroine to blame herself. But, to quote again James's famous description of George Eliot's heroine, 'The universe forcing itself with a slow inexorable pressure into a narrow complacent and yet after all extremely sensitive mind – This is Gwendolen's story.' In that sense, therefore, George Eliot's heroine is the more fully tragic *character* of the two.

The depth in George Eliot's novels is in such ways as these that of tragic experience, the tragedies of the individual soul, whereas the breadth (it might be said) is that of the sense of English life which the novels also convey, the comedy of life going on in whole communities of people.

The resemblances in George Eliot's novels to Shakespearian (and Greek) tragedy are striking and not to be accounted for simply by the profound impression which her reading of Shakespeare, Aeschylus and Sophocles made on her. They come from the centre of her own personal experience of life. The tragic experience of the race is experienced again in a 19th-century context, lived through again imaginatively in her novels of 19th-century England. Some of the greatest things in her novels – among the greatest things in English literature outside Shakespeare – arise from her tragic sense of nemesis ('what's done cannot be undone'), her recognition that things done have consequences which are inexorable, which may come back on the doer years after. This element of tragic experience is present already in *Adam Bede* and the other early novels and is developed and explored in George Eliot's greatest imaginative art. It unmistakably comes (as I said) from the novelist's deepest experience of life. This tragic insight into the complexities and conflicts of the individual soul is beyond anything in the 18th-century novel, not excepting *Clarissa*. (Scott's earliest 19th-century experiment in a Shakespearian tragedy in novel form, *The Bride of Lammermoor*, has not this degree of insight into the complex workings of the mind. *The Heart of Midlothian* comes nearer to real tragedy.)

There are passages in George Eliot's novels which, in their sense of tragedy (as well as imagery), may well recall the poetry of Keats's vision of Moneta, if they recall anything outside Shakespeare. In the opening chapters of *Felix Holt*, for example, Mrs. Transome, in her aristocratic Englishness, attains strikingly something like the stature and dignity of a Greek tragic heroine, as in this very English scene and setting (yet also as in a Greek tragedy) she awaits her son's return after a long absence of years – the son who is (she hopes) to restore the fallen fortunes of the house. As in a Shakespearian tragic soliloquy – again by a use of language essentially dramatic poetic – we are taken into and through the shifting complexities of her mental agony, her sense of the inexorable involvements, the unexpected developments and bitter disappointments of her situation as she alone, in the solitude of her mind, knows what that situation is. Mrs. Transome is felt to be a tragic personality because she is a proud woman inescapably involved in the error of her youthful past, not because she has 'a root of conscience in her'. This is more purely (again as in a Greek tragedy) a study of nemesis and of hubris without repentance. Mrs. Transome is an aristocratic nature, by temperament as well as by birth and place (in a Greek or Shakespearian tragedy she would be royal), accustomed to command, to impose her will. There is the part played by heredity in the tragedy too. Her son Harold, who has become 'a stranger to her', proves to have inherited from her a will of his own, too, stronger even than hers. He is also, as his mother is, a tragic character, with the uncompromising single-mindedness which often (as in the Greek tragedies) lays a character open to tragedy. By insisting on investigating the old lawyer's (Jermyn's) conduct of the family affairs and by pressing the investigation (like Oedipus) to its limits, he brings about his own undoing, the discovery that he is

Jermyn's son. Such is the bare outline of his tragedy, as one recalls it. But though such an outline is sufficient perhaps to indicate the resemblance to a Greek tragedy, the greatness of the effect depends on the dramatic-poetic specificity of the novel, the imaginative insight into the minds of the Transomes and the sense of the whole life of England within which their individual tragedy is an element.

But the study of the Transomes, memorable as it is, is little more than a tragic sketch compared to the study of Gwendolen Harleth in *Daniel Deronda*, one of the great things in literature. The rest of *Felix Holt* is a comparative failure, and not the achieved great whole that *Middlemarch* is.

In *Middlemarch* there are the three large-scale tragedies of individual lives. Each of these tragedies of individual lives has its own characteristics, as each of the great Shakespearian tragedies has. Lydgate's tragedy, for example, is not simply that of the progressive young doctor, the practical idealist, defeated by the prejudices of a stagnant provincial society, though it is partly that. He too is cast in the heroic tragic mould, nobly capable of disinterested 'intellectual passion'. The flaw, the Aristotelian hamartia which exposes him to tragedy, is 'the spot of commonness' which lays him open to the humming-bird attractiveness of Rosamund (the Mayor's daughter in a small provincial town). In the end the force of her triviality proves stronger than he is. The finer personality is destroyed by the inferior, by the obstinate hard core of her narrow wilful egoism ('her torpedo contact').

Bulstrode acquires a tragic dimension because (in his case) he *has* a conscience, an exacting Puritan conscience. He tries to live the good life according to his light (combining it with 'lawful gain'). He begins his life all over again in Middlemarch where he is successful both in a worldly sense and as an exemplary Puritan character. The temptations of worldly power, now that he occupies the seat of the mighty (the great Middlemarch banker) begin to get the upper hand, hubris as well as the Puritan vices of self-righteousness and hypocrisy. His tragedy is again one of nemesis. His past (his guilt of many years ago) comes back at him unexpectedly, just when he has arrived at the apex of wealth, power and respectability (though unloved) in Middlemarch.

'Into this second life his past had now risen, only the pleasures of it seeming to have lost their quality. Night and day, without interruption save of brief sleep which only wove retrospect and fear into a fantastic present, he felt the scenes of his earlier life coming between him and everything else, as obstinately as, when we look through the window from a lighted room, the objects we turn our backs on are still before us, instead of the grass and the trees. The successive events inward and outward were there in one view: though each might be dwelt on in turn, the rest still kept their hold in the consciousness.'

These, then, are still the ancient and universal ingredients (hubris, nemesis) in the tragedy of the 19th century bourgeois Bulstrode. But again his tragedy is lived through imaginatively – experienced as Bulstrode himself, in his innermost mind, experiences it – through the dramatic-poetic art of a great novelist. There is the rendering, for example, of his Macbeth-like inner conflict which develops when the conception of murder – it is essentially murder – begins to form itself compulsively in the obscure depths of his tormented mind as a proffered loophole of escape from the closing-in of his nemesis. These tragedies of individual souls are comparable to the Shakespearian because of George Eliot's profound imaginative understanding – 'seeing what is' – which brings home again (with 'pity and terror') the fullness of the truth that to know all is to forgive all.

But, if it is these tragedies of individual souls which give their Shakespearian tragic depth to the novels, there is their corresponding Shakespearian breadth, the sense conveyed throughout the novels of the whole life of England. We lose this sense – the sense of the whole human comedy – if we simply single out these individual tragedies from their context in the whole novel. These tragedies of individual souls are involved, and are shown in the fullest detail to be involved, in the general life of a whole society, 'the private life' involved in 'the public life'. The Shakespearian (or Tolstoyan) comprehensiveness of *Middlemarch* and the other novels of George Eliot (especially if we take them all together) is in their rendering of the depth of individual lives together with the sense of a whole society and the whole range of human life. This sense of a whole human society is imaginatively created largely through a multiplicity and diversity of minor characters, individual lives interconnected with one another and with the main characters in a complexity of interrelationships, people of different social and cultural strata, different occupations, interests and purposes, different generations. They make up the full sense of a human society, the sense of a whole people, and the sense, more particularly, of what it was actually like to live in such a community as Middlemarch in the England of the 19th century. The comedy of the novels belongs largely to this aspect of them. There is the tragedy of individual lives within the comedy of the social life in which all the characters are together involved, the life that goes on continuously from one generation to another.

We can see George Eliot therefore as, in some of her qualities and interests, the successor of Jane Austen. There is particularly the presence of an irony expressive of delicate moral and psychological discriminations, shades of characterization (for example, in the portrayal of Casaubon and of *his* egoism). The irony is, of course, not confined in George Eliot to the comedy, it is present also in the tragedy. But in the Shakespearian depth and breadth of her novels we can see George Eliot as the great successor not only of Jane Austen (and Scott) but of Wordsworth and the poets.

NOTE

In George Eliot's shorter masterpiece *Silas Marner*, with its wonderful combination of traditional folk-tale elements and novelistic realism, the study of the isolation of Silas in some ways foreshadows one of the main Conradian themes. The solitary weaver, an alien migrant in the Raveloe countryside (his innocent faith and love having been crushed in Lantern Lane), is at first an object of superstitious folk imaginings, fear and repulsion among the country people. But there *is* a real human community there, in that neighbourhood, a traditional English village life (fully and solidly presented in this, as in the other, George Eliot novels) into which the recluse is ultimately drawn and, as a consequence, *liberated* and restored to humanity. This is the effect on Silas of the child who, as if by a miracle, is found in the place of his vanished gold, the hoarded produce of his daily weaving, stolen away from him, the miser's gold that had engrossed his affections and still further constricted his withered life.

'. . . the child created fresh and fresh links between his life and the lives from which he had hitherto shrunk continually into narrower isolation. Unlike the gold which needed nothing, and must be worshipped in close-locked solitude – which was hidden away from the daylight, was deaf to the song of birds, and started to no human tones – Eppie was a creature of endless claims and ever-growing desires, seeking and loving sunshine, and living sounds, and living movements; making trial of everything, with trust in new joy, and stirring the human kindness in all eyes that looked on her. The gold had kept his thoughts in an ever-repeated circle, leading to nothing beyond itself; but Eppie was an object compacted of changes and hopes that forced his thoughts onward, and carried them far away from their old eager pacing towards the same blank limit – carried them away to the new things that would come with the coming years, when Eppie would have learned to understand how her father Silas cared for her; and made him look for images of that time in the ties and charities that bound together the families of his neighbours. The gold had asked that he should sit weaving longer and longer, deafened and blinded more and more to all things except the monotony of his loom and the repetition of his web; but Eppie called him away from his weaving, and made him think all its pauses a holiday, re-awakening his senses with her fresh life . . .

'As the child's mind was growing into knowledge, his mind was growing into memory: as her life unfolded, his soul, long stupefied in a cold narrow prison, was unfolding too, and trembling gradually into full consciousness.'

V

The index of a great living tradition seems to be not simply that it imposes resemblances but that it allows a large scope, that it promotes individual differences. The immediate successors of Dickens and George Eliot in the 'great tradition' of the English novel are James and Conrad, two novelists as different from one another as they are from their two great predecessors, and as are their predecessors from one another. James and Conrad may be said, for example, to have given the English novel new European and American relations or dimensions.

James's American predecessor is, of course, Hawthorne (though James himself was a New Yorker not a New Englander). The fact that Hawthorne called his novels 'romances' may itself indicate not simply conformity with the early 19th-century fashion for 'romance' but that he intended his novels and tales to be read more as poems than as 'realistic' novels. When Melville called Hawthorne 'the American Shakespeare' he may also have intended to emphasize the poetic-creativeness of his work, not simply to accord it superlative praise. The clue to what Hawthorne was attempting to do in his own work may in fact be found in what he himself says of Shakespeare (in *Our Old Home*).

'Shakespeare has surface beneath surface to an immeasurable depth ... There is no exhausting the various interpretations of his symbols.'

Hawthorne's literary ancestors, whom he himself was most conscious of as such, are in fact Chaucer and Shakespeare, the Bible, Spenser, Milton and Bunyan. In particular the elements of allegory and symbolism in his work derive mainly from the pre-18th-century authors.

But though James has a distinguished New England predecessor in Hawthorne, it is an equally important fact that his imagination was steeped from boyhood (as he recalls in *A Small Boy and Others*) in Dickens. England, on his arrival there, was already familiar to him, recognizably Dickensian England. *The Bostonians*, his most comprehensive ironic comedy of the varieties of life in the American scene, has its relation, of course, to Hawthorne's *Blithdale Romance*. But it may also be described as, in many of its qualities, Dickensian, more spontaneously so than is his novel with a London scene, *The Princess Casamassima*. *The Bostonians* is abounding with Dickensian 'characters', in the obvious sense, created out of a comic imaginative fertility. Here, for example, is part of the initial presentation of Miss Birdseye:

'She had a sad, soft, pale face, which (and it was the effect of her whole head) looked as if it had been soaked, blurred, and made vague by exposure to some slow dissolvent. The long practice of philanthropy had not given accent to her features; it had rubbed out their transitions, their meanings. The waves of sympathy, of enthusiasm, had wrought upon them in the same way in which the waves of time finally modify the surface of old marble busts, gradually washing away their sharpness, their details. In her large countenance her dim little smile scarcely showed. It was a mere sketch of a smile, a kind of instalment, or payment on account; it seemed to say that she would smile more if she had time, but that you could see, without this, that she was gentle and easy to beguile.'

We may recall for the sake of the comparison the phrases (with their images) which initially present Miss Tox (*Dombey and Son*, ch. I):

'The lady thus specially presented, was a long lean figure, wearing such a faded air that she seemed not to have been made in what linen-drapers call "fast colours" originally, and to have, by little and little, washed out. But for this she might have been described as the very pink of general propitiation and politeness. From a long habit of listening admiringly to everything that was said in her presence, and looking at the speakers as if she were mentally engaged in taking off impressions of their images upon her soul, never to part with the same but with life, her head had quite settled on one side ... Her dress, though perfectly genteel and good, had a certain character of angularity and scantiness. She was accustomed to wear odd weedy little flowers in her bonnets and caps. Strange grasses were sometimes perceived in her hair; and it was observed by the curious, of all her collars, frills, tuckers, wristbands, and other gossamer articles – indeed of everything she wore which had two ends to it intended to unite – that the two ends were never on good terms, and wouldn't quite meet without a struggle. She had furry articles for winter wear, as tippets, boas, and muffs, which stood up on end in a rampant manner, and were not at all sleek. She was much given to the carrying about of small bags with snaps to them, that went off like little pistols when they were shut up; and when fully-dressed, she wore round her neck the barrenest of lockets, representing a fishy old eye, with no approach to speculation in it. These and other appearances of a similar nature, had served to propagate the opinion, that she was a lady of what is called a limited independence, which she turned to the best account. Possibly her mincing gait encouraged the belief, and suggested that her

clipping a step of ordinary compass into two or three, origina-
ted in her habit of making the most of everything.'
or Mrs. General (*Little Dorrit*):

'. . . If her countenance and hair had rather a floury appearance,
as though from living in some transcendently genteel Mill, it
was rather because she was a chalky creation altogether, than
because she mended her complexion with violet powder, or
had turned grey. If her eyes had no expression, it was probably
because they had nothing to express. If she had few wrinkles,
it was because her mind had never traced its name or any other
inscription on her face. A cool, waxy, blown-out woman, who
had never lighted well.

'Mrs. General had no opinions. Her way of forming a mind
was to prevent it from forming opinions. She had a little
circular set of mental grooves or rails on which she started
little trains of other people's opinions, which never overtook
one another, and never got anywhere.'

Miss Birdseye, Miss Tox, Mrs. General are characters very differ-
ent from one another. The resemblance is in the art of language
which creates them and the multitude of other diverse characters
in the novels of James and of Dickens. The comic imaginativeness
of *The Bostonians* is, of course, held firmly in place, contained
within its ordered structure, its classic design, and controlled by
the irony. It is possible to see the great Jamesian novel as, in some
of its qualities, also in the line from Jane Austen and Crabbe
and Pope.

I have earlier suggested that there are resemblances – at least
in subject-matter and even, in some respects, in treatment –
between James's witty ironic comedy of 'London society' at the
end of the century in *What Maisie Knew* and *The Awkward Age*
(and some of the short stories) and Byron's comedy of Regency
society as he recollects it in *Don Juan*. If there are these resem-
blances, there are also, of course, essential differences. There is no
impression of the 'slap-dash' conveyed by James's art any more
than by Pope's art. But James in creating his own unique individ-
ual novels takes in the larger whole of English tradition. Compari-
sons and contrasts with Byron do not therefore preclude our
seeing aspects of *What Maisie Knew* and *The Awkward Age* –
again the classic design and ironic wit – as also in the line from

Jane Austen, nor does it preclude our finding in these novels
again a Dickensian imaginative-comic fertility. Even James has
his comic monsters, his grotesques (e.g. Countess Gemini in *A
Portrait of a Lady*). Indeed they come thick and fast in *What
Maisie Knew*, as they present themselves, her elders, to the child.
They include the child's own mother, whose appearance can
change so bewilderingly (ch. IX):

'her ladyship's remarkable appearance, her violent splendour,
the wonderful colour of her lips and even the hard stare, the
stare of some gorgeous idol described in a story-book, that
had come into her eyes in consequence of a curious thickening
of their already rich circumference. Her professions and ex-
planations were mixed with eager challenges and sudden drops,
in the midst of which Maisie recognised as a memory of other
years the rattle of her trinkets and the scratch of her endear-
ments, the odour of her clothes and the jumps of her conversa-
tion. She had all her old clever way – Mrs. Wix said it was
"aristocratic" – of changing the subject as she might have
slammed the door in your face. The principal thing that was
different was the tint of her golden hair, which had changed to
a coppery red and, with the head it profusely covered, struck
the child as now lifted still further aloft. This picturesque
parent showed literally a grander stature and a nobler presence,
things which, with some others that might have been bewilder-
ing, were handsomely accounted for by the romantic state of
her affections.'

There is the child's encounter, in Kensington Gardens, with her
mother (ch. XV):

' "My own child," Ida murmured in a voice – a voice of sudden
confused tenderness – that it seemed to her she heard for the
first time. She wavered but an instant, thrilled with the first
direct appeal, as distinguished from the mere maternal pull,
she had ever had from lips that, even in the old vociferous
years, had always been sharp. The next moment she was on
her mother's breast, where, amid a wilderness of trinkets, she
felt as if she had suddenly been thrust, with a smash of glass,
into a jeweller's shop-front, but only to be as suddenly ejected
with a push and the brisk injunction: "Now go to the Cap-
tain!" '

What Maisie Knew is thus simultaneously comedy and tragedy, the comedy of the London 'fast set' at the end of the century, the tragedy of the involvement in it of the child. *What Maisie Knew* and *The Awkward Age*, in addition to being astringent criticisms of aspects of English life and society, are further explorations of the Blakeian and Wordsworthian subjects of the child and the adult, innocence and experience. In *What Maisie Knew* it is the adults who are misbehaving outrageously, whereas the innocence of Maisie proves invulnerable. The point of the novel is the innocence of the child in spite of what she 'knew', and the influence shed by her innocence on some of her elders. The characteristically Jamesian consciousness of the complexities of life could only have been rendered in language in which creative imagination and irony are associated.

It will be remembered that James had in his early years of learning the practice of his art gone to school, as it were, with the French novelists (meeting several of them personally, together with Turgenev, in Paris). His critical essays on Flaubert, Balzac, etc. show how seriously he took their art. In Paris, at a decisive stage in his own development into a novelist, the young American found a discussion of the art of the novel, the novel discussed seriously as art, as it was scarcely as yet discussed, it seemed to him, in London (see his essay, *The Art of Fiction*, 1884). Yet for James, American and, therefore, also English, the art of the novel was not in some ways regarded seriously enough by the French novelists, as an art related to life. In his criticism, he finds it necessary to dissociate the art of the novel from Art for Art's sake. James in fact himself discovered that his most profound affinity was not with the French novelists but with George Eliot and the novelists in the English language. His supreme admiration for George Eliot is clear in what he says about her, though (as he also recognizes) Dickens had from an earlier time, from boyhood on, worked powerfully on his imagination. As an American, whose language and tradition was English, he found in George Eliot a depth of 'moral interest' that was congenial to him, an imaginative understanding of human nature, together with a reverence for human life. It emerges from his essays that these qualities are felt by him to be in some measure missing in the great French novelists composing in the French sceptical tradition or in the French rhetorical (rather than poetic) tradition. Formidable as is the French sceptical intelligence, James could also recognize its limitations. His acquaintance with the French novelists certainly helped to give him in his own novels and tales his European – as well as English and American – viewpoint. But it is also clear that the great novels of George Eliot had a liberating effect on his imagination and showed him the larger possibilities and scope of the novel in realizing the complexities of human individuals and the situations, both comic and tragic in aspect, in which they involve themselves or become involved.

There are, of course, also significant differences between James and his English predecessors. There is the sense that James in his novels and tales is 'in search of a society' in ways in which George Eliot or Jane Austen had no need to be, conscious as they are of a surrounding and sustaining society (its 'rich density') as well as of its constrictive pressures on individual lives. Here is one respect in which it is possible to associate James and Conrad. Apart from the fact that James is exceptionally qualified – from his observations of American, English and European life and from the consequent detachment of his viewpoint – to make comparisons between people of different nations, cultures and traditions, he is the first of the great novelists to convey a sense of the absence anywhere of a fully civilized, humane society, a sense of its dissolution or vanishing, if it ever existed, a sense of its elusiveness, a sense that it has become difficult to identify or recover. The implication is that it is needful to discover or define, by means of his novelist's art, an ideal of civilized, humane living. An ideal of living had, of course, for James (as for Jane Austen) to be an ideal of civilized living. This is not the same as saying that he is preoccupied with the portrayal of 'manners'; he could not, any more than could Jane Austen, have dissociated 'manners' from 'morals'. His concern for civilized, humane living is inseparable from the kind of moral and psychological interest that associates him both with George Eliot and Jane Austen. It is inseparable also from 'the sense of life' which is an essential characteristic of the novelist and the poet from Chaucer onwards. The 'air of reality', James also calls it, and he speaks of 'solidity of specification' in the presentation of life as the primary requirement for any novelist. To convey 'the sense of life' – not only its external appearances but also life going on in the minds of his characters – commits James, as it commits Dickens and George Eliot, to an art of fully imaginative or poetic dramatic presentation.

We may take as a Jamesian example the opening of *The Europeans* (James's earliest fully mature or classic presentation of the 'international theme', apart from one or two short masterpieces among the earlier short stories). The newly arrived European cousins – a brother and sister, themselves surprisingly different from one another, contrasted products of Europe – look out from their Boston hotel on a wintry, meagre townscape with a graveyard, their first discouraging impressions of the New World. Then there is an irruption of life, a crowd round a street-car.[1] The scene and the moods of the two spectators keep shifting and changing. Apart from the controlling presence of the Jamesian irony and wit, the symbolism here compares with (if indeed it was not suggested by) that of the opening of *The Scarlet Letter*, the graveyard and the prison of the 17th century New England Puritan township, a rose-bush incongruously flowering, with its life and colour, at the prison-door. The poetic use of such correspondences between an outward scene and states of the mind is clearly the kind of thing that has been taken over by the 19th-century novelists from the earlier poets. That initial impression of New England is displaced in the second chapter of *The Europeans* by the enchantment (as it first strikes the visitor from Europe) of the house of the Wentworths (the American cousins) its beautiful harmonious simplicity, serenity and spaciousness, expressive of aspects of the lives and minds of those whose home it is, suggestive almost of an air of Garden of Eden innocence.

It may be compared with the enchantment of Old England in the opening chapters of *A Portrait of a Lady*, as the English scene unfolds for the first time to the young American visitor. These enchanting first impressions are to some extent borne out, not wholly dispelled by the facts on further exploration. There is

[1] Cf. how in the dead Dombey street outside the dead Dombey house there erupts a transient stream of life – water-carts with their refreshing sprinklings of water, 'old clothes men', 'people with geraniums', 'an umbrella mender', a motley succession that soon vanishes again, in the prevailing gloom and desolation. 'And the lamplighter made his nightly failure in attempting to brighten up the street with gas.'

found to be sufficient substance behind the beautiful appearances partially to justify these particular first impressions. It is not always so in James's novels. In contrast, the enchantment of Osmond's Florentine villa, as it is first presented to Isabel, deludes the girl as to Osmond's real character, proves to have been part of the deception. But life in New England and in Old England is discovered, in *The Europeans* and in *A Portrait of a Lady* at least, to embody certain real civilized values, though (and this is the point) they are contrasting or complementary values. It was possible for James critically to appreciate the best of both the Old and the New Worlds, while at the same time perceiving and portraying with remarkable lucidity the deficiencies and limitations in the civilization of each. The ideal of civilized, humane living he profoundly seeks to define in the novels, in all their shades and nuances, is to be found nowhere fully in any one place or region of the world (he recognizes), though there are hints, intimations, partial realizations of it in many places, in America, in England, in Europe, in the lives of individuals and the relationships between them (e.g. the Touchetts, father and son). The poetry of the Jamesian novels and short stories subtly conveys this meaning.

VI

No two novelists could be more different than James and Conrad. Yet (if we think of *Nostromo*) Conrad is in his different way also an explorer of 'the international theme'. The 'international theme' had, of course, been introduced into the English novel occasionally before. There is the effect of the presence of Herr Klesmer among the English aristocracy in *Daniel Deronda*. But a wide personal acquaintance with different countries and peoples, traditions, cultures, civilizations provided the later novelists, James, Conrad, Lawrence with material for observations, comparisons and assessments of the different ways in which different people in the world live. Conrad's peculiar intensity, however, is in expressing also, in the midst of vivid impressions of a diversity of people and places, a sense of the fundamental isolation of each individual. This, as well as some of Conrad's other differences from James, differences of temperament, may be partly accounted for from their differences of origin and circumstances. A Pole by origin – remaining always something of a Pole in exile – and a cosmopolitan by circumstances and experience, Conrad was, perhaps, drawn more deeply into the French mind and sceptical tradition than James, though like James he consciously detached himself from it in the process of becoming an English novelist.

There had already been the exiles – or poets who imagined themselves to be so – among the early 19th-century English poets, Byron, Shelley, perpetual travellers not only through countries but (like Goethe's Faust) experiences, 'busily ranging in perpetual change'. But if these poets felt themselves to be isolated individuals, it was partly because they wanted to isolate themselves, to break away from their particular society. But by the end of the century and the beginning of the 20th what has begun to force itself on the imagination, notably of Conrad, is the possibility that the individual can discover himself to be radically detached and alone, not simply accidentally separated or estranged from a particular human society that exists. He can discover himself to be without even a society to rebel against. This is different from the sense of a constrictive or oppressive society against which the individual feels he must assert and liberate himself in becoming conscious of himself as an individual. The need for an individual to enter into relationships with other individuals in some kind of civilized society can thus become intensely the concern of an individual who discovers himself to be isolated.

In some such way the 19th-century interest in the individual has altered. Not the pressure of civilized society on the individual, as in Jane Austen, but rather its felt absence is what concerns Conrad. Jane Austen's concern is, of course, both with the inadequacies of individuals to civilized society and also with the inadequacies of society – the particular society she herself belonged to and knew – to particular individuals. Jane Austen's discomforting perceptions in these respects are extended in the novels of George Eliot. The limitations and deficiencies of the provincial town community (of Middlemarch) are found to have much to do with Lydgate's tragedy, as that is analysed in the novel. Dickens – in this respect more like Blake and Byron in their different ways – characteristically presents individual lives as oppressed, or at least impeded, by social conventions and institutions as well as by their own false values. In James there is still at least the sense of

individuals living always in a social milieu – there being different
kinds of civilized society, or vestiges of it, actually observable
everywhere – even though often a rather rarefied or tenuous
social milieu. It would scarcely (one feels from the novels of
James) have been possible for him, even if he had wished, to
imagine individuals as living dissociated from a social milieu,
outside some kind of civilized ethos, in which they could meet
and communicate, could form with one another at least the sem-
blance of a civilized human society or even its reality (as do the
Touchetts, father and son, a happy almost accidental combination
of both the American and English finer qualities). But in Conrad we
are presented with the phenomenon of the individual who dis-
covers himself to be radically isolated even among his fellow-
men, who rediscovers (as Conrad felt it) the essential solitude of
the human soul. We enter imaginatively in Conrad's novels and
short stories into new extremes and varieties of experiences of
isolation, not simply physical isolation on the sea and in tropical
places among alien peoples, but depths of moral and metaphysical
isolation. There are, of course, great tragic instances of moral (and
physical) isolation throughout literature, in Shakespeare (Mac-
beth) in George Eliot (Bulstrode). But in Conrad the whole
subject of isolation has for the first time become almost the main
concern of the novelist. The nearest to Conrad in this respect is
perhaps Coleridge (*The Ancient Mariner*). Poe in a minor way is
perhaps another such.

Related to these experiences of isolation in Conrad's novels is
the element of unsettling scepticism in them – undermining
beliefs – which strikes the reader as un-English, and is identifiable
as, at least partly, French (going back to Montaigne). Decoud in
Nostromo is unmistakably close to Conrad himself, or to one very
considerable element in his mind. This element may be accounted
for by the fact that, as a Pole, Conrad's second language had at
first been French. Nevertheless Conrad became and is an English
novelist, as such a great successor of Dickens and George Eliot.
We may ask again what was the impulse in Conrad himself which
caused him deliberately to choose English for his creative work
or why (as he himself expressed it) he felt that it was the English
language which chose him, not accidentally. The simplest account
is that it was, to begin with, for much the same reason as he felt

himself drawn towards the British Merchant Service, which not only necessitated his learning to speak English but appealed to him because of its traditions, traditions of discipline and of loyalty to ship and crew. By the time he had begun to make himself a novelist in English Conrad had (we may conjecture) not only himself experienced an inner and an outer solitude on strange seas, by strange shores, among strange peoples, he had lived with and come to value the traditions of the Merchant Service and learned what they could do to sustain and maintain a man even in extremity.[1] These traditions of a hazardous profession continue throughout Conrad's novels and short stories to stand for tradition as a whole, regard for decency and order, a sense of moral responsibility. A traditional discipline or even routine (as he often shows in his novels and short stories) can keep a man going in the last extremity not only against external stresses but also against internal stresses, even an undermining scepticism, sapping a man's faith in life.

But this is still much too simple an account of Conrad. There is much more in Conrad's complex art than this account by itself suggests. There is the tradition embodied in the English language itself. Conrad had come to live not only with the British Merchant Service but, more profoundly, with the language of Shakespeare and Dickens. For one thing the English language gives Conrad the scope his genius required for vivid dramatic enactment, a Dickensian (or Shakespearian) imaginative energy of presentation characteristic of his novels and short stories. An English characteristic, too, we may say, is the profound 'moral interest', interest in 'the conduct of life' that is also congenial to Conrad and shapes his novels. Spectacular as his novels are, violent, even melodramatic, in action, flamboyant in gesture and attitude, the art of presentation is firmly controlled by a central 'moral interest' that associates Conrad with the English novelists. But in Conrad the 'moral interest' is associated also with a metaphysical interest which is perhaps not so English, a curiosity about what can be believed in, a preoccupation with each individual's neces-

[1] There is, for example, in *Typhoon* the apparent ordinariness of Captain McWhirr, nothing apparently heroic about him and his home background in England. Yet, in the centre of the typhoon, his ordinariness is heroic when he simply maintains his traditions, is and continues to be what he is in these extraordinary and critical circumstances.

sity for finding a belief by which to live. What gives both form and substance to Conrad's novels is that physical, moral and metaphysical conjunction. (Cf. Yeats's 'blood, imagination, intellect running together'.)

There is thus present in Conrad's novels (as there is, in a very different way, in Lawrence) the sense of a need even more fundamental than the need to discover a human society. There is the primary human need for meaning or for a belief for an individual to live with or for a whole people to create or re-create its society with. Some such sense of a failure of belief or meaning seems to have come over Shelley the idealist towards the end, if we may judge by the mood of disenchantment expressed in *The Triumph of Life*. The romantic sense of travelling through strange countries of the world, or through experiences that perpetually change, has been expressed from time to time throughout imaginative literature, from the *Odyssey* on, and can, it seems, result in the sense that experiencing for its own sake cannot by itself provide meaning. In some of the most imaginative passages in the second half of *Little Dorrit*, for instance, we share the consciousness of Little Dorrit that in journeying across the Alps and through Italian scenes the Dorrits are passing through an unreal dream, the shadow of the Marshalsea accompanying them still through those dazzling new regions. The prison, which had after all been her home, seems more real to her. She recognizes, too, that they – and all the rich tourists – take their mental prison with them, their false values of money and social position, from which they have not been liberated.[1] This sense of unreality culminates in the nightmarishness (with its echoes of *Macbeth*, e.g. the banquet scene) of Mr. Dorrit's death scene amidst the grandeur of Rome, a death scene that in the grandeur of its setting might be that of an Emperor. Thus ironically have Mr. Dorrit's delusions of grandeur been fulfilled. The final irony is that in his dying moments he imagines his Roman palace to be again the Marshalsea, the palace to be his prison which, in the sense the novel portrays, it is.

Somewhat similarly, the spectacle of life and the world which Conrad evokes with such Dickensian vividness in the poetry of his novels is accompanied always by a sense of its illusoriness (not generally characteristic of Dickens). It is (in Conrad) as if the

[1] Cf. *A Portrait of a Lady*, chapter LIII, Isabel travelling back through Italy.

splendid spectacle were suspended over a central emptiness, an inner hollowness. This feeling is unmistakably associated with the scepticism (expressed in *Nostromo* by Decoud) which so powerfully appealed to Conrad in the French tradition. It is counterbalanced in Conrad by the recognition that men need beliefs of some kind and, consequently, by the interest in his novels in the different kinds of beliefs (or illusions) that different men find to sustain them and do in actual fact live by. But there is in Conrad's novels no Wordsworthian or Lawrentian religious sense of a living connection or relationship between the human being and the non-human universe. Thus, in each of Conrad's greater novels, in each differently, whether in the dazzling worlds of *Nostromo* or *Victory*, or in the murky Dickensian London of *The Secret Agent*, or the snow-muffled St. Petersburg of the opening section of *Under Western Eyes*, the intensest concern is with the physical, metaphysical or moral isolation of the individual.

Already in *Heart of Darkness*, the poetry of which is so heavily charged as to be perhaps overcharged, the voyage up the African river into the heart of darkness is felt to be more than a geographical voyage, to be also a voyage into the central darkness and isolation of the human soul. The civilized mind of Kurtz ('All Europe contributed to the making of Kurtz') is discovered to have been corrupted and disintegrated by his isolation in the dark heart of the African continent. The emissary of the civilization and enlightenment of Europe, having rashly exposed himself to that alien environment, ceases to be a European, nor ever could become an African, and loses his identity. The impact of Europe – its mixture of profit-making and progress, enlightenment and commercial enterprise – on Africa and of Africa on the European consciousness proves to be mutually destructive (symbolized, for example, by the derelict machinery in the jungle or the futility of the warship firing shells into a continent). In these ways the voyage up the river is not simply a voyage into the African continent marvellously described. The descriptions themselves become poetic symbolism suggesting a darkness at the heart of the civilized consciousness. The primitive is discovered to have a sinister appeal to something corresponding to it within the civilized consciousness itself. Kurtz – not simply lost in the alien vastness of the external African continent – crumbles and dissolves into a central darkness and nothingness within himself.[1]

No novel, not even another novel of Conrad, creates a more vivid impression of the spectacle of life and the world – or of life and the world as a spectacle – dazzling, yet strangely illusory, than *Nostromo*. The action of the novel – and the gestures and poses of the human actors in the novel – may strike the reader, the modern English reader, as violent, extravagant, even melodramatic, as in an Elizabethan or Jacobean play. Yet, at the same time, the novel conveys this Conradian sense of the bright and varied spectacle and all that animated action as suspended over a central hollow darkness. The black gulf across which Decoud and his fellow-passengers glide in the lighter, like dead souls in limbo, becomes in the poetry of the novel a darkness that is felt to be both physical and metaphysical, symbolical of a central darkness that Decoud's intelligence cannot penetrate. The element of scepticism – the undermining, unsettling suggestion that the human actors are only kept in continuing motion by ideals or beliefs that are perhaps themselves illusions – is impersonated in the novel by Decoud, significantly a cosmopolite of French culture. Decoud is perilously near the heart of the great novel, if not of the novelist himself. But it is one of the magnificent ironies of the novel that the sceptic himself, with his brilliant intelligence, the product of the conversation of the boulevards and cafés, is discovered to be himself nothing if not 'social', for whom an audience is indispensable. He has to have other people to converse with, to express or relieve his scepticism in witty ironical conversation, as in his youth in the cafés on the boulevards of Paris, even in the last extremity writing at least a journal

[1] Cf. *A Passage to India*. Forster's novel is not simply about India at that particular historical moment, not simply about different kinds of Englishmen and different kinds of Indians. It is not only an ironic comedy of contrasting human beings and their failure to understand one another, though the strength of Forster is in the Jane Austen line. But the novel further projects Forster's imaginative vision of the human situation against the background of the sub-continent – which assumes in the passages about the Marabar Caves the proportions of a universal background – a situation in which the difficulties of human beings in understanding one another seem almost insuperable. The novel is in some ways Forster's equivalent, in the English liberal tradition, of Eliot's *Waste Land* or Lawrence's *St. Mawr*. The radical differences between these three works proceed from the radical differences of vision of their authors. Lawrence would have discovered profoundly different things about India than does Forster.

which he hopes will be read. The poetry of the novel renders in minute detail his consciousness as, alone on his island, he begins to lose his sense of his own identity, to dissolve into sea and sky, with no inner resource to hold him back from his personal annihilation. (Cf. Lawrence's short story, essentially also a poem, *The Man who Loved Islands*.)

But if the scepticism impersonated by Decoud is almost the most powerful single element in the great novel, it is balanced by an equally strong – or more than equally strong – 'moral interest', an interest in the actual 'conduct of life', which identifies Conrad with the English tradition of Shakespeare and the English novelists. The diversity of characters, presented with a Dickensian dramatic-poetic energy, is one of the most remarkable features of *Nostromo*. But the interest which gives the novel its classic form and structure, its pattern of significances, is the interest to discover, exhibit and examine the things that can seem to give life positive meaning for men and women. The vivid dramatization of diverse characters living and acting diversely is firmly controlled by the novelist's interest in elucidating and evaluating their motives and springs of action, their beliefs, ideals or illusions. This interest in discovering meanings in the lives of people is the relevance of 'the international theme' which Conrad shares, though their treatments of the theme are so different, with James. Costaguana, Conrad's imaginary Central American state, is, as it were, the whole world with its contrasting and conflicting nationalities, cultures and traditions focused in a single work of art. The theme is presented in the way of a novelist or dramatist, the Chaucerian way, by means of a grouping or confluence of individual characters, producing a single impression of a multitude of diverse people.

In the pattern of significances Decoud's opposite is significantly the Englishman, Charles Gould. With his belief in 'progress', a 'romantic idealist', not 'a materialist', Charles Gould is nevertheless ironically drawn into a fatal identification with 'material interests' through his enterprise and work which he believes to be in the interests of humanity. This is one of the grim tragic ironies of the novel, associated with the poetic symbolism of the corrupting effect on so many lives of the silver of the mine. The great modern illusion to which Charles Gould devotes and sacrifices his own life and that of others is that conditions of material well-being will necessarily promote moral well-being, liberal enlightenment, tolerance, a more civilized humane life throughout a whole land and people. Charles Gould's life-time's effort thus implied, to begin with, a touching innocent romantic faith, the 19th century faith, in the essential goodness of human nature. In the end – the end of *Nostromo* – 'material interests' have triumphed in backward Costaguana but at the expense of humanity. The triumph proves to be in fact an inhuman one.

Throughout the novel Mrs. Gould has largely expressed, by her understanding and sympathy, her capacity (and need) for humane personal relationships, the spirit of humanity. In the poetry of the novel, the Casa Gould, because of her presence in it and because it is her house, visibly expresses, in the midst of the encroaching brutalities, her humane spirit and aspirations, a spacious, gracious place, glowing with light and colour, but also gently refreshing with its coolness and shade in a hot land. But, at the end, Mrs. Gould is (and lingers in the memory after the novel is read) a sad, forlorn, lonely figure – understood only by the good Dr. Monygham (an apparently cynical, maligned, maimed, misunderstood character, but his own harshest critic).

'She leaned back in the shade of the big trees planted in a circle. She leaned back with her eyes closed and her white hands lying idle on the arms of her seat. The half-light under the thick mass of leaves brought out the youthful prettiness of her face; made the clear, light fabrics and white lace of her dress appear luminous. Small and dainty, as if radiating a light of her own in the deep shade of the interlaced boughs, she resembled a good fairy, weary with a long career of well-doing, touched by the withering suspicion of the uselessness of her labours, the powerlessness of her magic.

'Had anybody asked her of what she was thinking, alone in the garden of the Casa, with her husband at the mine and the house closed to the street like an empty dwelling, her frankness would have had to evade the question. It had come into her mind that for life to be large and full, it must contain the care of the past and of the future in every passing moment of the present. Our daily work must be done to the glory of the dead, and for the good of those who come after. She thought that, and sighed without opening her eyes – without moving at all. Her face became set and rigid for a second, as if to receive, without flinching, a great wave of loneliness that swept over her head . . . An immense desolation, the dread of her own continued life, descended upon the first lady of Sulaco. With a prophetic vision she saw herself surviving alone the degradation of her young ideal of life, of love, of work – all alone in the Treasure House of the World. The profound, blind, suffering expression of a painful dream settled on her face with its closed eyes. In the indistinct voice of an unlucky sleeper, lying passive in the grip of a merciless nightmare, she stammered out aimlessly the words –

' "Material interest." '

There is no need to recall here in any detail the main outlines and features of the other great novels of Conrad, except to indicate how each novel in its different way illustrates this essential concern with the isolation of the individual. The London of *The Secret Agent* could not be more different, as a setting for the drama of human life, than the Costaguana of *Nostromo*. But *The Secret Agent* is a further exploration of that basic Conradian theme of isolation. Each character in the novel is conceived as carrying about with him through the London scene his own condition and situation, disparate and divergent from any other, each a centre of consciousness of which no one else is conscious. Consequently, each individual is discovered to be liable to harbour erroneous assumptions about the thoughts and feelings of others, even of someone with whom he or she has lived in the closest proximity, mutual convenience and amiability, for a lifetime. This is the case of Mr. and Mrs. Verloc, comfortably living their respectable, if somewhat squalid, married lives till things go wrong unexpectedly. But their case is presented as not exceptional. What each individual assumes he (or she) knows of the mind of another is presented as guesswork that can prove comically or tragically wrong, resulting on occasions, at moments of crisis, in disconcerting revelations of fundamental misunderstanding. The world of *The Secret Agent* is peopled with such characters. Complacent in their ignorance of one another, each moving in the enclosed sphere of his individuality, taking for granted that their viewpoints are as a matter of course shared by others, they talk and act at cross purposes – until the moment when their situation is revealed as shockingly different from that which they had assumed. This is the basis of the grim irony of *The Secret Agent*, breakdowns of communication, failures of understanding which can force upon an individual at last a sense of his own isolation even from those among whom he has lived familiarly his accustomed life.

There are the many characters in Conrad's novels who remain complacently unconscious of isolation (Captain Mitchell in *Nostromo*, for example) and who thereby contribute the more to the ironic comedy. But the central interest in the great novels is invariably in those individuals whose consciousness of isolation (as the reader is made imaginatively to share it) becomes intense. There are in fact many different forms and varieties of isolation, or the consciousness of isolation, physical and moral, expressed in the novels. In *Under Western Eyes*, the St. Petersburg student, Razumov ('as lonely as a fish swimming in the sea') would prefer to be left alone, would preserve the detachment necessary for his studies. He has only his ambition (to make himself independent, to make his own way in the world) to sustain him. But when his comfortable degree of isolation is violated by the unwelcome intrusion of the anarchist student, Haldin, he discovers he has not recovered it by giving up – in fact betraying – Haldin to the Police. He finds on the contrary – this is the terrible Conradian irony here – that he has involved himself irrevocably in both the opposed networks, that of the Revolutionaries and that of the Secret Police. His involvements with both organizations, involving him in complicated misunderstandings and incomprehension, force upon him a consciousness of more profound forms of isolation than anything he had wished to secure by his act of betrayal. The deeper his involvements the more total and finally unendurable becomes his consciousness of moral isolation. He discovers finally that the degree of physical isolation produced by the brutal destruction of his sense of hearing is much less unendurable than had been his consciousness of moral isolation. It was Conrad who said that a 'moral discovery' should be the end of every novel. The 'moral discovery' which is the end of *Under Western Eyes* is that the human being cannot live without love of some kind, without some kind of human relationship.

This is very much the 'moral discovery' which is the end also of

Victory. But the particular form which an individual's consciousness of isolation takes in this novel is different again. Heyst's distrust of life, the philosophic scepticism inherited or acquired from his philosopher father, isolates him and causes him to endeavour to isolate himself from life, his particular prescription for detachment being a perpetual wandering through the countries and across the seas of the world, attaching himself nowhere or to anyone. The poetry of *Victory* conveys the impression of a shifting, dazzling succession of seas, shores, islands – 'What seas, what shores . . .' – though they are specifically those of South East Asia. Heyst's failures of detachment are in fact, though he himself does not recognize them as such, victories of his own nature ('No decent feeling was ever scorned by Heyst'). He never fails to respond chivalrously to appeals for help from others in distress, the climax of these being his rescue of Lena (of course, misunderstood).

'The world' finally and fatally breaks in again on Heyst on his island – where he has sought to detach himself and Lena – breaks in, this time, in grotesque and evil shapes.[1] 'Nothing can break in on us here' – Heyst's reassuring remark to Lena is dramatically followed – a characteristic Conradian irony – by his abrupt 'He's here'. Who's here is the ghostly Chinaman, Wang, who has for once materialized at the wrong moment. Something must have gone seriously wrong to produce such an aberration. Others besides the innocuous Wang are in fact 'here', a landfall from 'the world of men' – monstrous caricatures of mankind – a man like a cat, a man like an ape, a man like a spectre of death. But the victory which gives the novel its title is a moral victory – at the very moment of physical death – a victory of life and love, expressed by Lena's deliberate heroic sacrifice, over the distrust of life in Heyst which had inhibited his relationship with her. Thus each novel and short story of Conrad projects, as a kind of poem, its variation of a Conradian vision of life.

VII

Hardy has been seen as the direct successor of George Eliot, as well as of Scott. In some respects he is so, a successor of George Eliot as a novelist of provincial life, a successor also of Words-

[1] There are some resemblances here with *The Tempest*.

worth as a tragedian of humble lives set in traditional rural communities against the huge background of the universe (though Hardy's universe is not Wordsworth's but the 'neutralized nature' or mechanical universe suggested to him by 19th-century science).

The composition of Hardy's novels proved to have been an episode in a lifetime of composing poems. The two – the novelist and the poet – are never (I think) quite one throughout any one of the novels as a whole. He is characteristically a poet of sharply poignant moments, memories and regrets, and, therefore, of short poems. In a few of these poems he is unmistakably a great poet in the expression of insight into common or universal human experience, achieving an authentic note of tragedy. In these poems Hardy's ghosts, for example, are characteristically remembered images such as may haunt the mind of anyone from his personal past. They belong to the psychology of the individual as often as (in other poems of Hardy) they are the ghosts of the superstitions, legends and traditions of the country people. In this respect Hardy belongs both with the poets and the novelists of the 19th century. In *After a Journey*, for example (the subject of one of Mr. Leavis's classic analyses), he – the poem is autobiographical – revisits the place where forty years ago, as young lovers, 'we haunted here together'. There are 'lovers' haunts', and also ghosts haunt. She is there again in the same place as vivid as she was when alive and young, there and yet not there, an image in the mind (she is dead). He is 'just the same', yet not the same (he is now an old man). The poem conveys a sense of the complexities of time and place in the consciousness, a sense of the immediate presence of the past in a place which is the same place it was 'at the then fair hour in the then fair weather'. The poem conveys, of course, more than that, the tragedy of a human relationship. But Hardy is less certainly a great poet in this way in the novels. The novels are the more limited as novels for that reason, for all their extension compared with the short poems – more limited than the novels of George Eliot or the poetry of Wordsworth (if one thinks in particular of *The Prelude*).

On the other hand, Hardy's sense of a non-human world, between which and man there is no Wordsworthian sense of a living connection, produces its own authentic poetry in the novels as well as in the short poems. There are in *The Return of the*

Native, for example, passages (in the section called 'The Fascination' chapter 5, and in 'The Closed Door' chapters 2, 5, 6) in which Egdon Heath seems to expand in the imagination both in the spatial and temporal dimensions, its proliferating ferns magnified into the semblance of primaeval forests, its prolific insect life seeming not only to multiply infinitely but to extend back through ages of the evolutionary process.

Lawrence significantly seizes on this feature in Hardy's novels – it is among the remarkable Lawrentian insights into Hardy's imaginative vision (and its peculiar limitations) to be found in his *Study of Thomas Hardy*. Lawrence's understanding of Hardy clearly emerges from his own profound vision of the non-human world, one difference with Hardy (and resemblance with Wordsworth) being Lawrence's sense that the human individual can enter into a relationship with, realize his living connection with the non-human world.

'This is a constant revelation in Hardy's novels: that there exists a great background, vital and vivid, which matters more than the people who move upon it . . . Upon the vast, incomprehensible pattern of some primal morality greater than ever the human mind can grasp, is drawn the little, pathetic pattern of man's moral life and struggle, pathetic, almost ridiculous. The little fold of law and order, the little walled city within which man has to defend himself from the waste enormity of nature, becomes always too small, and the pioneers venturing out with the code of the walled city upon them, die in the bonds of that code, free and yet unfree, preaching the walled city and looking to the waste.

'This is the wonder of Hardy's novels, and gives them their beauty. The vast, unexplored morality of life itself, what we call the immorality of nature, surrounds us in its eternal incomprehensibility, and in its midst goes on the little human morality play, with its queer frame of morality and its mechanised movement . . .

'And this is the quality Hardy shares with the great writers, Shakespeare or Sophocles or Tolstoi, this setting behind the small action of his protagonists the terrific action of unfathomed nature; setting a smaller system of morality, the one grasped and formulated by the human consciousness within the vast,

uncomprehended and incomprehensible morality of nature or
of life itself, surpassing human consciousness. The difference is,
that whereas in Shakespeare or Sophocles the greater, uncom-
prehended morality, or fate, is actively transgressed and gives
active punishment, in Hardy . . . the lesser, human morality,
the mechanical system is actively transgressed, and holds, and
punishes the protagonist, whilst the greater morality is only
passively, negatively transgressed, it is represented merely as
being present in background, in scenery, not taking any active
part, having no direct connexion with the protagonist.'
Earlier in his *Study of Thomas Hardy* Lawrence had already
remarked:

'This is the tragedy of Hardy, always the same: the tragedy
of those who, more or less pioneers, have died in the wilder-
ness, whither they had escaped for free action, after having left
the walled security, and the comparative imprisonment, of the
established convention. . . . Remain quite within the convention
and you are good, safe, and happy in the long run, though you
never have the vivid pang of sympathy on your side: or, on the
other hand, be passionate, individual, wilful, you will find the
security of the convention a walled prison, you will escape, and
you will die, either of your own lack of strength to bear the
isolation and the exposure, or by direct revenge from the com-
munity, or from both. This is the tragedy, and only this: it is
nothing more metaphysical than the division of a man against
himself in such a way: first, that he is a member of the com-
munity, and must, upon his honour, in no way move to disin-
tegrate the community, either in its moral or its practical form;
second, that the convention of the community is a prison . . .'

Hardy has, of course, followed George Eliot in being consci-
ous, as a novelist, of Greek Tragedy. But, unlike George Eliot's
tragedies, if we consider her imaginative insight into and analysis
of the processes of the mind in relation, for example, to the theme
of nemesis, Hardy's tragedies scarcely measure up (as Lawrence
recognizes) to the Greek or Shakespearian tragedies, even in the
role he accords to fate or necessity in them. Hardy's 'neutralized
nature' is, of course, identified by him with fate (or 'the gods')
and has much to do both with the sense of a relentless march of
events and with the pervasive element of pity for men and women

in his work. They are conceived generally as in the end helpless creatures, however violently they aspire and struggle to be free, caught and broken inevitably in the wheels of the universal machinery. But the universal machinery (as Lawrence perceives) tends in Hardy (in contrast to the wild Egdon Heath) to become too simply a symbolical extension of the social machinery, 'the great self-preservation system', the system of social conventions which exceptional individuals attempt in vain to break out of and, in so doing, are either punished by it or perish in the open. They have not the strength, it seems, to stand alone, not enough fight in them in their conflicts to be fully tragic, as are the tragic heroes of Aeschylus, Sophocles and Shakespeare. 'They are pathetic rather than tragic figures.'

Lawrence also refers in this connection to 'Hardy's metaphysic' as intruding into and interfering with his art. Certainly Hardy's sense of injustice suffered by human individuals as inevitably victims, a sense of grievance about the human lot, is an obtrusive element in his novels as in many of his poems. In this respect he lacks the free range, the breadth and depth, the largeness of vision which George Eliot to some extent shares with the Greek tragedians and with Shakespeare. The fact that discussion of Hardy returns so often to what is called his 'pessimism' suggests a limitation, a comparative narrowness, if occasional intensity, of vision. The word 'pessimism' like 'optimism' indicates a one-sided view. It would be less easy to categorize George Eliot as either 'pessimist' or 'optimist'. Her novels, we recognize, take in a more inclusive view of human life in the world. Hardy's 'pessimism' – or pessimistic 'metaphysic' – as it affects his art, or in so far as it does so, provokes remonstrance, rouses the reader to protest. Things very often do go wrong in life but (the reader protests) not all, or nearly all, the time. But Hardy seems often to have deliberately contrived in his art – in that sense 'interfered' with his art – to show that things do invariably and inveterately tend to go wrong. It is this element of contrivance in his plots – not the fact that unlucky accidents and coincidences are an element in human life and are, therefore, necessarily part of the subject-matter of art, part of the truth about things which art must not shirk, but the suspicion that the artist, in order to illustrate his 'metaphysic' is persistently contriving unlikely successions of such events – it is this element of contrivance that produces an impression of life distorted or twisted to illustrate a pessimistic metaphysic. Yet, when all is said, we are left with the sense that Hardy truly is endeavouring to express in his art his own genuine, highly idiosyncratic, wry vision of life, that his art is the authentic expression of his independence and honesty, if naïveté, of mind and character and that that is its great distinction. Nevertheless in the comparison it still remains undeniable that George Eliot is able to take a larger, freer view of life as a whole and to explore more deeply the minds of individuals. To that extent, she is the greater novelist, the greater artist. As a consequence her tragedies are the more tragic, as her comedy seems the more spontaneous.

But Hardy's novels do convey with greater or less artistic success – as do the poems – not only a highly personal vision of human life but a sense of an immemorial rural life as it was in a specific locality of England, together with a sense of a vast non-human background. Hardy has his place as one of the last recorders of a vanishing rural England, in the line (in that respect) from Wordsworth and George Eliot (as well as from Scott as recorder of his older Scotland). He is also an early recorder of the impact of a modern urban mentality on that traditional rural life, the presence of intruders from the modern towns, incongruous new forms of life, among the country people. This again makes it possible to associate Hardy not only with George Eliot but with Lawrence.

VIII

But the great successor of George Eliot – and of a greater novelist still, though Lawrence would not himself acknowledge this fact of his own profound indebtedness, particularly in *The Rainbow*, to Tolstoy – is not Hardy but Lawrence. We need only recall the consciousness in *The Rainbow* of the processes of change in England, the contrasts with the older traditional local life of the farms and villages that the emergence of the industrial England of machine production and modern education were producing – the consciousness of these changes as they profoundly affected and altered individual lives and the fundamental relationships between men and women. *The Rainbow* conveys, as only a novel (as distinct from a play) can convey, this sense of the gradual movement and shift of one generation into the next, this sense of the vast, slow, complex process of history, as 19th-century England (and with it an England much older than the 19th century) changes into the England of the 20th century. But this sense is conveyed in the novel not in the historian's way but in the novelist's, the poet's way, through a sense of sharing imaginatively the innermost experiences of individual lives as they struggle, grow and develop from childhood – and the world of their childhood – into manhood or womanhood in a world that by the time they have grown up has itself undergone changes, is itself become a new unfamiliar world for them to find new bearings in, form new relations with. If *The Rainbow* thus conveys, through the imagined experiences of individual men and women, the sense of an older world in process of becoming a different world, *Women in Love*, its successor but by no means its sequel, produces a sense of the modern world already in being. *Women in Love* may perhaps be described as a comprehensive analysis of civilization – or the failure of civilization – in the 20th century, of the kind of thing civilization had in fact already become (in the contemporary world of the novelist). The word that may readily occur to the reader as describing *Women in Love* is 'diagnosis'. The novel may well strike him as the most searching 'diagnosis' we have of the condition of modern civilization. Yet if 'history' (or 'social history') in the ordinary sense is an inadequate word for *The Rainbow*, 'analysis' or 'diagnosis' are also inadequate words for *Women in Love*. The process by which the 'analysis' resulting in the 'diagnosis' is carried out is again creative or dramatic poetic, searching out and revealing in imagined experiences of imagined individual lives the complexities, difficulties and possibilities of human relationships, particularly the fundamental relationships between men and women, in the context of modern civilization, the difficulties (to borrow Yeats's words) of attaining 'unity of being' in 'a much-divided civilization'.

But the moral and psychological insights characteristic of George Eliot, Lawrence's great predecessor among the English novelists, are developed in Lawrence's novels and short stories (many of them marvellous essential poems) in a way that is, in at least one important respect, uncharacteristic of George Eliot (as well as of James). They are developed in association with an exploring re-examination of the foundations and basis of human life, the connection and relationship of the individual human being with the non-human sources and springs of life both in himself, and outside himself in the non-human universe. There is the difference made by Lawrence's intuitive recognition that relationships between individuals cannot be dissociated from their relationships with the non-human levels of themselves and with the non-human universe outside themselves. It is in this respect in particular that we are reminded that Lawrence's affinities with Blake and Wordsworth are in some ways still more profound than with the novelists who more immediately preceded him. The differences between Lawrence and James (whose interest is focused in the civilized consciousness) and Conrad (whose intensest concern is the isolation of each individual in the midst of the vast spectacle of life and the world) need no stressing. But the differences between Lawrence and George Eliot may be indicated by our noting that the intense ethical interest which he shares with her (and with the other great English novelists and Tolstoy) is associated in his case also with what is, perhaps, an essentially religious, Wordsworthian sense of 'the mystery, the depth of human souls' and of the human individual as having his individual being deeply implanted in, drawing its life from, a reality other than his human self. In this respect Lawrence's creative work can be recognized as a new and further development from *The Prelude*. There is again (notably in *The Rainbow*) the Lawrentian sense of the struggle of each new human individual from childhood towards completeness or wholeness of being in manhood or womanhood, towards maturity in relationships with other human beings and in relationships with things (including birds, beasts, fishes, plants), and with the non-human reality within and outside itself.

This seems to include the significance of the Lawrentian recognition of what had by his time come to be called the unconscious levels beneath the conscious, the Lawrentian re-creation in his novels, short stories and other work of the conception of the unconscious as not the limbo of the consciousness, the dustbin of suppressed ideas or impulses, but the roots of conscious life, the source and springs of life rising up from the darkness (of unconsciousness) into the light of consciousness. But Lawrence's whole concern as a novelist is, of course, not simply with the unconscious any more than simply with the conscious minds of his characters but with their struggle towards – whether with success or failure – wholeness of being, the living completeness of what he calls 'man alive'. How, then, could Lawrence's sense of this wholeness, or potential wholeness, of life – the potentially whole living man or woman in each of his characters in their ever-changing relationships – have been portrayed, rendered, suggested and explored in any other way than, as it is in *Sons and Lovers*, *The Rainbow*, *Women in Love* and the other novels and short stories (a variety and abundance of short stories each of which is a poem) – in any other way than through a creative-poetic (or Shakespearian) development of the English language? Lawrence seems to have been the culmination of that 19th-century line of great novelist poets, each of whom projects an individual vision of life, yet all of whom can properly be regarded as the successors of the poets (as well as of the earlier novelists) and of Shakespeare.

IX

There is a sense, of course, in which, as works of imaginative literature, all novels are poems. Aristotle himself would have endorsed this classification. The novels of Richardson and Fielding are in this sense poems as much as are the novels of Dickens and George Eliot. But this does not affect our recognition that in the 19th century the poetic imagination has enlarged and deepened the novel in its renderings of the comedy and the tragedy of human life. This is the great achievement of the 19th century. By comparison with the greater novels of Dickens and George Eliot, the poetry of their Victorian contemporaries, including the poetry of Tennyson, seems marginal. (The later poets are no longer the explorers the earlier 19th-century poets are,[1] though they concentrate more consciously on their 'art'.) Dickens and George Eliot create more fully than the more deliberately prosaic 18th-century novelists out of the whole range and resources of the English language. In this respect they are the successors of

[1] And as T. S. Eliot again is, supremely in *Four Quartets*, the great 20th-century creative achievement.

Shakespeare and the poets and not simply of the earlier novelists. It is by means of the fullest poetic use of the English language that in the novels of Dickens or George Eliot or Lawrence, as in the plays of Shakespeare, the sense of complex living characters, their shifting, changing conscious (and unconscious) states of mind is created. The 'history of prose fiction' throughout the centuries would not account for *Little Dorrit, Great Expectations, Wuthering Heights, Middlemarch* or *The Rainbow*, as the history of pre-Shakespearian drama would not account for Shakespeare. These novels should be viewed as new creative developments out of the whole of English language, literature and tradition.

¹ The line of 'great' novelists is the line first boldly and justly distinguished as such in *The Great Tradition* (1948).

INDEX

(Individual works are listed under their authors, approximately in chronological order.)

Arnold, 49, 72, 81, 111, 143, 149 n, 239; *Stanzas from the Grande Chartreuse*, 111; *Friendship's Garland*, 239

Austen, Jane, 11, 50, 52, 153–5, 202–3, 238, 247, 257, 285–6, 288, 294, 298, 304, 308, 311, 314; *Northanger Abbey*, 257, 288; *Mansfield Park*, 50, 257; *Emma*, 50

Balzac, 310

Bible, The, 12, 15, 60, 66, 68, 72, 77, 106, 124, 132

Blake, 11–20, 21, 27, 30, 32, 35, 42, 45, 49, 79, 115, 128, 132, 148, 203, 216, 235, 241, 283, 285–8, 290–1, 310, 314, 331; *Poetical Sketches*, 13–14; *Songs of Innocence*, 14–16; *Songs of Experience*, 13–14, 16–20; *Auguries of Innocence*, 21

Brontë, Charlotte and Emily, 11, 45, 64 n, 285, 293–5, 296; *Wuthering Heights*, 45, 64 n, 294; *Jane Eyre*, 294–5; *Villette*, 294

Browning, 201 n

Bunyan, 12–13, 22, 186, 290, 306; *Pilgrim's Progress*, 12–13, 22

Burns, 77, 205, 241, 276, 286, 290

Butler, *Hudibras*, 200

Byron, 49, 98, 116, 121, 199, 200–82, 283, 285–6, 290, 308, 314; *English Bards and Scotch Reviewers*, 201–4; *Childe Harold*, 202, 206, 209, 216; *Beppo*, 200–2, 206–12; *Vision of Judgement*, 200–5, 212–16; *Don Juan*, 116, 200–6, 216–82, 285–6

Cervantes, *Don Quixote*, 216, 252

Chaucer, 11, 78, 98, 103, 153–4, 158–9, 162, 166, 170, 188–9, 193–4, 197, 206, 220, 222, 289, 306, 311

Classics, The (Greek and Latin), 149 n, 218, 225

Clough, *Amours de Voyage*, 201

Cobbett, 161, 181

Coleridge, 20–7, 30, 32, 35, 38, 42, 50, 79, 103, 135 n, 179, 287, 315; *This Lime-Tree Bower*, 22; *Frost at Midnight*, 22; *The Ancient Mariner*, 21–4, 42, 315; *Christabel*, 25; *The Circassian Love Chant*, 25; *Kubla Khan*, 25; *Dejection: an Ode*, 22, 26–7, 30, 135 n; *Biographia Literaria*, 22, 142

Collins, 13 n

Conrad, 11, 24, 305, 313–24, 331; *Heart of Darkness*, 318–19; *Typhoon*, 316 n; *Nostromo*, 313, 319–22; *The Secret Agent*, 318, 322–3; *Under Western Eyes*, 318, 323; *Victory*, 318, 324; *The Shadow Line*, 24

Cowper, 158

Crabbe, 61–2, 70 n, 78, 131, 141, 146, 153–99, 202–3, 206, 238, 241, 283, 285–6; *The Village*, 157–8; *The Parish Register*, 158–60; *The Borough*, 160–166; *Tales in Verse*, 70 n, 153, 166–199, 285

Dante, 46, 104, 111, 118, 214

De Quincey, 20, 71 n, 286–7

Dickens, 11, 17 n, 20 n, 49, 83, 122, 138 n, 148, 158–60, 163, 196, 203, 214–16, 241–2, 247, 254, 287–93, 295, 306–8, 310, 314, 316–18, 332–3; *Dombey and Son*, 17 n, 20 n, 83, 160,

288, 290 n, 307, 312 n; *Bleak House*, 290 n; *Hard Times*, 290 n; *Little Dorrit*, 20 n, 160, 290 n, 292–3, 308, 317; *Great Expectations*, 20 n, 138 n, 290 n, 295

Donne, 81–2, 151–2

Dryden, 155, 158–9, 186, 258, 279–80

Dunbar, *Lament for the Makars*, 149 n

Eliot, George, 11, 45, 49, 55, 83, 153, 160, 186, 239, 257, 283–5, 295–305, 310–11, 313–15, 324, 329–33; *Adam Bede*, 300; *The Mill on the Floss*, 295; *Silas Marner*, 304–5; *Felix Holt*, 301–2; *Middlemarch*, 160, 295–6, 302–4, 314–15; *Daniel Deronda*, 239, 297–300, 313

Eliot, T. S., 32, 40–1, 43, 84, 104, 118, 288, 319 n, 332 n; *Prufrock*, 41; *The Waste Land*, 118, 319 n; *Ash-Wednesday*, 43; *Burnt Norton*, 32; *The Dry Salvages*, 84; *Little Gidding*, 104, 118; *Four Quartets*, 332 n

Fielding, 200, 203, 241, 262, 286–7; *Tom Jones*, 200

Flaubert, 310

Forster, *Where Angels Fear to Tread*, 207; *A Passage to India*, 319 n

Galt, 200; *The Entail*, 200 n

Gillray, 234

Goethe, *Faust*, 201–2, 215, 314

Goldsmith, *The Deserted Village*, 158; *The Citizen of the World*, 238

Gothicism, 94, 105, 214, 256–7, 271–5, 287–8

Greek Tragedy (Aeschylus, Sophocles), 67, 147, 300–2, 327–8

Hardy, 49, 106, 134 n, 141–2, 149, 273, 324–9; *The Return of the Native*, 326; *Neutral Tones*, 134 n; *A Broken Appointment*, 142; *After a Journey*, 325

Hawthorne, 11, 13, 109 n, 306, 312; *The Scarlet Letter*, 312; *Blithedale Romance*, 109 n, 306

Hazlitt, 287

Herbert, George, 162

Hogarth, 120, 156–8, 162–3, 167, 185

Homer, 214, 225–6, 270, 273, 317

Hopkins, 49, 92, 120 n

Horace and Horatianism, 12, 78, 158, 271

James, Henry, 11, 42, 151, 193, 217, 239, 248–9, 257, 278, 298–300, 305–13, 314–15, 331; *The Art of Fiction*, 310; *The Europeans*, 312–13; *A Portrait of a Lady*, 278, 298–300, 312–13, 315; *The Bostonians*, 306–8; *Princess Casamassima*, 306; *What Maisie Knew*, 239, 308–10; *The Awkward Age*, 239, 248, 308, 310

Jeffrey, 206

Johnson, Sam, 21, 45, 50–1, 77, 120, 146, 153–8, 163, 169, 175, 180, 183, 185, 203, 251; *London*, 120, 153, 157; *The Vanity of Human Wishes*, 51, 183; *Rasselas*, 155; *Lines on Death of Levet*, 77, 175

Jonson, Ben, 162, 257, 289; *To Penshurst*, 257

Juvenal, 120, 158, 185

Keats, 27–48, 49, 119 n, 132 n, 301; *Endymion*, 27, 29; *Odes*, 30–45; *Hyperion* (Revised Version), 42, 45–8, 119 n, 301

Lamb, 286–7

Lawrence, 11, 20, 27, 35, 49, 96, 148, 161, 284–5, 319 n, 320, 326–7, 329–332, 333; *Study of Thomas Hardy*, 326–7; *Sons and Lovers*, 332; *The Rainbow*, 295, 329–32; *Women in Love*, 330–2; *St. Mawr*, 319 n; *The Man Who Loved Islands*, 320

Leavis, 13, 36, 44, 95–6, 152 n, 212, 295 n, 325; *Revaluation*, 152 n, 212; *The Great Tradition*, 333 n.

Marvell, 18, 155, 257, 260 n

Melville, 11, 13, 306

Milton, 12, 26–8, 30, 46, 54, 72, 82, 95, 99, 111, 146, 149 n, 158, 161, 202, 214–15, 283, 306; *Il Penseroso*, 12; *Lycidas*, 158; *Paradise Lost*, 12

Molière, 289

Montaigne, 237, 315
Mozart, 201

Ovid, 43

Pastoralism, 12, 77, 158
Peacock, 201, 257, 259, 288; *Headlong Hall*, 201; *Nightmare Abbey*, 201, 257, 288
Pope, 12, 15, 98, 99 n, *153–8*, 162, 164, 180, 182, 186, 200, *203–5*, 211, 213–214, 216, 223, 250, 257, 280, 286, 308; *The Rape of the Lock*, 200; *Elegy on an Unfortunate Lady*, 213; *Moral Essays (Epistle 4)*, 154, 182, 257; *Dunciad*, 12, 99 n, 200
Pushkin, *Eugene Onegin*, 202 n

Racine, 26
Richardson, 11, 26, 126, 301; *Clarissa*, 301
Rilke, 96
Rousseau, 26, 79

Santayana, *Three Philosophical Poets*, 201 n, 285 n
Scott, 154, 159, 200 n, 258, 273, 301, 304, 324, 329; *The Heart of Midlothian*, 200 n, 301; *The Bride of Lammermoor*, 301
Shakespeare, 11–12, 14–15, 17–18, 21, 23, 25–9, 30, 32, 36–7, 39, 42, 45–7, 51–4, 63, 70–2, 75–6, 78, 84–6, 99, 122, 126, 136, 141 n, 146–7, 151–2, 154, 166, 186, 188–9, 216–17, 236–7, 241, 260, 263, 283, 288–9, 295–6, 300–4, 306, 315–17, 328, 332–3; *Love's Labour's Lost*, 28; *Romeo and Juliet*, 17, 28, 147; *A Midsummer Night's Dream*, 28, 289; *Richard III*, 186, 289; *Richard II*, 146; *Henry IV Parts 1 and 2*, 216–17, 289; *The Merchant of Venice*, 32; *As You Like It*, 14, 52, 260; *Twelfth Night*, 18; *Hamlet*, 14, 17–18, 25, 236–7, 289; *King Lear*, 14, 15, 53, 71, 136; *Macbeth*, 17, 21, 23, 51, 53, 84–6, 126, 166, 186, 289, 303, 315, 317; *Othello*, 39, 141 n; *Antony and Cleopatra*, 36–7, 39, 286; *A Winter's Tale*, 14–15, 70; *The Tempest*, 23, 324 n

Shelley, 46, 49, 116, 118–19, 201, *214–216*, *218–219*, 235, 247, 314, 317; *The Mask of Anarchy*, 216, 235, 247; *Peter Bell the Third*, 116, 201, *214–216*; *Adonais*, 119; *The Triumph of Life*, 46, *118–19*, 317
Smollett, 11, 241, 287
Spenser, 15, 27–9, 43, 93, 98, 108 n, 110, 283, 306; *The Faerie Queene*, 15, 29, 43, 93, 108 n
Stendhal, *Le Rouge et le Noir*, 219; *La Chartreuse de Parme*, 230
Swift, 162, 169

Tatler and *Spectator*, 287
Tennyson, 43–4, 49, 144, 332
Thomas, Edward, 72 n
Tolstoy, 72, 230, 303, 329, 331
Turgenev, 310

Vaughan, 90
Voltaire, *Candide*, 201

Wordsworth, 20, 26, 30, 32, 35, 45, *49–152*, *153–5*, 161, 179–80, 217, *283–5*, 287, 295, 304, 310, 324–5, 329; *Guilt and Sorrow*, *50–1*, 136; *Lines Left on a Seat in a Yew Tree*, *51–2*; *The Borderers*, *53–6*, 136, 283; *Margaret or The Ruined Cottage*, *56–66*; *Lyrical Ballads*, 49, 56, 66, 72, 78; *Preface to Lyrical Ballads*, 78; 'Strange fits of passion', *140–2*; 'A slumber did my spirit seal', *141–2*; *Old Cumberland Beggar*, *72–4*; *Michael*, *66–72*; *The Brothers*, *74–6*; *Nutting*, *91*; *Yew Trees*, *91*; *Resolution and Independence or The Leechgatherer*, *105–8*; *The Prelude*, 20, 30, *79–139*, 199, 217, 285, 295, 331; *Ode on Intimations of Immortality*, 85, 135 n; *Upon Westminster Bridge*, *121* n; *The Excursion*, 56, 64, 81, *142–9*; *Extempore Effusion on Death of Hogg*, 149 n; 'Surprised by joy', *149–51*; 'Why art thou silent', 149, *151–2*

Yeats, 12, 25, 30–1, 39, 40, 66, 149, 317, 330; *Sailing to Byzantium*, 30–1